POLISH MUSIC HISTORY SERIES

1

Wanda Wilk

Karol Szymanowski: A Guide (1982)

2

Judith Rosen

Grażyna Bacewicz: Her Life and Works (19. .)

Grażyna Bacewicz: Chamber and Orchestral Music (1985)

4

Kornel Michałowski and Gillian Olechno-Huszcza

Polish Music Literature (1515-1990):
A Selected Annotated Bibliography (1991)

5

Teresa Chylińska

Karol Szymanowski: His Life and Works (1993)

6

Maja Trochimczyk

After Chopin: Essays in Polish Music (2000)

Published by: Polish Music Center
(vol. 1-5: Friends of Polish Music)
Flora L. Thornton School of Music
University of Southern California
Los Angeles, CA 90089-0851

AFTER CHOPIN:

ESSAYS IN POLISH MUSIC

Maja Trochimczyk

Editor

Polish Music History Series, vol. 6
Polish Music Center at USC
Los Angeles; 2000

POLISH MUSIC HISTORY SERIES
Wanda Wilk, Editor (vols. 1-6)
Maja Trochimczyk, Editor (vols. 7 -)

ISSN 0741-9945
ISBN 0-916545-059

After Chopin: Essays in Polish Music
Maja Trochimczyk, Editor

Library of Congress Cataloging-in-Publication Data

After Chopin: Essays in Polish Music / edited by Maja Trochimczyk

Includes bibliographical references and index.
ISBN 0-916545-059 (pbk.: alk.paper)
1. Music - History and criticism. 2. National identity and music.
I. Trochimczyk, Maja (Harley, Maria Anna), 1957 -

Published by the Polish Music Center
Flora L. Thornton School of Music; University of Southern California;
Los Angeles, 840 West 34th Street; California 90089-0851, USA.
<http://www.usc.edu/go/polish_music>
e-mail: polmusic@usc.edu

Distributed by Pendragon Press
P.O. Box 190, Hillsdale, New York 12529-5839
<http://www.pendragonpress.com>
e-mail: penpress@taconic.net

MANUFACTURED IN THE UNITED STATES OF AMERICA

To my parents,
Aleksy and Henryka Trochimczyk,
with gratitude.

Table of Contents

APPENDIX

Portrait of Fryderyk Chopin. Anonymous postcard.
Kraków: S.A. Krzyżanowski, n.d. (late 19th c.).
Collection of the Polish Music Center, Los Angeles.

Introduction:
Music for the Nation or the Nation for Music?

by Maja Trochimczyk

Love no country: countries soon disappear.
Love no city: cities are soon rubble. . . .
Do not gaze into the pools of the past.
Their corroded surface will mirror
A face different from the one you expected.[1]

I decided to begin this exploration of two centuries of Polish music by quoting Czesław Miłosz's somber warning - uttered in 1946, in the shadow of the Holocaust and the destruction of the past that called for a new beginning for the whole of Europe and each of its inhabitants. Miłosz wrote these words in New York, a temporary home before his permanent residence in California. Paradoxically, he soon proceeded to "gaze into the pools of the past" while serving his "faithful mother tongue" in its political misfortunes through his poetry which brought "a little order and beauty" to a tormented culture.[2] Nonetheless, Polish intellectuals had to deal with the fragility of their country long before Miłosz: Poland had disappeared from the map of Europe in 1795 only to return in 1918, and then be recast in a different shape in 1945.[3] Culture, especially literature, played a unique role in the survival of national identity through over 100 years of statelessness; music, particularly that composed by Fryderyk Chopin, was construed as highly important.

---

[1]Czesław Miłosz, *Child of Europe,* Part 6, in *The Collected Poems: 1931-1987* (New York: The Ecco Press, 1988), 88.

[2]Phrases quoted from Czesław Miłosz, *My Faithful Mother Tongue,* a poem written in 1968 in reaction to the dire political events of that year in Poland: Polish participation in the invasion of Czechoslovakia, student protests, and a virulent anti-Semitic campaign leading to the exodus of thousands of Poles of Jewish descent. See *The Collected Poems,* 217.

[3]The country was partitioned between Russia, Prussia and Austria in 1772, 1791 and 1795; it regained sovereignty as the result of World War I. See Norman Davies, *God's Playground: A History of Poland*, 2 vols. (New York: Columbia University Press, 1982).

Chopin was assigned a particular place in the national pantheon as a poet-prophet [*wieszcz*] whose musical statements equaled in significance the proclamations of Adam Mickiewicz (1798-1855) and expressed the true spirit of the nation.[4] This was, at least, the opinion of Polish composers - Zygmunt Noskowski (1846-1909), Władysław Żeleński (1837-1921), Stanisław Niewiadomski (1859-1936), and Karol Szymanowski (1881-1937).[5] Their essays, selected for the first part of this book ("100 Years of Defining Chopin"), exemplify a Polish tradition of constructing Chopin's identity, a tradition that is little known outside of the country. Reflections about the significance of Chopin in the history of Polish music take into account issues of his originality and individual talent as well as questions of tradition and personal reception. These themes are prominent in the text by Szymanowski as well as two articles that complement the first part of this volume, by musicologist Mateusz Gliński (1892-1976) and composer Witold Lutosławski (1913-1994).

Though Chopin became Poland's foremost national composer, having a French father did not help to establish this reputation. In the patriarchal world of Western Europe, the French last name and patrilineal genealogy (as well as a host of other factors, such as Parisian residence for most of his mature life, etc.) continue to be invoked as proofs that Chopin is, at best, international, if not "truly French" or even "Parisian," as Peter J. Pirie claimed in the

---

[4]See Maria Janion and Maria Zmigrodzka, "Fryderyk Chopin wśród bohaterów egzystencji polskiego romantyzmu" [Chopin as a hero of Polish romanticism], *Rocznik chopinowski* 19 (1987): 33-48. For an English language overview of 19th-century Chopin reception see Zofia Chechlińska, "Chopin Reception in Nineteenth-Century Poland," in *The Cambridge Companion to Chopin*, Jim Samson, ed. (Cambridge and New York: Cambridge University Press, 1992), 206-221.

[5]For biographical information about these composers see the notes to individual essays; their short biographies are also included in the Appendix, "Notes on Contributors." Many of these essays have been collected in *Kompozytorzy polscy o Chopinie. Antologia* [Polish composers about Chopin: an anthology], Mieczysław Tomaszewski, ed. (Kraków: PWM Edition, 1980). Certain issues and the views of some of these writers are discussed by Leszek Polony, *Polski kształt sporu o istotę muzyki* [The Polish shape of the argument about the essence of music] (Kraków: Akademia Muzyczna, 1991).

mid-1970s.[6] A nationalist appropriation of the composer required the "polonization" of his name that, consequently, transformed Chopin to Szopen. Niewiadomski's article "Ch or Sz" highlights a number of arguments in favor of this change, to which, as Niewiadomski maintains, even the composer would not have objected. Repeated and concerted efforts to claim Chopin for Poland have preoccupied Polish writers and musicians since the composer's death; essays brought together in the first part of the present volume highlight the earlier stages of this process. Some of these writings suggest the existence of conceptual links with European writers on nationhood and the arts, especially German romantic philosopher and critic, Johann Gottfried Herder (1744-1803), whose ideas were borrowed by Noskowski and Żeleński, and a French historian of social-Darwinist orientation, Hippolyte Taine (1828-1893), who was cited by Niewiadomski and Szymanowski.

Similarly to Herder, Polish composers sought to define national identity as a spiritual phenomenon, centered on the experiences and productions of the Folk, the people of the countryside who created and lived in close connection to nature, "the fields and meadows" of Poland. Chopin's music was valued not in and of itself; instead, its quality was construed as stemming from its closeness to Polish folk song and the landscape. Reverberations of such ideas may be heard even in the famous dictum of poet Cyprian Kamil Norwid (1821-1883) who described Chopin in the following words:[7]

> Varsovian by birth, a Pole by heart and a citizen of the world by talent, Fryderyk Chopin knew how to gather field flowers, without shaking off even a slightest drop of dew, or a smallest

---

[6]Janusz Szprot, ed., "Spór wokół Chopina" [Controversy surrounding Chopin], *Ruch Muzyczny* no. 18 (16-30 September 1973): 8-9. In this exchange of ideas, Peter J. Pirie was opposed by Adam Harasowski and Alistair Wightman.

[7]Cyprian Kamil Norwid, *Promethidion*, quoted from *Myśli o Polsce i Polakach* [Thoughts about Poland and Poles], Marian Dobrosielski, ed. (Białystok: Krajowa Agencja Wydawnicza, 1983), 46. "Rodem warszawianin, sercem Polak, a talentem świata obywatel, Fryderyk Chopin . . . umiał zbierać kwiaty polne, rosy z nich ani puchu nie otrząsając najlżejszego. . . . Przezeń Ludu polskiego porozrzucane łzy po polach w dyjademie ludzkości się zebrały na dyjament piękna, kryształami harmonii osobliwej."

speck of dust from them. He gathered the tears of the Polish peasantry, scattered on the fields, in a diadem of humankind; they became diamonds of beauty, crystals of unusual harmony.

An emphasis on the role of Polish folk music in Chopin's output is a common thread through all the essays defining him as a national composer. A newer conceptual strain arises from Taine's philosophy of art which emphasized the "racial" unity of ethnic groups, shaped by their genetic kinship, their natural environment and their location in historical time. Taine's speculations about the origins of aesthetic traits of national art in that nation's geographic-climactic conditions were not questioned by any of the writers, who embraced his holistic explanation of national identity in art and extended his ideas into the domain of music. In the interwar period, Taine's "racial" terminology, so jarring today, was used without remorse or apology by Szymanowski, Niewiadomski, and Gliński.[8]

The next phase of Chopin reception (with distinct characteristics) took place after World War II, in communist Poland.[9] In a study of "Chopin as a National Composer," published in a volume on ethnicity, identity and music, Zdzisław Mach described the propaganda mechanism used by the post-1945 government to elevate the "folk-loving" Chopin to the status of a

---

[8]Zofia Helman discusses Szymanowski's connection to Taine in her study published in the third part of the present volume. I focus on the use of "racial" terminology in reference to Chopin in "Chopin and 'The Polish Race:' On Political Dimensions of Chopin Reception," paper read at *The Age of Chopin: A Sesquicentenial Chopin Symposium,* Bloomington, Indiana University, September 1999 (publication forthcoming in the conference proceedings).

[9]The most extensive studies of Chopin reception in Poland have been conducted by Mieczysław Tomaszewski. His award-winning monograph, *Chopin: Człowiek, dzieło, rezonans* [Chopin: Man, work, resonance] (Poznań: Podsiedlik, Raniowski i Spółka, 1998) presents issues of Chopin reception (among composers, scholars, performers, and the public) on pp. 735-800. Tomaszewski's 1959 introduction to the anthology *Kompozytorzy polscy o Chopinie* outlines the main directions of Chopin reception since the 19th century, yet, for obvious reasons, it does not contain any critiques of the "official appropriation" of the composer by the communist government.

national hero.[10] He suggested that the marriage of communist
ideology with nationalist rhetoric required a shift in emphasis to
social class. In the 19th and early 20th century the reception of
Chopin as a national composer occurred mostly among Poland's
gentry and intelligentsia. After World War II, his links to the ari-
stocracy and upper nobility had to be discounted and his love of the
common man emphasized in order to open the path to his canoni-
zation as a national symbol in the Polish People's Republic (PRL).
The peasantry was then endowed with the role of carrying the
essence of national identity; Chopin's links to folk song and his
mythical childhood in Żelazowa Wola served to articulate that
connection. It is not difficult to argue, however, that contemporary
composers did not share this vision of a "peasant Chopin;" the
article by Witold Lutosławski illustrates their tendency to converse
with the great predecessor as a composer and musician, to ponder
those aspects of his art that might be relevant to their own. The
communal issues of national identity and the use of music in its
service are replaced here by a focus on individual creativity: a
national (or not), but certainly great - and greatly revered - composer of the past provides a link to the tradition and an inspiration
for the future of music-making, not nation-constructing.

* * *

Is it because of "Polish" or because of "music" that we
study "Polish music"? How does one draw the line and where
should the emphasis be placed? The title of my introduction attracts
attention to these issues of identity and shifting focus: "constructing
national identity" serves as the main thematic thread for the first and
the third part of this collection. National (and ethnic) belonging is
a basic human characteristic, if only because of the necessity to
express identity in language. As Agnes Heller writes in *A Theory of
Modernity*, identity is always complex. People are both "identical
with themselves" (i.e. with their psychosomatic beings) and "identical with at least one group, the so-called 'social *a priori*' into

---

[10]Zdzisław Mach, "National Anthems: The Case of Chopin as a National
Composer," in *Ethnicity, Identity and Music: The Musical Construction of Place*,
Zdzisław Mach, ed. (Oxford: Berg, 1994).

which their 'genetic *a priori*' had been thrown and with which it needs to be dovetailed in the process of becoming a certain kind of person."[11] Heller continues:

> Identity . . . is also temporal and spatial. It includes identity with a place (or with a few representative places) and identity through time. Identity in place and identity through time is the geography and narrative of a people's, or group of people's life. The meanings that a group of people attribute to its way of life - its language, rules, and norms, beliefs, ceremonies, and so on - are homogenized - although not entirely - into one meaning; that is, into a world which includes the geography and the narrative of this people.

For Heller, historical consciousness presents a world; similarly, the historical consciousness of Poles presents a world of Poland, a world of Polish culture. Yet, as Heller argues elsewhere, we live in the times of diaspora, a time of non-belonging, of exile: "since we are born contingent - and are also aware of our contingency - we are strangers, aliens, wherever we are born."[12] Immigrants, with roots in one country and residency in another, articulate this estrangement in their own being: they live out the nostalgia for a lost homeland by constructing an image of their idealized *patria* that reaches mythical proportions. The construction of Chopin as all-Polish, a Slavic soul with an accidentally misspelled name, is a particular manifestation of such a myth-making, a process of "national imaginings" that in the 19th-century compensated for the actual, political loss of national self.[13] At that time, music seemed to exist "for the nation," the artistic was subject to the ideological, and the universal values of Chopin's contributions to "high culture" were subsumed by his capacity to create markers for national identity.
      The "national" ideals seem suspicious in our time of inter-, trans-, and supra-national philosophies, a time when criticizing

---

[11]Agnes Heller, *A Theory of Modernity* (Oxford: Blackwell Publishers, 1999), 2.

[12]Heller, *A Theory of Modernity*, 194.

[13]The phrase "national imaginings" comes from the title of Barbara Milewski's doctoral dissertation on the history of the mazurka (*Mazurka and National Imaginings;* Princeton University, in progress).

ethnocentricity seems of paramount importance.[14] Similarly, the notion of "high culture" has been under attack by critics who fully embrace the "anthropological concept" of culture according to which "every way of life is a culture. Every people has a culture and every tribe as well. Moreover, cultures are divided into 'subcultures' - urban subcultures, religious subcultures, sexual subcultures, and so on."[15] Agnes Heller reminds us that, in contrast to this "empirical universality" of the anthropological culture, "high culture" is a "normative universal" and the inclusion of artefacts in this culture depends on aesthetic standards.[16] The works of "high culture,"[17]

> are placed high because they have the potential to serve for infinite interpretability, and they have already been interpreted from various perspectives again and again. They perform a function - the function of rendering meaning and evoking the feelings of nostalgia and closeness.

The "infinite interpretability" of music is possible when musical compositions are accessible as notated texts, continuously available for study and interpretation. A Polish philosopher of art, Roman Ingarden (1893-1970) argued that the notation provides the work of music with an ontological basis while the work itself exists in a peculiar, intersubjective and intentional manner. My discussion of his concept was awarded the Wilk Prize for Research in Polish Music in 1994 (Professional Prize; more on the "Wilk Prizes"

---

[14]Agnes Heller writes: "The term 'ethnocentrism' was coined in the modern culture and only those cultures that accept that all cultures have a legitimate claim for recognition can be ethnocentric. It is first the modern/Western/European world that relativizes itself, its own culture, its own tradition, and its own truth, simply by coining the anthropological concept of culture, an empirical universal as a norm that Europeans should accept by relativizing themselves." See Heller, *A Theory of Modernity*, the chapter "Culture and Civilization I," p. 138.

[15]Heller, *A Theory of Modernity*, 134.

[16]Heller, *A Theory of Modernity*, 134: "'High' culture is a normative universal (it provides a yardstick) and 'cultural discourse' is an optative universal (it provides equal opportunity), whereas the third concept of culture [anthropological concept] is an empirical universal (it encompasses everything that in fact exists)."

[17]Heller, *A Theory of Modernity*, 125.

themselves will be said later). Its inclusion in the second part of the book, entitled "Essays on Polish Music" paradoxically shifts the volume's emphasis from "Polishness" to "music" (before returning to an extended treatment of national issues in the third part of *After Chopin*). In addition to the Ingarden study, the second part of the book consists of papers dealing with the music of Karol Szymanowski and Witold Lutosławski. These papers form a sample of results of a scholarly competition, the Wilk Prizes for Research in Polish Music. Here we encounter detailed examinations of individual pieces: Karol Szymanowski's Piano Sonata in A major, Op. 21 studied by Stephen Downes (a British musicologist; Student Prize in 1987/88), Szymanowski's choral *Stabat Mater* reviewed by Richard Zielinski (an American choral conductor of Polish descent; Professional Prize in 1991), and Witold Lutosławski's *Partita* for violin and piano analyzed by Michael L. Klein (an American music theorist; Professional Prize in 1995).

The scholars chose these works themselves; attracted by the musical and aesthetic values, they searched to illuminate the significance of these compositions in the world of high culture. Downes, Zielinski, and Klein focused on features of individual "works of music" and, by doing so, expressed their allegiance to the concept of "high culture" and simultaneously took upon themselves the role of arbiters of this culture. They decided (to paraphrase Heller) that these particular compositions are "the carriers of authority and the keepers of secrets."[18] Thus, they ventured into the domain of interpretation and engaged in a modern form of "devotion." Agnes Heller stated: "Interpretation of works of art (and of cultural objects) is a devotional practice. The object of devotion is the this-ness, the *ipseity* of the old text or the old thing - the interpretandum - and not its matter, content, or message alone."[19]

The focus shifts from the "ipseity" of music back to its "national content" in papers gathered in the third part of the book, "Music and National Identity," where issues of national myth-making are examined from a scholarly perspective. This segment begins with Zofia Helman's magisterial study of the "Dilemma of Polish Music in the 20th Century: National Style or Universal

---

[18]Heller, *A Theory of Modernity*, 146.

[19]Heller, *A Theory of Modernity*, 144.

Values." Helman reviews this subject from the triple point of view of the composers' writings, their musical oeuvres, and musicological interpretations (especially by Polish musicologists, such as Zofia Lissa and Anna Czekanowska). The article brings together the thematic threads of *After Chopin: Essays in Polish Music* - a collection juxtaposing florid essays about Chopin and compositional aesthetics with scholarly interpretations of the music by Polish composers. On a personal note, I also thought it fitting to complete the array of studies constituting my first edited book with an in-depth article by my first and most influential musicology professor (Institute of Musicology, University of Warsaw, 1976-1988), who directed me towards this academic discipline and away from more practical and far less intellectually stimulating occupations in the music industry and the media.

Two papers included in the third part of *After Chopin* apply the idea of "music-defining-nation" to specific repertories. My overview of the history of Polish national anthems highlights the ongoing debate, still distant from its conclusion, about the preferable definition of national identity as either secular or religious. The competing concepts of nationhood found direct expression in the choice of songs that have served as anthems. In the only ethno-musicological paper of this book, Timothy Cooley, a Wilk Prize laureate of 1998 (Student Prize), presents a fascinating instance of constructed "authenticity" in the music of the Tatra Mountains. As Cooley points out, the stylistic uniformity of the *górale* music emerged at a specific point in time that coincided with the onrush of Polish tourists and the genesis of tourist industry in that area at the end of the nineteenth century. His analysis of folk song collections suggests great differences in the repertoire of songs and their characteristics before and after the arrival of people from the plains. "Authenticity," like "identity," is a construct that can be unraveled and explained. The "archaicized" music of the mountains, seen as more robust, primitive and pure than the productions from other areas of the country, reflects yet another artistic tendency, one to-wards "exoticizing" realms of Western music.[20] There are also ob-vious parallels with the construction of "pure, strong and simple"

[20]See Jonathan Bellman, ed., *The Exotic in Western Music* (Boston: Northeastern University, 1998).

folk authenticity in American Appalachia and Argentina.[21]

In a recent article, a Polish-American historian, John J. Bukowczyk examined "Polish Americans, Ethnicity and Otherness," focusing on the formation of the sense of ethnic and national identity among Polish immigrants to the U.S.[22] As Bukowczyk writes, the historical multi-ethnicity of the Polish state (more than 1/3 of its interwar population was ethnically non-Polish) has not been reflected in the construction of a fictional, timeless and ethnically unified Polish Nation which the American Polonia saw as its idealized "Old World homeland." Simultaneously, Polish Americans found themselves at the bottom of the scale of "social status" assigned to various ethnic groups originating from Europe. Their colorful "Old World" mythology compensated for the drab "New World" reality. Members of the same ethnic group took it upon themselves to counter this myth-making process by providing access to scholarly, unbiased information about Poland, its history and culture via a host of cultural organizations: The Kościuszko Foundation in New York, the Polish Institute of Arts and Sciences of America, the American Center for Polish Culture in Washington, D. C., the Copernicus Foundation at the University of Michigan, Ann Arbor, and various Polish Studies departments across the U.S.

In the domain of music, the task of elucidating myths and providing knowledge is primarily entrusted to the Polish Music Reference Center at the University of Southern California.[23] The

---

[21]These issues were recently discussed at a special session "Music Making and Nation Making," the 1999 Meeting of the American Musicological Society, Kansas City, Missouri; especially in "Defining American Identity: Cultural Preservation, Presentation, and Transformation" by Ron Pen, and "Argentine Cultural Construction and the *Gauchesco* Tradition" by Deborah Schwartz-Kates. Recent studies of musical definitions of national identity have been greatly influenced by ideas of Richard Taruskin, esp. in *Defining Russia Musically: Historical and Hermeneutical Essays* (Princeton: Princeton University Press, 1997) and Michael Beckerman, e.g. in the collection of essays on *Dvorak and His World* (Princeton: Princeton University Press, 1993).

[22]John J. Bukowczyk: "Polish Americans, Ethnicity and Otherness," *The Polish Review* 43 no. 3 (1998): 299-313.

[23]In 1998, for instance, the PMRC, in collaboration with the Hebrew Union College, hosted the first ever *International Conference 'Polish/Jewish/Music!'* (15-16 November 1998, Los Angeles). Scholars from five countries presented papers on Polish/Jewish relations and Jewish contributions to Polish (musical)

Center was established at the USC Thornton School of Music in 1985 by Dr. Stefan and Wanda Wilk who envisioned for it a purpose of promoting music of Polish composers by providing information in English through publications (newsletters, books, web site), collecting scores, recordings, manuscripts, and ephemera, answering requests for information, and organizing special events.[24] In 1986 the Wilks moved one step further, and created a new research competition, the Stefan and Wanda Wilk Prizes for Research in Polish Music. The competition, by 1999 reaching its 13th edition, has resulted in a substantial collection of papers on Polish music, written by students and professional musicologists (two separate prizes). Until 1998, the majority of these papers remained unpublished while their copyright rested with the PMRC. Some authors have submitted their articles for publication in scholarly journals and essay collections (a full list of these publications accompanies the list of prize-winning papers in the appendix). Winners of the 1998 and 1999 competitions saw their essays published in electronic form: the *Polish Music Journal* (ISSN 1521-6039), a semi-annual online periodical, was created at the PMRC to provide a much needed venue for the Wilk Prize papers. The journal also includes translations of scholarly articles by Polish musicologists, mostly from the Polish musicological quarterly, *Muzyka*, and previously unpublished essays, as well as book reviews and reports. Readers interested in the future winners of the Wilk Prizes for Research in Polish Music are encouraged to look for this journal on the PMRC website.[25]

In order to memorialize the competition and publicize its existence, Ms. Wilk, who had served as the editor of the Polish

---

culture. Issues of identity, cultural assimilation and exclusion were a common thread. (Proceedings of this conference are currently being prepared for publication.) These topics recurred at a panel discussion on Polish identity in music that I organized for the 1999 Meeting of the American Musicological Society, Kansas City, Missouri (November 1999).

[24]The first of these events actually preceded the formation of the PMRC: the 1982 Szymanowski Centennial, organized by Wanda Wilk at USC, included symposia, lectures, concerts and exhibits. The PMRC manuscript collection consists of 22 scores by contemporary composers, including 5 major pieces of Witold Lutosławski, works by Baird, Bacewicz, Skrowaczewski, Ptaszyńska and others.

[25]URL: <http://www.usc.edu/go/polish_music/PMJ>

Music History Series published by the PMRC's fund-raising organization, Friends of Polish Music at USC, entrusted me with the task of preparing a selection of past prize-winning essays for publication in this series. I gladly accepted this challenge and, after reading through the array of papers, contacted prospective contributors. To provide the volume with a thematic thread I decided to limit the topics to papers on Chopin, Szymanowski and Lutosławski, the three Polish composers of the greatest international significance over the past two centuries. In addition, several other papers were to serve as thematic "interludes" enriching the variety of topics and methods presented in the volume. This framework lost its initial clarity when the "Chopin" section disappeared due to the prior publication of several important essays (most notably those by John Rink and Jeffrey Kallberg) in other books and journals. Instead, the first part of the finished book now contains texts highlighting certains stages in Chopin reception in Poland. Yet something of the original plan remains, if only in the presence of essays on Chopin by Szymanowski and Lutosławski which interconnect parts one and two of this volume. (Parts one and three are related through their common emphasis on "Polishness.")

The methodological diversity of approaches to the area of Polish music presented in *After Chopin: Essays in Polish Music* extends well beyond differences between popular essays by composers and strict analyses by scholars. The volume brings together various scholarly disciplines: historical musicology (Helman, Downes), music theory (Klein), philosophical aesthetics and popular music studies (Trochimczyk), and ethnomusicology (Cooley). The scholars represented here come from Poland, England and the U.S. They share neither their methods, nor academic backgrounds, yet they all belong to a single culture, "the culture of cultivated discourse."[26] They search for new meanings and provide new interpretations. With the hope that such enlightened discourse about Polish music will continue and flourish, I entrust this volume to our readers.

---

[26]Heller, *A Theory of Modernity*, 128-9. She uses this term as her "second concept of culture" located between the elitist "high culture" and the pragmatic "anthropological concept of culture."

* * *

As the editor of *After Chopin: Essays in Polish Music* I owe debts of gratitude to my collaborators and assistants: Dr. Linda Schubert of Los Angeles, who edited and proofread the whole collection (working as a volunteer); graduate students in the department of music history and literature of the USC Thornton School of Music - Anne Desler, Brian Harlan, as well as Junior Fulbright Scholar, Małgorzata Szyszkowska (at USC in the academic year 1998/1999) who helped with the translations; professional translators - Maria Piłatowicz, Joanna Niżyńska, and Peter J. Schertz; and editorial assistant, Magdalena Bedernik. My contributions to this volume benefitted from discussions with my professors (Susan McClary, Bo Alphonce at McGill University, 1992-4), colleagues at USC (Prof. Bruce Brown and Janet Johnson, 1996-) and elsewhere, especially participating in the same sessions at scholarly conferences (Prof. Michael Beckerman, University of California at Santa Barbara; Dr. Timothy Cooley, University of California at Santa Barbara; Dr. Halina Goldberg, Indiana University; Prof. Maciej Gołąb, University of Warsaw, Poland; Dr. Martina Homma, Cologne, Germany; Barbara Milewski, Princeton University; Prof. Margarita Mazo, Ohio State University; Prof. Dorothea Redepenning, Heidelberg University, Germany; Dr. Steve Sweeney-Turner, U.K.; Prof. Adrian Thomas, Cardiff University of Wales, U.K.; Prof. Mieczysław Tomaszewski, Jagiellonian University), and students, especially the participants in my musicology seminar (Spring 1999) devoted to "Polish identity in music." I am also grateful for the support from Dr. and Mrs. Wilk that made this work possible and for the enthusiasm of all the Friends of Polish Music who have contributed donations to the Polish Music Fund at the Flora L. Thornton School of Music, University of Southern California.

Maja Trochimczyk (Los Angeles)

Na grób Chopina
For the Tomb of Chopin

W obcej gdzieś krainie	*In a foreign country -*
Kamień twój grobowy,	*Your sepulchral tombstone.*
Cudze niebo płynie	*A foreign sky is shining*
Nad snem twojej głowy,	*Above your head's slumber,*
Cudze niebo chmurne	*The foreign sky is clouded,*
Rankiem grób twój rosi,	*It brings rain in the morning,*
Cudzy wiatr ci echo	*For you a foreign wind carries*
Cudzej pieśni nosi.	*The echo of a foreign song.*
Ani twej mogiły	*Your tomb is not guarded*
Nasza brzoza strzeże,	*By our birch-tree; there*
Ani świerk pochyły	*The crooked fir-trees do not*
Szepce tam pacierze,	*Whisper their daily prayers,*
Ani wierzby nasze	*Neither our willows*
żałosnemi szumy	*With sorrowful rustling*
Budzą ciebie nocą	*Awaken you nightly*
Z śmiertelnej zadumy.	*From the mortal dreams.*
Kurhanu twojego	*Your brothers did not carry*
Bracia nie sypali,	*Our soil for your cairn,*
Nasza złota zorza	*Our golden sunlight [dawn]*
Tobie się nie pali,	*For you does not burn,*
Nie palą się tobie	*Our trembling stars*
Nasze gwiazdy drżące,	*For you do not shine,*
Grobu twego nasze	*Your tomb is not brightened*
Nie srebrzą miesiące.	*By our silver moonrays.*
Oj, nie miała matka	*Oh, the mother did not*
Szczęścia w swoich progach,	*Have luck in her household,*
Oj, puściła synów	*Oh, she let her sons go*
Po rozstajnych drogach. . .	*By the distant cross-roads. . .*
Oj, żyły tam syny	*Oh, her sons long lived there*
W długiej poniewierce,	*In misery, abandoned,*
Oj oddały matce	*Oh, they gave her back*
Swe pęknięte serce.	*Their broken heart(s).*
Hej, hej!	*Hey, hey!*

Poem by Maria Konopnicka (1842-1910)
[set to music in Zygmunt Noskowski's Song Op. 76, No. 1]
English translation by Maja Trochimczyk

PART I

100 YEARS

OF DEFINING CHOPIN

On the 50th Anniversary of Chopin's Death

by Władysław Żeleński[1]

Fifty years have passed since the death of Chopin, and still he is so close to us as if death snatched him from among us only recently. The passage of time did not weaken the impression and influence made by the music of this master; it magnified these effects instead. Today the world's virtuosi could not exist without his music. Similarly, whoever yearns to penetrate the hearts of listeners, whoever would like to stir their emotions, that person must also play the works of Chopin. Certainly, Chopin is the most beloved musician. "He had the heart and he looked in the heart" and that is why he succeeds - according to Słowacki's famous expression - "in transforming bread-eaters into angels." Such a spiritual elevation is indeed the highest purpose of all the arts!

The delicate subtlety of his feelings, his melancholy mood, and the whole ideal direction that he gave to piano music, have joined together to create this unique, one-of-a-kind personality, which is clearly manifested in his musical style. While Chopin brought a new, fresh element into the treasure trove of the world's music, it is in our country that his name has become epochal because he created the new beginnings and the foundations for national music. He accomplished this by drawing from Polish melodies, rhythms and other material that had been accumulating for ages - giving them a renewed life, and a greater permanence. The songs that Chopin had heard during his youth in his native village sustained him in the foreign lands. It was from these songs that he developed his marvelous melodies for which the passage of time has only provided a test of quality.

---

[1]Władysław Żeleński (1837-1921) was a composer and composition professor of a neo-romantic orientation. His speech "On the 50th anniversary of Fryderyk Chopin's death" was delivered in 1899 in Cracow and published in *Echo Muzyczne, Teatralne i Artystyczne* no. 837 (15 October 1899). A slightly abbreviated version appeared in *Kompozytorzy polscy o Fryderyku Chopinie: Antologia* Mieczysław Tomaszewski, ed. (Kraków: PWM, 1980), 63-67. [This and all subsequent notes by the editor unless otherwise indicated].

With the most eminent creative individuals there is always a prominent national trait, especially in the compositions that are purely moody and subjective; works of a larger scope, however, often enter the domain of a universal, cosmopolitan style. This should not come as a surprise, because spiritual creativity cannot be constrained by geographic borders. Nevertheless, the greatest composers have often borrowed folk motives from the heritage of their nations, which has provided them with the most beautiful material and which remains an inexhaustible source of inspiration. Proof for this may be found in the creative outputs of Beethoven, Schubert, Schumann, and Weber. In Schubert's music everywhere one can sense this typically German *Gemütlichkeit*; in Schumann's works the characteristic *Träumerei* is set against a background of a somewhat morbid fantasy, stimulated by the writings of Jean Paul Richter and E.T.A. Hoffmann.[2] In Weber's music, particularly in the *Freischütz*, one can discern a true German tone throughout. Despite the fact that the style of German composers reveals their national attitudes and personalities, this style has been regarded as universal, known to the whole world. Meanwhile, the distinctions between the Italian, French, and German styles have gradually become less prominent. Since the latter style has established all the means of melody, rhythm, and harmony in their equality without any exceptions, and since it has led to the establishment of musical genres, one may state that this style should be called the only true, universal style.

In our music, a quality of longing [*tęskna nuta*][3] is apparent in every composition. Before Chopin this emotional tone was heard weakly, as it was not very prominent among earlier musicians who were either foreigners or who followed the paths of the Italian muse. Chopin was the first to consciously draw from the treasures of our folk songs, and he endowed his compositions with a purely Polish character (particularly in his dance pieces). He raised the form of the polonaise to the level of an unprecedented ideal; in the famous Polonaise in A major he gave us a true type of a Polish dance. In

---

[2]Jean Paul Richter (1763-1825) and Ernst Theodor Amadeus Hoffmann (1776-1812) are two prominent representatives of early romanticism in Germany. Some of their stories contain a strong element of the supernatural and the grotesque.

[3]The expression used by Żeleński, "tęskna nuta" means literally a "longing tone."

other polonaises, while preserving their proper character, he introduced a tone that was either martial or sorrowful and passionate, but always magnificent, proud, and noble. He brought the form of the polonaise to the summit of perfection in the Polonaise in F sharp minor and in the unparalleled Polonaise in A-flat major (*Polonaise-Fantaisie*). Chopin's mazurkas are a completely new type of salon music;[4] we can divide them into three categories in accordance to their character. Some mazurkas are completely dance-like, as they were written under an influence or an inspiration of a joyous moment - improvised with a group of friends, or composed for actual dancing. The second type, sustained in a sorrowful, lyrical tone, as if taken from the melody of a song, found the most numerous group of imitators; even the poets repeatedly attempted to provide appropriate words for these works so that the mazurkas could also be used for singing. The highest category, though, consists of such mazurkas that contain something more than lyricism, i.e., a certain ballad-like tone, for they are permeated by the feeling of a ballad. Among the most beautiful mazurkas of this kind I should include the famous Mazurka in C minor Op. 56, No. 3; the Mazurka in A minor Op. 59, No. 1; and both Mazurkas in C-sharp minor, i.e. Mazurkas Op. 50 No. 3 and Op. 41, No. 1. The first one from the latter pair (op. 50) is particularly marvelous because of its intricate polyphonic structure.

In the Mazurka in C minor the modulation from C minor to D minor and the return to C minor, resembling the old Dorian mode, is extraordinarily poignant. No matter how many times the late Princess Marcelina Czartoryska played this Mazurka for me, I repeatedly experienced simultaneous feelings of inexpressible pain and delight - because of the way this charming passage so miraculously emerged from under her hand.

In his book on Chopin, Niecks places the waltzes at the most elevated position and accuses the mazurkas of a certain lack of finish.[5] This opinion could be expressed only by a man who does

---

[4]Here, "salon music" refers to "chamber music" and does not bear negative connotations.

[5]Frederick Niecks, *Frederick Chopin as a Man and Musician*, 2 vols., (London, 1888). Reprint of the 1942 edition (New York: Vienna House, 1973). Niecks is also the author of *Robert Schumann* (New York: AMS, 1978) and *Programme*

not know and does not understand the meaning of our folk songs, someone unable to comprehend the harmonies that sometimes sound harsh, yet are so strangely original and beautiful. In my opinion, among all the works by Chopin his mazurkas should be placed in the highest position, as unparalleled masterpieces. In respect to their form, the nocturnes belong among his "universal" rather than "national" compositions, even though they express much longing and lyricism particular only to our character! The profound sorrow [*żal*], the quiet complaint [*skarga*], and even a forceful, dramatic element appear in the genre of the nocturne for the first time in the works by Chopin.

Moreover, in certain nocturnes Chopin touched upon the spirit of the mazurka, for example in the Nocturne in C-sharp minor Op. 27, No. 1. After a tempestuous *agitato* section the rhythmic pattern of the mazurka appears in full strength; later on, following a violent cadenza, the first motive returns. It is quiet, yet sorrowful, and the addition of D instead of D-sharp intensifies this sorrow even further. The tone of the mazurka also occurs in the Nocturne in F-sharp minor Op. 49, No. 2, however, it appears in a more constrained manner, and there is less passion here than in the previous nocturne. Finally to mention one more example, in the Nocturnes in G minor Op. 15, No. 3 and Op. 37, No. 1, and the magnificent Nocturne in C minor Op. 48, No. 1, one can see how strangely beautiful is the introduction of the "chorale" tone in Chopin's music.

Chopin always loved "fluid"[6] singing; his *cantabile* melodies flow in a broad stream, and it is well-known that the Italian way of singing was, for him, always an ideal. With the greatest delight he listened to the works of Bellini, which in the mouths of Rubini, Pasta, or Malibran, had a charm that we cannot even fathom

---

Music in the Last Four Centuries: A Contribution to the History of Musical Expression (New York: Haskell House, 1968, reprint of a 1908 edition).

[6]The exact word used here, "potoczysty" means "fluid, flowing, continuously moving, in a rolling motion." It could be applied to a person's dance movement, the dance itself, the character of a speech; the usage in reference to singing is rare.

today.[7] However, the art of beautiful singing (*bel canto*) died out gradually with the passage of time. Today the melody by itself cannot please; we seek dramatic effects, stirred by characteristic elements of harmony, timbre, and by the colors of the orchestra. Nonetheless, one can glean from the well-known Nocturne in E-flat major, Op. 9, No. 2 how great was Bellini's influence on Chopin's music. Yet, [in contrast with *bel canto*] the melodies of Chopin will never lose their appeal because our master inseparably connected them with strangely profound harmonies and with rhythmic patterns of a great originality.

Some people who are not aware of the difficult ways of creativity, imagine that the inspiration flowed from heaven to the artist's soul like a rainbow of divine tones, and that he only faced the task of writing down what had been marvelously sent to him from above. Obviously, Chopin received such inspiration - he expressed it in his improvisations. But as far as his manuscripts are concerned, they bear traces of numerous crossings out and changes, corrections and variants. Moreover, those who knew him and witnessed this process have revealed that it was a true spiritual suffering - this **completing**[8] and perfecting of an idea before it was ready to be printed in the form that entirely satisfied the creator of these works of genius. Similarly to a sculptor who smoothes out and perfects [*wypieszcza*][9] the marble before it reaches his ideal of perfection, so did Chopin work out his compositions in minute detail.

Being a poet, and a purely subjective one at that, Chopin wrote down only what sounded in his own soul - what he could right away perform at his instrument. He became so close to the piano that all other instrumental timbres were foreign to him. He never

---

[7]Giovanni Battista Rubini (1794-1854), Giuditta Pasta (1798-1865), and Maria Malibran (1808-1836) are famous Italian opera singers; Bellini wrote parts in *Norma* for Rubini and Pasta; Malibran was best known as a singer of Rossini (she also composed songs and was the sister of Pauline Viardot, Chopin's close associate). In Paris, Chopin had many opportunities of hearing their voices.

[8]This and several other words are set in bold font to reflect the emphasis of the author.

[9]The verb "wypieszczać" means literally to "caress, cherish" and is very difficult to translate [translators' note].

attempted to write for orchestra, and even the larger works in which he used orchestral accompaniment lose a lot in the fact that the orchestral score by itself is not sufficiently colorful and engaging. Nevertheless, Chopin will remain our unparalleled bard, a unique master that no other nation possesses! Grottger, too, did not paint large paintings, he did not have a feeling for colors, but with his pencil he created such masterpieces that he will remain the great Grottger forever.[10] Chopin's music did not give rise to a school; past experience has suggested that all the blind imitators who were devoted completely to the cult of Chopin, not only as creators but also as performers, have fallen prey to a manner of unwelcome sentimentality. They have forgotten that the master, despite his originality, despite the life he led, could not protect himself from a certain morbid melancholy, and that he could not see the truth clearly and express it in a healthy fashion. Whoever wants to understand Chopin and whoever wants to draw from his treasure chest, has to start learning a more healthy classical music. After such a preparation the disciple could approach with respect, and then begin to research these jewels. This will protect him from falling prey to a **manner**. While I highly respect Wagner as a composer, I am amazed by his greatness, but I am not delighted at all with the **Wagnerians.** An exclusive and exaggerated cult has to have a harmful effect on the fanatical devotees.

For Poles, the epoch of Romanticism begins in poetry with Mickiewicz, and in music with Chopin. He has to be called the turning point of a new era.

Translated by Małgorzata Szyszkowska and Brian Harlan

---

[10]Artur Grottger (1837-1867) is a Polish painter widely recognized for his expressive cycles of drawings on the themes of the war and the tragedy of the January Uprising (1863); see Tadeusz Dobrowolski, *Malarstwo Polskie* [Polish Painting] (Wrocław: Zakład Narodowy im. Ossolińskich, 1989), 118.

The Essence of Chopin's Works

by Zygmunt Noskowski[1]

The works of a genius have one highly significant characteristic: their meaning and value can be appreciated only by later
generations, and the greatness both of these works and their creators
increases in proportion to the distance from the epoch during which
a given master lived and was active.

More than 90 years have passed since the birth and 50 years
since the premature death of Fryderyk Chopin; in other words, it has
been half a century since the lyre of this incomparable singer of our
fields and meadows has become silent. Although the worship of
Chopin increases every year, it was not until now that the very
essence of his music has been adequately examined and brought to
light for the benefit of the wider circles of the master's admirers.
This is the case despite several excellent biographies (one of which,
written in England by Niecks,[2] could be called exemplary) and
despite the highly favorable contemporaneous judgment of Schumann[3] and a magnificent work by Franz Liszt.[4]

---

[1]Noskowski's article of 1899 was originally published as "Istota utworów
Chopina" (Warsaw: Saturnin Sikorski, 1902).   This translation by Maja
Trochimczyk and Anne Desler is based on the version included in Mieczysław
Tomaszewski, ed. *Kompozytorzy polscy o Chopinie: Antologia* [Polish com-
posers about Chopin: An anthology] (Kraków: PWM, 1980), 68-89. [This and
the majority of subsequent notes are by the editor unless otherwise indicated.]

[2]Frederick Niecks, *Frederick Chopin as a Man and Musician*, 2 vols. (London,
1888; reprint of a 1942 edition, New York: Vienna House, 1973).

[3]In the course of his abundant writings on music, Schumann deals extensively
with Chopin, interpreting his piano works in his peculiar fictitious way. In "An
Opus 2," Schumann discusses Chopin's *Variations on Là ci darem la mano,
Opus 2*. The "Report to Jeanquirit in Augsburg on the Editor's Last Art
Historian's Ball" contains comments on the *Bolero, Op. 19* and the Two
Polonaises, Op. 22. Schumann's opinion about Chopin's significance among
other great composers of h is time can be found in "Schubert, Mendelssohn, and
Chopin." In the collection of short essays entitled *The Museum*, Schumann deals
with the Twelve Études, Op. 25. Other works he reviews in newspaper articles,
essays, and letters include the following: Rondo à la Mazurka, Op. 21; the First
Piano Concerto in E minor, Op. 11; the Second Piano Concerto in F minor, Op.
21; the Variations for Piano on a Theme from *Ludovic* by Herold and Halévy, Op.

I believe, therefore, that one cannot celebrate the semi-centennial of Fryderyk Chopin's death in a more appropriate way than by reflecting on the creative output of his spirit, by searching for the essence of his inspiration, so different from what we encounter in other artists. I am not deluding myself, believing that I could say everything or that I could be able to treat this subject exhaustively in this short essay. I simply intend to make a beginning; therefore, managing to be equal to my task even to the least degree will be sufficient reward for my efforts.

Whoever intends to examine the essence of the oeuvre of our master needs to remind himself of the ways in which music has developed and what paths it has taken before it attained its present perfection. Music history teaches us that music as an art is a creation of recent times and that it is justly called the youngest of the fine arts. The reasons for such a late development are inherent in the nature of music, in its inborn features, namely that it is a direct reflection of the different states of the human soul, expressing these states by a means that is almost immaterial - sound. When we listen to singing, we are not at all interested in the anatomy of the throat or in the physiology of the vocal chords. We care equally little about the external shape of musical instruments - they are but tools. It matters little whether either a single artist performs or an entire orchestra, for our ear enjoys only what the artistry of the performers is able to produce with these tools; and the more the sound (that is

---

12; Two Nocturnes, Op. 27; Twenty-Four Preludes, Op. 28; Impromptu in A-flat Major, Op. 29; Four Mazurkas, Op. 30; Scherzo in B-flat Major, Op. 31; Mazurkas, Op. 33; Three Waltzes, Op. 34; Sonata in B-flat Minor, Op. 35; Two Nocturnes, Op. 37; Ballade in F Major, Op. 38; Waltz, Op. 42; Tarantelle, Op. 43; Concert Allegro, Op. 46; Ballade in A-flat Major, Op. 47; Two Nocturnes, Op. 48; Fantasy, Op. 49; Piano Trio in G Minor, Op. 8. Cf. *Robert Schumann's Gesammelte Schriften über Musik und Musiker* (Robert Schumann's complete writings on music and musicians), 5th ed, 2 vols., (Leipzig, 1914) and Herman Erler, ed., *Robert Schumanns Leben aus seinen Briefen*, 2 vols., (Berlin, 1886), as well as several collections and selections of Schumann's writings.

[4] Franz Liszt, *Frédéric Chopin.* Nicole Priollaud, ed., preface by Irena Poniatowska (Paris: Levi, 1990). Reedition of Liszt's text which appeared originally in the form of 17 articles in *La France musicale* (1852). English translation with an introduction by Edward N. Waters (New York: Vienna House, 1973). Please note that the entire second paragraph is one single sentence in the original. It has been broken up into several sentences for the sake of clarity .

created on an instrument or by the movement of vocal chords) flows from the soul, the more sincerity and internal power it has, the more strongly it talks to us and intensifies the emotions.

To a certain extent, music can be called an abstract art since matter or substance plays such a subordinate role in it; however, this abstractness has a different meaning in music than in philosophy, because musical thought ceases to be something detached and ephemeral as soon as it is given a proper form. It is this very form by means of which we remember the principal idea [of a musical work], in other words, the embodiment of the emotional essence; and therefore we nowadays attempt to express the particular principal idea in a comprehensible manner.

The latter is an achievement of more recent times. In the beginning of the emergence and during the early development of music, attention was paid especially to its external features, i.e., to the combinations of pitches and chords, to the good quality of sonorities, regardless of what these sonorities and chords could express. Those were the times of formalism: a formative and very necessary period in the development of art, but one that was deficient with regard to the distinctness of feelings and expression.

It was perhaps for this reason that in this initial stage so little attention was given to instrumental or "pure" music, i.e., music that is freed from its connection to the word, which continuously provided an object for the expression of musical thought. Musicians of the time could not do without this word because they did not possess the necessary spiritual independence - they were not even aware that such individuality could exist, and that it was the factor that distinguishes an artist from a mere producer of formalist works. Then they did not understand that music is more than an illustration of a secular or religious text, all-too-often a colorless illustration, a pale background deprived of the most beautiful feature in works of art: inspiration. Solely after a couple of centuries of this dry scholasticism, of this predilection for colorless combinations, of this turning in an unduly limited circle of consonant harmonies, music began to be freed from its narrow confines and the awakening of individualism was taken into account. It was, however, no earlier than in the 18th century (which witnessed the activity of great masters) that the final developments took place which then came to become the foundation of what was growing and increasing in power in the century under discussion.

The individuality of musical creators increased in proportion to the maturing of humankind. Simultaneously with the dawn of new ideas in social life, music was enriched with ever newer means of the expression of feelings. Haydn, filled with jovial humor and naiveté, made room for Mozart, who already knew how to pour sincere tears of sorrow, because, as he was suffering himself, he could perceive this suffering and express it in sound. However, only when humankind in its entirety was driven into new directions, when a struggle of rules with progress took place, did the great Beethoven appear. Only he could fight out these giant battles, wrestle for praise in his works, and it was he who, by propelling music onto new tracks, established its future direction for many years. A great symphonist and a profound thinker, Beethoven was undoubtedly one of the first enemies of the cold aesthetic principle *l'art pour l'art*. His quick mind and simmering temperament could not be satisfied with cool objectivity. Therefore he made the concept of "art for humankind" his own, and that is why all of humankind poured tears at his grave.

Simultaneously, during the period of Beethoven's most fertile activity, Chopin was born and from the very beginning his artistry (despite his exceptional individuality) entered the same path as the German master's and followed his ways, because our musician became a translator of the feelings and secrets of the human soul. He drowned his own pain in the universal suffering and for that reason his works became the property of the entire world as time passed. Chopin, gifted with boundless sensitivity, was able, with his subtle disposition, to ascend into ideal spheres, to superterrestial domains - he seemed to converse with the spirits, and from their country he drew his incomparable thoughts and inspirations. At the same time, however, he did not forget that he was a child of the earth. He remembered that he had emerged from a society of which he could express the feelings with ease, because they were part of his natural disposition and the result of everything that he experienced in his childhood, at which he looked with the eye of a true poet.

Today, it is beyond the slightest doubt that childhood and youthful impressions leave a mark that cannot be erased from the soul of an artist, in whose later works everything that sank into the soul early on in life and that found itself a sheltered nook at the bottom of the soul must necessarily resonate. Music as a pure and self-sufficient art is closer to a state of the ideal than its sister arts because it is its nature to express feelings and thoughts, i.e., concepts that are indefinite and not-concrete, and also because it creates expressions by means of that of the senses which is the least - let me put it this way - sensual. Through the sense of hearing, the impression directly enters the soul, without seeking assistance from imagination or reason. There is no need for an intermediary path; therefore, none other of the fine arts demands such treasures of sincerity as music.

Schiller said: "The fine arts breathe life; from a poet I demand thought, but the soul is expressed only by Polyhymnia."[5] The musical creator is able to capture the listener and has the power to stir his soul with his emotions only to the extent to which he draws his inspiration from the depth of his soul. It happens, however, - and quite often for that matter, that a trickster trades music for gold, that he deludes the crowd with deceitful brilliance, and that his works temporarily gain more recognition and attention than the inspired creations of a true genius. The history of music abounds with such cases. Thus, in his time, Salieri overshadowed Mozart. Although there was respectful recognition for Beethoven, he was not understood, because the contemporaneous and immediately following generations found a more accessible composer in Onslow, who, however, is almost forgotten today.[6]

Chopin was surrounded by a small circle of true admirers, but the general public could not appreciate him and in concerts virtuoso pianists preferred to show off with pieces by Thalberg or Henryk Herz.[7] Similarly, during Moniuszko's life, no one dared call him a great composer in public, although this honorable appellation is sometimes given to an artist of lesser rank who happens to be

---

[5]Johann Christoph Friedrich von Schiller (1759-1805), German Romantic poet and playwright. The source of the quotation has not been located.

[6]George Onslow (1784-1852) was an English composer active in France, the author of a large number of chamber pieces in an eclectic style.

[7]Sigismund Thalberg (1812-1871) and Henri Herz (1803-1888) were Chopin's contemporaries and well-known virtuoso pianists and composers.

fashionable at a particular moment.[8]

Therefore, if a genius-musician reflects his own soul in his pieces, and if in this soul treasures lie accumulated that dazzle when they are brought to the light, if in these spiritual treasures new thoughts appear, new trends and broadly-defined directions, then one should not be surprised that a just evaluation does not take place immediately, but rather in proportion to the measure in which the creations of the genius enter the human souls. Franz Liszt understood this perfectly, when he wrote at the beginning of his book on Chopin: "we doubt that the time has yet come for him . . . to hold the high position of universal regard that the future likely reserves as his." [9] Since it has been proven so often that one is not necessarily a prophet in one's own city, does it not happen also that those, who with prophetic intuition precede the passage of their own times with their works, are not always recognized by their contemporaries as priests of the truth?[10]

These words themselves, which were uttered years ago, I could boldly call prophetic - they were confirmed completely in reference to Chopin, whose importance in the temple of art begins to increase only now, after he was, for years and years, greatly diminished by being reckoned among the composers of character pieces for piano. Moreover, the emotions poured into his music were misunderstood as sentimentality, elegance in form was referred to as "salon quality," and the national character of the mazurkas was not recognized.

Yet using only one single musical tool in the expression of inspiration could not possibly decrease the value and general significance of an art work. For this reason, there is no need to deal

---

[8]Stanisław Moniuszko (1826-1872) was a Polish composer best known for his operas (he was considered the father of the national opera, with *Halka* and *The Haunted Manor*), and numerous and popular songs (*Śpiewnik Domowy*). He also composed symphonic and choral music.

[9]Liszt, *Frédéric Chopin*. This quotation is from a reprinted version (New York: Vienna House, 1973), p. 29.

[10]Here, Noskowski paraphrases Liszt, adding some of his own thoughts. The quotation in Liszt's *Frédéric Chopin* reads: "It has often been proven, *no man is a prophet in his own land,* is it not also known that those prophets, men who sense the future and announce it by their work, are not acknowledged as such in their own age?" (p. 29).

with this matter of secondary importance. Chopin loved the piano and made it an interpreter of his thoughts. Nowadays the piano recital cannot exist without Chopin's music and a pianist whose repertory does not include the works of the master exposes himself to ridicule. Now that the performance of piano music is so wide-spread and popular, people are no longer surprised by the exceptional quality of Chopin's music, and it fills us Poles with pride when we contemplate how the master, born at the waves of the Utrata river, was instrumental in the enormous development of piano playing, and that his name resounds everywhere to our glory.

There are different opinions about the nature of the predominant feeling which permeates the works of our master. In this respect, one encounters many views that are contradictory or, even worse, false. Some call that feeling sentimentality, others melancholy, still others tearfulness, and some finally call it an elegiac quality. Yet it is universally known that Chopin himself gave the most accurate description of the mood in which inspiration came to him most often - the expression *żałość* [sorrow].[11] It is also common knowledge that he liked to repeat this word at every occasion, as though he wished to burn into his soul this feeling which is not known to foreign peoples (like the word itself which is difficult, or even impossible, to translate into other languages).

Żałość [sorrow] is neither longing nor pain [*boleść*], neither pensiveness [*zaduma*], nor complaint [*skarga*]. It is different from melancholy and completely different from an elegiac quality. This feeling of sorrow may be discerned in almost all of Chopin's melodies, both in minor and in major; it is the main thread of his thought, and it is what makes him original in his ideas.

The sorrow permeating Chopin's works is far from som-berness and pessimism. The master longs, laments and pours out his tears; in moments of pain he surrenders to despair, painting it with progressions of unusual, sometimes sharply dissonant, chords, but even in the moment of the greatest doubt he does not utter complaint or blasphemy. Thanks to this, he does not evoke such feelings in others, feelings that are neither beneficial nor honorable for humankind. At times, however, one notices an undue softness or

---

[11]The word *żałość* [sorrow] is closely related to *żal* which denotes a confluence of negative feelings including sorrow, regret, sadness, and pity.

hears a boyish whimpering instead of manly mourning; but such was Chopin's disposition, such were his intrinsic characteristics which can neither be eliminated nor changed. The extreme sensitivity and the great extent of the subtlety of his emotional life are important features of our master. His path of life, i.e., his mental and physical suffering still amplified this sensitivity, which necessarily had to be reflected in his works.

Whatever we call the mood in Chopin's works, be it "elegiac quality," "longing," or "sorrowfulness," it is of primary importance to state that, above all, the purest poetry prevails in them and that the breath of this poetry captures the hearts in a way that cannot be described with words. If I used the expression "the purest poetry," I did not do so accidentally, but after careful consideration and reflection, and I wish to especially emphasize the quality of "purity" of the poetry. Poetry in its purest form resides in nature of which it is the reflection; it is a crystal-clear spring which has its purest source in the bosom of nature, the mistress of all the arts and all artists.

The more sensitive the "conjurer"[12] is to the wonders surrounding him, the more willingly he imbibes these wonders with his soul and heart, thus enriching the treasure chest of his imagination with the impressions drawn from these marvels, the more sensitive he is, the stronger will his connection to nature be expressed in the creations of his spirit and the more prominent will be the freshness of his inspiration. And this purity and freshness are so evident in art works that even those who have had little experience with art are able to feel them clearly and to distinguish them easily from everything which, especially more recently, has become so widespread in music, i.e., the attempt to convert the arts themselves into artificiality. In order to explain the previous sentence and to make it more understandable, I will allow myself to illustrate it with an example from the world of plants. We all know flowers that grow in the wild and that delight us with their manifold shapes as well as with their fragrances. Take, for instance, a violet or a lily-of-the-valley - how much delight do these tiny flowers with their modest appearance give in springtime, how many dreams do they bring of the meadows in which they grew.

---

[12]The Polish term "sztukmistrz" means literally "magician" or "trickster."

The art of gardening has taken these tiny creatures to the greenhouse and owing to expert breeding, both the violet and the lily-of-the-valley have beautified their dresses and look more lovely; at the same time, their fragrances, too, have become more intense. However, in wintertime, when we see these flowers growing behind the glass of a hothouse, how different is our delight from that which we experience in our hearts at the sight of a meadow covered with flowers growing at the bosom of nature under the life-giving rays of the sun. If we do already sense a certain artificiality in the so-called "improvement" or "perfection" of nature, what then could happen once the human hand tries to make something mimicking a flower, attempting to endow its products with the features of the real thing by means of piecing together multicolored materials? When artificiality tries to replace nature it will deceive the eye for a moment, but it cannot, even remotely, awaken in us the feelings that we experience seeing a live flower. For a rather long period of time now, something similar has been happening to music - namely since the emergence of the so-called "salon music."

When was it born and who was its father...? It is impossible to obtain a satisfactory answer to these questions, as no one is able to decree when and how salon life itself emerged, a life filled with exaggeration and banality, a life that is a distortion of what took place in the famous salons of the past in which the most eminent representatives of the sciences and the arts used to gather. In places where, instead of having conversations about serious matters of importance, people exchange shallow opinions and preoccupy themselves with everyday concerns, where instead of expressions of [genuine] joy over a manifestation of great creativity, everything is dealt with by means of empty compliments, there is no room for good music. The sonata, quartet, and classical aria, as well as free compositions [i.e. free in terms of form but still filled with content], could not gain adequate recognition in this sterile environment, and therefore they had to give way to the various *galanteries* with pretentious titles and decorative covers. The salons became populated with the miscellaneous serenades, nocturnes, *melancholies*, rains of pearls, bouquets of melodies, and finally waltzes and mazurkas, the latter with the essential addition "de salon." These pieces were written by a different kind of musician at times even gifted, but brought up on the cobblestones of the city, and therefore deprived of the impression that can only be found in the embrace of nature. Where is one to look for poetry in the middle of the noise of the streets, within a life that is limited by the narrow confines of working for one's daily bread, in the never-ending struggle for - most often momentary and fleeting - success, in the strife for fame or for a short-lived glory?

Urban life, ordinary and Philistine as it is, kills art and brings forth artificiality of the kind I have mentioned earlier. Salon pieces as a result of such life may therefore be compared with greenhouse flowers, or even worse, with the products of a milliner, i.e., with artificial roses, violets, or lilies-of-the-valley. The emergence of Chopin in this world necessarily had to incite contrary opinions and reactions, expressing bewilderment at the truly different, when the artist was seen entering the arena with nocturnes, waltzes, and mazurkas, or in other words, with the types of works that are also considered salon pieces.

What happened to Chopin is what frequently happens in similar cases too: musicians that considered themselves authorities, judged him by the titles of his works, without giving our master's ideas any in-depth consideration. For them, Chopin was nothing more than a salon composer. His sterner critics even called him a dilettante modulating in an amateurish fashion without much knowledge of harmony.

And how was he received in the salons...? It is there where he was truly misunderstood. The artist brought a strong disappointment to the salon circles, because when listening to his nocturnes and mazurkas one could not remain thoughtless and indifferent, one could not continue quietly to digest a tasty dinner, as one easily can to the sounds of a *Rêverie* or of the *Virgin's Prayer* [*La Prière d'une vierge*].[13]

Chopin entered the salons holding a bouquet of wild flowers in his hands, he brought a breeze of fresh air, unknown to that atmosphere of exotic fragrances. The mere novelty and direction of his ideas and his soaring above transitory ordinariness, in other words, the very two properties that were the least welcome in a

---

[13]Popular salon piece composed in 1856 by Tekla Bądarzewska (1834-1861). It is commonly used a symbol of musical Kitsch - issued in thousands of copies by 80 publishers around the world.

world of appearances and triteness, introduced and recommended him to little benefit. This is the very reason why Chopin's works were seldom used as display pieces by contemporary pianists. However, this happened also because the majority of the concerts from this period bears a sad testimony to public taste. The *virtuosi* of the first half of the century included in their programs pieces that were worthless and banal, sterile in both their contents and their presentation. If an artist in our times dared to play something similar in public, he would expose himself to ridicule not only from the critics but even from the most patient listeners.

From this, despite the positivistic principles of the eminent Taine[14], it is obvious that Chopin's creations are not for his contemporaries but that he lived before his time, and only future generations could evaluate him adequately and offer him worship; the reason for this delay in paying him homage was the course of times - fashions had to fall and to be outlived in order to make room for newer and more profound directions.

Today, almost no one denies that there are nationalistic distinctions in music - an idea with which even great musicians did not want concur in earlier times. On the same token, no one acts surprised at the notion that not only dance rhythms, but also the general mood which reflects the spiritual properties of any given people, gives music a national flavor. That this is indeed so, we owe to the genius of Chopin who gathered his thoughts and melodies from our meadows, fields, and forests. They sang hymns to him and nurtured his poetic soul with tunes full of simplicity and unforced gracefulness. And this is why the essence of our master's very being lies in his impressions from childhood and early youth. Nature was his first mistress; her brilliance and beauty entranced him and left

---

[14]Hyppolyte Taine (1828-1893) is the author of *La philosophie de l'art*, a positivistic work that emphasizes the dependence of art on race, epoch, and environment. The book had 14 editions and was translated into several languages. English translation by John Durand, *The Philosophy of Art* (New York: Holt & Williams, 1873). Henryk Markiewicz studied the reception of his thoughts in Poland in "Les Avatars polonais de l'esthetique de Taine" in *Litteratures sans frontieres: Melanges offerts à Jean Perus,* Jacques Gaucheron and Philippe Ozouf, eds. (Clermont-Ferrand, France: Adosa, 1991), 121-28. For a study of Taine's literary criticism see Jean-Thomas Nordmann, *Taine et la critique scientifique* (Paris: Presses Universitaires de France, 1992).

their traces deep in the soul of this great artist, traces that could not be removed by such a long distance of time and space.

Chopin's melodies are poetic transformations of the sights that the master absorbed in his youth; they are their lucid reflections. From many a mazurka one can guess the color and light filling a landscape that the master saw with the eyes of his soul while writing his beautiful poem. Not only does the choice of a particular key alone already give us an approximate idea of the mood of the soul of our artist, but it also allows us to feel the overall color - let me even say - the "season" during which the ideal image, dreamed of by Chopin, unfolds itself.

Does the famous Mazurka in B-flat Minor, Op. 24,[15] No. 4 not evoke the beginning of fall, this all-pervading melancholy mood, result of the increasingly paler rays of the September sun? The leaves on the trees begin to turn red, the plains grow gray and the fields become empty; all foretells the imminent demise of nature. And when finally, at the end of the mazurka, the melody in B-flat major resounds, does one not, inevitably without a conscious effort, imagine a shepherd playing a farewell song to summer on his pipe?

How different is the sorrow gushing out in the Mazurka in C-sharp Minor, Op.41, No.1! The key itself captivates us and makes us dream of winter, and the beginning of the melody, in which the lowered supertonic (from D-sharp to D) is reiterated obstinately, seems to paint not only the somber sight of the snow-covered earth with clouds above, but simultaneously it expresses a longing for spring and its green meadows. The sudden change of mood from minor to major is like a surge of hope that God's little sun will return to revive the petrified nature. Before this may come true, however, the ending of the mazurka again recalls the presence [of winter] - the sorrow returns and the soul is immersed in gloomy reflections … about snow and ice.

When I discussed above the feeling of a certain color in connection with a certain key, I did not talk about a paradox, because musicians have agreed for a long time that every tonality has an analogous color in painting and that the musical creator, in skillfully combining these tonalities works on the same effect as an eminent painter who selects harmonizing hues. A painter, by com-

---

[15]Noskowski polonizes the word *opus* into "work" (i.e., *dzieło*) in Chopin's title.

posing an image in a certain palette of colors, adjusts the painting to the subject that he intends to portray; only then does a painting make an impression when the palette of colors is in complete agreement with its content. Similarly a musician only reaches the intended goal when the tonalities chosen are well suited to the idea, content, and mood of the piece.

For this reason, musical creators usually utilize the strong keys of E-flat major and B-flat major for expressing triumph or heroism, while A-flat, D-flat, and G-flat only appear in their works for moments of dreaming or the delight of love. A pastoral mood is best represented with F and G major, longing and sorrow are best captured with G and F-sharp minor, and complaint with A minor.

The last few remarks are only very general and superficial - this subject demands a separate study, and I only included these observations because I wanted to prove Chopin's infinite sensitivity to the use of keys that are adequate to his marvelous ideas. In this respect, i.e., as a painter, Chopin stands on a par with Mickiewicz, who represents even small scenes with such distinctiveness that one can see everything as though it were real.[16] The feature of Chopin's music most closely related to this accuracy of coloring by means of tonality is the rhythm of the melody, which is full of subtleties and differentiation and always applied to perfection in every piece.

Chopin, who had the opportunity to hear the *mazur*, *kujawiak*, and *oberek* in various areas of the country, intuitively grasped and varied their rhythms. Close examination of these three dances reveals many fundamental differences, however akin they may seem in terms of their rhythmic patterns and apparent similarities. I explored this subject years ago in an essay,[17] which, however, went largely unnoticed at the time, so that I will have to discuss this matter right now, because learning about the rhythmic properties of our dances will make Chopin's importance even more evident. Many a composer has erroneous ideas about our dances and believes with certainty that it suffices to write a lively melody

---

[16]Adam Mickiewicz (1798-1855), a romantic poet and playwright, belongs to a group of Poland's three most important poets of the 19th century (with Zygmunt Krasiński and Juliusz Słowacki).

[17]Zygmunt Noskowski, "O tańcach polskich" [About Polish dances], *Echo muzyczne i teatralne*, 1878.

in triple meter and baptize it *oberek* or *mazur* to gain the title of a "national" artist.[18]   And how often one hears the rhythms of Schubert's *Ländlers* in these so-called mazurkas!

The central difference between our three dances in triple meter lies not only in the tempo but also, and perhaps most importantly, in the relationships between accents, i.e., the stresses [of the beats].

The *mazur*, born on the Mazovian plains, abounds with verve and exuberance and rhythmic emphases occur in a capricious and whimsical fashion as if to contradict the monotony of the landscape. At one time, the first beat in a measure is stronger, then, unexpectedly, the emphasis is stronger on the second or third beat; finally, we sometimes encounter two accents in one measure, always in a free fashion, on beats one and three, one and two, or on two and three, and occasionally there even are accents on all three beats. In the last-mentioned case, it sounds like three hearty foot stomps which can often be observed during a moment of great excitement during the dance.

The tempo of the *mazur* should be moderately fast; despite its exuberance, there is a certain seriousness to the dance, and it is impossible to rush when accenting the clicking of the heels, because one would loose track of the beat. However, in recent years, the *mazur* began to be danced so quickly that the impetuousness was irrevocably lost, and only some jumping and mincing steps remained that excite no more than a smile of pity and contempt.

The characteristics of the *kujawiak* are completely different: it is slower in tempo and the accents are distributed more evenly. The division into four-measure phrases is very easily recognizable and the strongest emphasis can be found in every fourth measure on the first, second, or third beat, depending on the particular melody. As if in opposition to the lively *mazur*, the mood in the *kujawiak* is lyrical, often even sorrowful and sad [*smętny i żałosny*]. On the sensitive and tender soul of Chopin this tenderness [*rzewność*], poured out in *Kujawy* melodies, must have had an unparalleled impression, and its unusual richness could dazzle him without doubt, if only in terms of quantity. One can count thousands of *kujawiaks*, and they are full of charm, all very different in terms of intervallic

---

[18]Literally: "swojski" - i.e., "ours" or "local."

relationships as well as rhythms. This is the dance that had the greatest influence on Chopin's music, and even though the master called many of his marvelous poems mazurkas, one has to confess that three quarters of them are really *kujawiaks*, as is apparent from their mood, rhythms and accents.

Of the three dances the most easily distinguishable is the *oberek* with its extremely fast tempo and completely regular accents which occur on the last beat of every second measure. This dance then consists of a series of two-measure fragments (with the exception of one exceedingly famous *oberek* which begins with four fragments of three measures and only then changes into the usual division).

Therefore, the content of several of Chopin's mazurkas consists of three quintessentially different dances, and regardless of what they really are, they are named the same, proving that the master without knowing the distinctions [between the three dances] combined all of their different rhythms in one piece. The Mazurka in F Major, Op. 68, No. 3 is a *mazur* throughout the first two sections, and undoubtedly an *oberek* in the trio. The Kujawiak in D Major, Op. 33, No. 2 changes to *mazur* rhythms in the central sections.[19] It is quite easy to find such rhythmic differences in many other mazurkas; I only quoted the best known and most characteristic examples.

However, this combining of dances could also be and most certainly was, a faithful reflection of the lives of the people, who liked frequent changes in singing and dance and usually moved from a *mazur* to an *oberek*. In the Kujawy region this succession of dances even had a usual order: first a "walking dance," then a faster one, i.e., the *kujawiak* itself, and finally, at the end, an *odsibka*, i.e, an *oberek*.[20]

In Chopin's memory and imagination the individual memories of real folk scenes blended together in one whole, and by

---

[19]Chopin called this work a mazurka; the change of the title comes from Noskowski.

[20] "Walking dance" [*chodzony*] is a folk version of the polonaise. At the end of the sentence Noskowski uses a rare folk term in Mazovian dialect that is not typically encountered in ethnomusicological literature; "odsibka" comes from "od siebie," i.e., "from self."

calling all these dances the generic name of the mazurka, our great song-master created a new artistic form with new harmonic and melodic patterns. In this domain he will remain the model forever as is the case of the polonaise in the composition of which he is unsurpassed: he expanded the dimensions and introduced heroic rhythms into this noble dance.

The circumstance however, that the master, endowed with such sensitivity for folk music, dealt so little with the *krakowiak* deserves some consideration. I do not think that he did not like the *krakowiak* rhythms, but rather that he did not know very many melodies, because he lived in Mazowsze and Kujawy throughout his youth and never visited the Kraków area for an extended period of time, so that he did not have an opportunity to listen to these melodies at their source. In addition, because of the contemporary means of transportation, trips were inconvenient and difficult; these same circumstances were the reason that the *krakowiak* was disseminated but little in other regions. Only one very popular tune was known everywhere, and in Kujawy, too, the *krakowiak* "Leć głosie, po rosie" [Fly, voice, over the dew] was sung; in this song, however, only some of the rhythmic features of the dance are touched upon, but the whole dance is not fully represented. Only much later, thanks to the unquenched zeal of Oskar Kolberg, could people learn about the unusual abundance of Kraków melodies.[21] Their rise in popularity in Warsaw was aided by Rajczak,[22] a trumpet virtuoso who is, for the most part, forgotten today.

Since Chopin did not know the *krakowiak* well enough, he could not immortalize this dance in his music as he had done with other dances in triple meter. The finale of the Piano Concerto in E Minor is not a *krakowiak* because the melodies in this otherwise enchanting piece do not possess the prominent syncopations on the second eighth-note, which provides the [rhythmic] pulse which distinguishes the *krakowiak* from the Galician dances as well as from the *csardas* and the polka, the latter of which our peasants dance in the whole country. Be this as it may, what Chopin con-

---

[21]Oskar Kolberg, *Dzieła Wszystkie* [Complete works], vols. 5-8, *Krakowskie* (Wrocław: Polskie Towarzystwo Ludoznawcze, 1962).

[22]Andrzej Rajczak (1808-1861), also composer of popular music, *mazurs*, and *krakowiaks*, was active in Warsaw in the 1850s and 1860s.

tributed in other dances is such a faithful reflection of our character, such a powerful "poeticization" of the rhythms of folk music that only this small portion of his achievements is already perfectly sufficient to immortalize the great master's fame.

Nonetheless, we should not forget that in the works of Chopin, beside the rhythmic characteristics yet another important feature was revealed: the distinct mood, representative only of our people. If we take, for instance, the Impromptu in F-sharp Major, already in the first couple of measures we get the impression that the master gathered this melody in the green fields, like a bee gathers nectar from a flower, such are the fragrances and the freshness that it breathes. It bears some similarity to a certain shepherd's song that I heard sung in Kurpie.

For a long time I was thinking of this marvelous poem under the name "Sunday in a village;" Józef Chełmoński's wonderful painting by the same title which I saw later on, strengthened my conviction, so that I found the courage to call this *Impromptu* by its accurate [poetic] name.

Let us imagine a beautiful summer morning: the rays of sunshine bathe the fields that are covered with newly ripened wheat, gently swaying under a slight breeze. All of this can be seen in the sounds of this captivating melody; one can also feel the solemn mood underlying the whole scene. Suddenly, the master modulates to D major, and with the mighty octaves in the bass he seems to imitate the voices of church bells calling to the service, and, in time, when these low sonorities subside and the first thought returns, we can feel that something is developing in the airy figurations, like the mild stroking of the gentle wind of the wheat fields. Nature in its entirety is praying in this moment, the ears of wheat bow down to worship God's majesty, the holiday sentiment pervades everything, and the last chords, carefully tuned to the scene, conclude this musical image in a wonderful way.

The mood in such profound pieces as the Ballade in G Minor, where there is nothing even close to the kind of rhythms that might suggest national subjects, is very different. Here we enter into the domain of pure feeling outpoured in these sublime works, we feel an intimacy that is closely familiar to us and that provides the overall sentiment of the ballade, disturbed only in the middle section by a passionate outburst.

However, in the course of this poem as well as in the two other Ballades in F major and in F minor, we discover still more elements that move us profoundly, besides the mood which is reflective of our spirit. As in poetry, a ballade narrates specific events, usually with a tragic ending; Chopin too, as if with living words, unfolds stories that are undoubtedly filled with magnificent things and end in sorrow, giving listeners the freedom to find their own explanation of the content according to their tastes and the state of their souls. In every one of these ballades, one can sense the gradual development of action until finally the catastrophe strikes, and afterwards all is dissolved in pain and longing.

Only the Ballade in A-flat Major differs from her sisters in mood and spirit because its overall scenery and general features are not ours. Chopin's contemporaries and acquaintances claimed that this work tells the story of the Lorelei, which seems plausible to one who listens to its wonderful melody, full of gracefulness with its gentle rocking motion, its seductiveness and charm.... The singing of the magic maiden could have sounded like this, when she was sitting high above the Rhine river, awaiting a careless sailor who, seduced by the deceiver's song, would die in the treacherous waves of the river. We are confirmed in this conviction by the whole de-velopment of the ballade, by the growing anxious tension, by the increase in speed of the left-hand figurations, by the unusual turn to the sinister key of C-sharp minor, and finally by the closing *fortissimo*, expressing as it were, the witch's triumphant cry after luring the hapless victim into the deadly abyss. Chopin's ballades, in terms of idea and form, create a completely new form of music that was not known until then, and for this reason as well as because of the vastness of the dimensions of these works and the unusual diversity with regard to the proportions between individual phrases and sections, I consider them to be the most complete and most self-sufficient component of the master's oeuvre. That this statement is not unduly bold is easily proved: it suffices to analyze every one of Chopin's ballades in order to arrive at the conviction that the form of each is different, the sequence of its parts distinct, and the thematical development is particular [to each composition].

In the other large-scale works, e.g., the sonatas, scherzi and polonaises, Chopin adhered to traditional forms, only changing them on his own once in a while. But again, we are less interested in the external features than in the exceedingly rich contents, i.e., the depth of the melodic and harmonic ideas. It is this internal aspect that makes these works completely new and fills them with individuality. It would exceed the scope of this essay to discuss every single one of these compositions individually, although each of them deserves a separate analysis. I will only call your attention to the Sonata in B- flat Minor with regard to what I said earlier about the colors of certain keys. This sonata is a great autumn poem; one can perceive or guess events and images in it of the kind that could take place only in this season brimming with sorrow. Does not the brief finale, consisting of expansive and swiftly-moving scalar figures, represent the blasting wind that shakes the last remnants of reddish leaves from the trees onto the tombs? Are not the last two movements of the sonata two scenes cast in gloomy shades, for a depiction of which the key of B-flat minor is so very suitable?

While touching upon no more than the most outstanding moments of Chopin's creativity, I need to mention those of his poems that are somewhat smaller in dimension but no less profound and intense in terms of content, works which the master, overly modestly, called etudes. Indeed, these pieces do serve the purpose of developing a pianist's technique; however, while in the case of many other composers the development of technique is the entire goal, with Chopin it only serves as an opportunity to express marvelous musical ideas. These etudes remain etudes, but their purpose is - let me put it this way - the spiritualization of the fingers, the transformation [of the pianist's hands] into tools not just suitable for perfectly performing the technical aspects of any given composition, but also for expressing its essence, which abounds with poetic ideas and the inspiration that Chopin poured into all his works and which he always drew primarily from Polish nature. This nature was continually before the eyes of his soul; he idealized it in his imagination and painted its wonders by means of sound.

Even when new sights and images appeared before his eyes, even when a visit to Mallorca offered him a series of impressions very different from those of his childhood, even then, I repeat, Chopin never stopped being himself, and he crystallized the whole power of his poetic genius in a series of short, but magnificent images, which together make one masterpiece with the general and simple label: Twenty-four Preludes.

Because of works like these, Chopin became great with small things, similarly to Meissonier.[23] The preludes crown his output and are unfailing reflections of what the splendid nature surrounding him on the island[24] had to offer him, for example the sounds of the waves of the Mediterranean, the shimmering of the leaves on the trees that are so unlike our willows and firs, or the drops of rain falling from the rooftop of the old monastery. But these impressions were transformed within our master's soul, they blended with his longing and sorrow and were transfigured into dreams about something beyond comprehension, about things past and irrevocably lost, dreams also about the kingdom which the master's soul was slowly approaching, foreboding his premature death.

Is the Prelude in C minor not a proof of this premonition...? These few measures filled with a series of solemn chords, do they not depict vividly a funeral procession, albeit not out of this world...? While listening to this piece it seems to us that we may see the opening gates of eternity. Among the images and poems filled with profound meaning, the Prelude in A major appears as a lost ray of sunlight, shining upon our meadows and fields that the master did not forget even among the miracles of the wonderful nature in the South.

My quick survey of several parts of Chopin's creative output is not capable of encompassing everything, but this was not the purpose of my undertaking. I did not intend to present a detailed consideration of the meaning and value of each and every work by this genius; instead, I wanted to grasp the whole of his musical activity, to discover the very essence contained in the works by this master and, finally, to reach the source from which sprang this series of inspired thoughts.

It is easy to conclude from my words where this source and essence have their true origin, because even the mood of Chopin's works proves to us beyond any doubt that he had drawn his inspiration from nature. Different images of nature have wrought themselves into the soul of the artist, who, after concentrating in

---

[23] Juste-Aurèle Meissonier (1695-1750), one of the co-creators of the French rococo.

[24] As is well known, the preludes were composed on Mallorca in 1839, or, they were at least finished there [author's note].

himself an array of such impressions, transformed them through the prism of his imagination, scattering about a rainbow of brilliance.

Chopin is a poet and a prophet of his country, and this is known to all; he became such through capturing and purifying the simple folk song, which, thanks to the genius of this artist, was dressed in magnificent robes and entered - as if a queen - the temple of art. This song was born on the bosom of nature and it remains nature's faithful reflection. In general, the mood of a folk song is in complete agreement with its surroundings; its character reflects not only the features of a given country, but also almost each one of its distinct regions.

A *tarantella* filled with wildness or a jumpy *saltarella*, and, in general, songs following the meter of six-eight, are a faithful reflection of the Neapolitan area, highlighted by the hot rays of a southern sun and breathed upon by the burning gusts of *sirocco*. Spanish melodies distinguish themselves with completely different features, though one cannot doubt their southern origin even for a moment. These songs are permeated with the fiery temperament of the tribe,[25] but besides that, they are saturated with poetry and often display a lyrical mood full of longing.

Let us now move to the north and compare songs from Scotland and from Scandinavia in order to convince ourselves to what extent the images of the countryside influence song types. Scottish melodies are filled with poetic swaying, they are tranquil and tender because this mountainous landscape has nothing in it that is hard or wild. In contrast, in Scandinavian melodies, in their rhythms and intervals, tenderness disappears to reveal all that may be found in the images and the general mood of this country. In these songs, we seem to hear sharp gusts of wind scattered upon the fjords and the naked rocks. The melodies are brisk and filled with energy; sometimes they give an impression of being carved in stone by a giant's hand.

Turning our attention to our home country, we notice in our songs a completely different background. A pastoral quality provides their basis, but that does not mean that the melodies of our people are to dissolve in soft melodic turns and that the only mood expressed in them is that of quiet satisfaction. Our pastoral quality

---

[25]Noskowski uses the term "tribe" to refer to the nation, i.e. Spanish people.

contains a variety of feelings, and every region has its own particular character from which the mood of the song arises. Though many of these songs are known everywhere, it still may be known from which area they originated.

On the undulating hills of the Kraków region, filled with a variety of shapes, the boisterous *krakoviak* came to being: each of its lively melodies, sometimes ascending, sometimes rapidly descending, is a faithful representation of the landscape. The Mazovian plains are the crib of the *mazur* and while this dance is free in the domain of rhythm, yet its flowing melody, developing in small, conjunct intervallic steps, well agrees with the surrounding nature.

The *kujawiak* has many similar features to the *mazur*, because the area of Kujawy also possesses many common characteristics with Mazovia. Yet the lyricism and tenderness that permeates the charming songs of the Kujawy area remains in close relationship to the images of nature, to the slightly misty vistas in which the shorter distance to the Baltic sea and its sharper winds may be distinguished. There are villages in Kujawy where it is always windy, even if the sun is shining and warming the air. Whoever knows the lullaby from this area, a lullaby which develops on the minor tonic chord with an added seventh, may surely hear in this song the noise of the northern wind and may feel that this lullaby could be created only in a region less abundant in fair and warm days.

In these areas Chopin spent most of the time during his childhood and youth; thus he had an opportunity to absorb all these characteristics of the songs and dances from these regions, and his genius, his bold and original talent, by raising above the conventional tastes of his contemporaries, was able to create a new art, to introduce in it new elements.[26]

The essence of Chopin's works lies in his ability to base his inspirations on the background of a folk motive. How much vividness, how much - if I may say so - historical and social necessity rests in it may be proved by the turn in this direction of many different nations who, during the past decades, have been able

---

[26]"Elements" - the term used in plural is *żywioły* meaning literally the elements of nature, i.e. wind, water, fire, etc.

to develop and distinguish their own music based on the same foundation. Chopin therefore, while ascending to the dignity of the premier master of his country, simultaneously became the model for other countries. In this phenomenon precisely resides his universal importance, in this is his glory that fills us with pride and joy at the thought - about which his immortal works continue to testify - that a mind so sublime, a spirit so unique and powerful belongs to us.

Translated by Maja Trochimczyk and Anne Desler

Example 1: First page of Noskowski's song "Na grób Chopina" [For the tomb of Chopin] to a poem of Maria Konopnicka. From *Trzy Pieśni,* Op. 76, No. 1. (Kraków: A. Piwarski i Ska, ca. 1900). Collection of the Polish Music Center, USC, Los Angeles.

Fryderyk Chopin

by Karol Szymanowski

How much we have written, spoken and thought about
Fryderyk Chopin![1] How many colorful, rhetorical wreaths have
been placed at his feet! Yet the questions surrounding his work still
remain unresolved. We are drowning in the depth of the issue, yet
we are still afraid to break the magic aura of the superhuman valor
which we characteristically ascribe to those from our past who, like
giant majestic statues, rise above the shoulders of their epoch.

Such reverence would have been worthy of admiration if it
had not been the cause of a very undesirable phenomenon. Rather
than leading to the heart of the great artist's mystery, the chronic
meandering along emotive and emphatic paths obscures the way,
leading instead into an often inexplicable conceptual labyrinth. The
inability to clearly grasp the objective essence of this aspect of
national creative activity remains a roadblock to the emergence in
our society of, what might be called a **national cultural awareness**.[2]

The anemic state of this "awareness"[3] is particularly pro-

---

[1]This is Szymanowski's first essay devoted to Fryderyk Chopin; it was drafted in
1921-1922, and completed it in February 1923. It first appeared in two issues,
(April and May-June) of the Warsaw monthly *Skamander* in 1923 (no.28, p.22-
27 and no.29/30, p.106-10). Reprinted in: Stanisław Golachowski, *Karol
Szymanowski o Fryderyku Chopinie* (Kraków: PWM, 1949); Teresa Chylińska,
ed., *Karol Szymanowski: Z pism* ,(Kraków: PWM, 1958); Mieczysław Tomaszewski, ed. *Kompozytorzy polscy o Chopinie,* (Kraków: PWM, 1959,
1964,1980). Fragments of the essay in English and German appeared in the
quarterly *Polish Music/Polnische Musik* no.3 (1977); this version trans. Maria
Pilatowicz from "Fryderyk Chopin," in Karol Szymanowski, *Pisma*, vol. 1, *Pisma
muzyczne* [Writings about music] Kornel Michałowski, ed. (Kraków: PWM,
1984), 89-103. [This and all subsequent notes prepared by the editor unless
otherwise indicated.]

[2]Bold font is used here to reflect Szymanowski's emphasis (marked by wide
spacing in Polish).

[3]The quotation marks come from Szymanowski; this is his second method of
emphasis used throughout the article. These marks have been preserved in the
English translation to reveal Szymanowski's choices of concepts and vocabulary.
Occasionally, the exact word and its English translation are inserted in the text

minent in the area of Polish music. The comprehensive theory of its evolution and the logic underlying the relationships between individual facts do not exist at all. The history of Polish music, especially of the 19th century, has not yet been written. At present it exists only as a chronological collection of biographies of its practitioners; as a more-or-less accurate analysis of each individual's achievement. Yet it lacks any conclusions concerning organic relationships and influences, or any discovery of dependencies-- it lacks any clear-cut, unambiguous, solid scheme. There seems to have been a general tacit agreement to keep silent about the fact (sad, as it may be, beyond expression) that the evolution of our music has taken place in a somewhat reverse fashion, *à rebours*, beginning at the unattainable heights of Chopin's genius and then gradually descending - step by step - into gray, somber valleys. . .

I boldly claim that it is a paradox that, to a large extent, the cause of this phenomenon is the uncritical, almost religious cult of Chopin as a **national hero**, which has prevented him from being truly understood as a great **Polish artist.**[4] As a result, the whole body of his priceless work has remained infertile, of value only to itself, as if on the margins of the subsequent developments in Polish music.

The work of a great artist never ceases to be an eternal source of a life-giving, creative power when (and only when) it occupies a precisely defined place (a place that it deserves) in the **national cultural awareness**, and if it is approached without sentimentalism.

* * *

It was an unusual, yet, immeasurably fruitful event in the history our culture when we "rediscovered" Juliusz Słowacki.[5]

---

in square brackets; all the expressions in such brackets are editorial additions.

[4]Here, as in many further passages, Szymanowski's sentence is extremely long and complicated. It has been divided into the two sentences forming this paragraph [translator's note].

[5]Juliusz Słowacki (1809-1849) was one of the three "prophets" [wieszcz], i.e the most important Polish poets of the romantic era - with Adam Mickiewicz and Zygmunt Krasiński. Słowacki's poetry is more difficult conceptually and lin-

There had never been any doubts as to his genius and greatness, but he did not descend from his lofty heights until the time of the *Young Poland* [Młoda Polska].[6] He suffered no loss of his greatness; however, from behind the exalted, tragic mask of the "prophet" [*wieszcz*], glittered the eyes of a "mortal man."[7] Suddenly - and most importantly - we beheld the face of an "artist", and we understood the marvelous mystery of his craft; his compositional *métier*; his magical artistry; his mindful, meticulous handiwork, persistently sculpting wondrous shapes from the raw substance of "language" [literally "słowo," i.e. "word"]. We were even able to recognize the rare moments when his hands, carefully bearing the unearthly weight of Beauty, trembled suddenly from the pain filling his heart.

At that moment the deep, utterly organic connection between Słowacki's verse and the birth of modern poetry in Poland became evident. From then on his work ceased to be exclusively a priceless relic, a lifeless memento of past greatness. It became something very much "alive," a mainspring and engine of new values, fresh new blood feeding the withered cerebral tissue. The rediscovery, this new "consciousness" of Juliusz Słowacki brought forth a new, and previously unknown, creative power, which pointed us in a new direction.

Unquestionably, the most crucial challenge for the future of *Young Poland* in music - a challenge which is nearly the *sine qua non* condition of its existence - is the analogous "rediscovery" of Fryderyk Chopin; the final unveiling of the mummy from the layers of emotional rhetoric accumulated over the centuries; the rational and practical realization of the possible paths leading to the

---

guistically than that of his colleagues, for this reason (as well as because of his tragically short life, of a span comparable to Chopin's), the recognition of his talent and his role in Polish literature was gradual.

[6]A group of progressive musicians formed at the beginning of the 20th century; they advocated a renewal of Polish music transforming it into a "modern" and "European" realm. The group included Karol Szymanowski, Mieczysław Karłowicz (1876-1909), Grzegorz Fitelberg (1879-1953), Ludomir Różycki (1884-1953), and Apolinary Szeluto (1884-1966). Cf. Stefan Jarociński, ed. *Polish Music* (Warszawa: PWN, Polish Scientific Publishers, 1965), 124-127.

[7]In this sentence and the continuation of the passage, quotation marks come from Szymanowski.

independence of Polish music, which **no one**, except for Chopin himself, wished or was able to follow.

Thus far Polish literature concerning Chopin - whether eulogistic, biographical, or even professional-musicological - was occasionally able to illuminate certain episodes of his life and work. Yet, none have been able to cast a sufficiently strong and constant light which would reveal his essence and capture the immutable, eternal quality of his work. Perhaps, one day, an ideal biographer and a creative critic of Chopin's work will materialize in the same, single person. While proceeding without fear along the path leading to the heart of the mystery of Chopin's great artistry, that person will ultimately be able to fuse in the flame of his zeal the greatest admiration of Chopin's work with the deepest understanding of Chopin's art yielding the stainless substance of true knowledge. **Today**, the path we should follow to understand the greatness of Chopin becomes ever more clear. And since these are our first steps on this path, it is quite understandable that they are very timid, indeed.

* * *

During discussions in "revolutionary" music circles, which by nature encompass hotly debated arguments against the music of the past, the question often arises which of "yesterday's" composers are truly worthy of their lofty pedestals? The answer which typically follows is a series of famous names which frequently varies except for two: Wolfgang Amadeus Mozart and Fryderyk Chopin. The simultaneous citing of the two names and their repeated juxtaposition side by side is extremely characteristic. It suggests that there exists an affinity between the work of the "classicist" Mozart and Chopin, the "romantic." Clearly, this link-age is not based only on a comparison of the magnitude of both the artists' individual talents; in spite of the fact that each talent is truly monumental. For many musicians, the "depth" of Beethoven or the "spontaneous power" of Wagner is a hundred-fold more convincing than the strangely balanced, and often aloof, music of Mozart. Perhaps the affinity between Mozart and Chopin originates from a much deeper, spiritual source. It likely stems from the most essential relationship between the artist and his creation, i.e. from the **manner** in which the raw material of music is transformed into an absolute work of art.

In this light, doubts arise concerning the extent to which the accepted, official labels of a "classical" or a "romantic" composer essentially correspond with reality. Is the dogmatic classification of creative individuals into a ready-made historical framework, and their subordination to the most general characteristics of a given historical period, sufficient to reveal the deepest nature of their work? These doubts are magnified by a second conclusion, resulting from such rigid categorization and selection of two terms only from the whole musical past: the "classical" and the "romantic." The two terms appear to be contrasted, in a seemingly polar opposition that articulates the ideological character of the respective historical periods. However, for the music being created **today**, both terms provide an essential and absolute value. The works of "classical" or "romantic" composers may serve either as signposts or as a solid bedrock upon which the development of contemporary music can firmly and securely rest; [I refer here to] the music which recently has begun to defiantly flourish beyond its official German homeland. Because today's music is growing as a protest against "Romanticism" (which particularly in German music reached its ultimate heights), it leads to the suspicion that it is not the peculiar brand of Chopin's "Romanticism" that makes him so close to us, but rather other qualities of his genius, undoubtedly these which make him akin to Mozart.[8]

Neither the somewhat distorting influence of historical perspective nor the deep disparities between artistic ideologies of various historical epochs have been able to eliminate the intimate connection which exists between certain creative personalities, and which is evident in the essential relationship of the artist and his

---

[8]Michałowski notes here that the manuscript contains another passage following this statement. In the deleted passage, Szymanowski discusses the apparent break of continuity in the development of contemporary music and the emergence of new trends and ideas that he compared to "flowers of a fragrance and color that has not been known earlier." He underscores the uniqueness of Mozart's talent by comparing him to a "lonely, slender tree bringing forth the most fragrant colors and the most colorful flowers in the whole kingdom of music." The "soil" for both Chopin and Mozart was the music of J. S. Bach (Szymanowski, "Fryderyk Chopin," op.cit., Michałowski's note 4, p. 99).

work. What sort of relationship existed between Mozart and his music? It is beyond doubt that the category of "depth" which was born in the age of German Romanticism and which anachronistically still wanders through the contemporary critical studies is now a worn-out, unintelligible symbol of works of dubious authenticity. This category cannot be justly applied to the art of Mozart.

His music, characterized by an abstruse, almost southern lightness and bathed in its own clear, absolute depth of formal perfection, still seems to be chiseled from a stainless and timeless metal. Apparently, Mozart's creative process takes place beyond the sphere of his direct, internal experience. Like Benvenuto Cellini,[9] who with infinite joy cast his Perseus or carved the golden chalice for his patron, the Pope, so has Mozart held his masterpieces in his hand and viewed them with eyes brightened by the joy of creation. His creations were always meticulously and critically crafted resulting in final, definite shapes, equally excellent whether the work was a symphony, the *Marriage of Figaro*, or only a trivial song.

Invariably, this somewhat "objective" approach by the artist to his work holds the secret to its perpetual excellence of form. A work of art, magically brought forth from a resistant lump of "matter" - expressing **nothing** else but itself - is an infinitely "plastic" and "positive" formation, "organized" according to its own internal logic, and thus "limited" in its perfectly harmonized dimensions. It exists independently, **beyond** the turbulent and ever-changing current of its creator's life.

Here lies the fundamental difference between Mozart's approach to his work and that of - say - his antithesis, Richard Wagner, whose unstoppable, ripping, and powerful onrush of emotion never allowed any definite form or given shape to solidify. Wagner exploded and destroyed and as a result produced art which is an eternal fiery flow. In a certain sense, his art cannot be considered "pure art" but may be defined as an objectified function of his truly titanic, yet, undeniably creative temperament.

---

[9]Benvenuto Cellini (1500-1571) was an Italian sculptor and creator of gold jewelry. "Perseus with the head of Medusa" is one of his best known sculptures, kept in Florence, Loggia dei Lanzi. The pope is probably Clemens VII, mentioned in Cellini's memoirs.

* * *

Fryderyk Chopin regarded Beethoven, the great loner, with respect but also with a certain uneasiness, an unambiguous reserve. He positively disliked Robert Schumann, an affectionate "perpetual youth" (*der ewige Jüngling* - in the words of Nietzsche) and treated him - how ungrateful! - in a clearly haughty and somewhat disdainful manner of a master. But Chopin admired and worshiped Mozart throughout his life.[10]

Chopin was the musical "futurist" of the Romantic period, who in his seemingly humble piano compositions had been laying the core foundations of the music still to come. Yet, he was almost horrified at Hector Berlioz pounding with romantic fury at the gates of great art, creating still more new, brilliant monstrosities. [In reaction to these romantic excesses] he conjured from the past an apparition of a graciously smiling "cherub" of music and placed him closest to his heart. There seemed to be a certain, mysterious understanding between Mozart and Chopin, as to what is the essence of music.

This "classical" passion of Chopin in the midst of the artistic atmosphere of Romanticism that surrounded him is both distinct and remarkable. Romanticism, in the sense of ideological coloring of the times, always served as a backdrop against which Chopin's psychological make-up was continually considered. Romanticism created this insurmountable, predetermined point of view, which has influenced all appraisals of Chopin and his work. It has given Chopin's persona a peculiar tinge, magnified still by the somber backdrop of Poland's national history. Until recently we were still unable to objectively account for the virtual explosion of Polish creative arts in the midst of the darkest period in Polish history. In the past, we had attempted to capture the essential, objective values of our art through the black, funereal shroud of national tragedy. Today, the reality of those times becomes increasingly clear and we can see Chopin's persona in a fresh, new light. By the same token the view of his relationship to his milieu

---

[10]He also worshiped Bach. However, it would not be possible to find two musicians whose outlooks differed in a most extreme fashion, but who would not agree with each other about this issue [Szymanowski's note].

should undergo a substantial modification. The essential value of his art seems to be much closer to us today than the entire era of Romanticism. Thus, during his lifetime he might have been more "isolated" and "misunderstood" than it now seems; he might also have been "less understanding" himself, and more bewildered by the feverish artistic atmosphere of Paris in those days. As is often the case in the snobbish circles of the great metropolis, he was probably more "fashionable" than "understood."

The "romantic" pathos of many of Chopin's compositions seems to be a reflection of a raging fire seen from the **outside**, an echo of a lament reaching us from a **distance**. Yet, the magic of his music was not in its **pathos.** Nonetheless, this very pathos was the source of the legends that grew around Chopin - a mysterious man, living in an enchanted circle of spiritual solitude. His **undeniable** loneliness, contradicting a seemingly busy social life and fashionable appearance of this *petit maître,* was incomprehensible even to Adam Mickiewicz.[11] The same pathos of Chopin's works became the source of tales about their "literary" origins, as the talkative elderly ladies - "students of the artist's students" - in empty, shallow chit-chat marred his works by attributing to them alien and banal content. There was talk of a portrayal of a "tavern scene" in one of the mazurkas, or of the appearance of "flying cavalry in winged armor" in the Polonaise in A major, or of Jankiel's cymbals[12] in *Polonaise-Fantasie*, or of the Etude in C minor as "revolutionary."

The fundamental characteristics of Chopin's attitude towards his own work acquires a particular significance when perceived against the background of his epoch and of its peculiar ideology of art. During this age of tremendous expansion of Western influence, the broadening of opportunities and the scope of life, including an uncommon explosion of cultural life, the creative man - the artist - became a central figure. He was an actor on the stage, playing his part in the drama of life, having a direct, normative influence upon the unfolding of the events in the whole

[11]The great Polish poet of the Romantic age (1798 -1855) contemporary of Chopin, who also lived in Paris at the time.

[12]Jankiel is a symbolic figure of the virtuoso musician (a Jewish cymbal-performer and a Polish patriot) from *Pan Tadeusz,* the pastoral epic by Adam Mickiewicz.

drama. However, the active social role of the artist bound [literally: "shackled"] him to the dramatic context of his own historical epoch, and he necessarily became the one who articulated the ideological content of the period. As never before, the artist became a typical representative of his epoch.[13] Thus pure art and its formal, objective value became secondary to the immediate, intense experience of life as reflected in the art; and this, despite the concept of metaphysical depths, was introduced to art from beyond its realm during this very period (Romanticism) in Germany. The artist was, in a manner of speaking, consumed on the stage of art and life while attempting - often in vain - to grapple in his work with the immensity of such existential content. How distant was the Ro-mantic art from the objective creation of finished art forms of the eighteenth century! How different it was from, for instance, the music of Mozart or even Bach (the latter's impenetrable pathos, though, somehow reaching the outer limits of reality).

The theatrical [literally "aktywno-aktorski" i.e. "active-actor's"] element in the make-up of the artist-creator is nowhere else more evident that in the compositions of Wagner, for whom music constituted only the means of expression. As a consequence of such an approach (and not because of its own inherent and externally theatrical nature), the work of art as a form in itself had to move to the background because of its author coming to the forefront as a living man and creator, to perform on the art scene his own existential-creative role of a protagonist. It is conceivable that such a capacity for the dramatization of one's own soul was Wagner's individual trait - indeed he was a genius in this respect! - yet, it also happened to most vividly reflect the relationship of the artist to his work that was characteristic of the Romantic Age in general. Chopin's music as a whole is entirely devoid of this theatrical element; it seems as if his psychic persona, *spirius movens*

---

[13]Szymanowski's theory that artists are "typical representatives" of modern times is indebted to the philosophy of art proposed by Hippolyte Adolphe Taine (1828-1893), often described as a "social Darwinist." Taine put forward an idea that each historical period and geographic-ecological location has its characteristic "representative man" who encapsulates in his psycho-physical being the main features of that epoch (all of his examples are male). See Taine, *Philosophie de l'art* (Paris: Hachette et cie, 1881, 3rd ed.). For a view of Szymanowski's dependance on Taine's ideas see the article by Zofia Helman in this volume.

of his creative will, has remained in the shadow of his music. Instead, his creation itself sparkles with a stunning light - a strange magic which makes its own worlds of beauty that have their independent existence. Chopin's music, liberated from all direct links to his psychic life (from which it emerged), reveals itself as a play of forms, pure and absolute; forms which in the invariable harmony of their individual elements give expression only to **themselves**.[14] His creative energy, free from any incidental connections, and his will to shape absolute forms, are what constitutes the characteristic "depth" of Chopin's music. The terms such as "depth" and "absolute" in this context are entirely unrelated to the recently fashionable aesthetic and metaphysical interpretation of music as the "means of expression." On the contrary - the characteristic "depth" of Chopin's compositions is a function of his concrete approach to the question of the so-called *métier*. The French, who usually formulate their critical and aesthetic ideas so clearly and concisely, often make use of this term. The mere introduction of the term "craft" into the realm of high art is an expression of a positivistic attitude and an indication of a healthy instinct. It is a statement of the fact that genuine quality of art lies in the craftsman's absolute control over his material. In the creative process the most important above all, is the **how** - to be much later followed by the **what.** No external elements introduced to the musical composition will ever be able to elevate its "spiritual value".... .

Here, the use of such solemn terms as "depth," "spiritual value," "absolute," etc., is not incidental, but premeditated. These words are found at almost every step in our critical ideas about music. During the last few decades our critical opinions about music were subject to evolution in a much lesser degree than the criticism of poetry or plastic arts. Our musical criticism, with a few rare exceptions, still relies upon the leading ideas borrowed from a distant past. The underlying cause of this might be the persistence of the Wagnerian paradigm - "music as the expression of. . ."[15]

---

[14]Literally "same siebie," i.e. "self by self."

[15]This expression reflects Wagner's use of music in his theory of drama; the expression is also a title of a book by Friedrich von Hausegger, *Music als Ausdruck* (1885). Hausegger's approach is usually construed as a polar

Today it is still troublesome for the emerging critical ideas about music to entirely dismiss the spellbinding influence of Wagner's powerful personality. The ambiguity of the "music as expression" paradigm may lead to numerous misunderstandings as to the definition of the absolute musical qualities of the composition, because it inherently downplays the importance of the structural and formal content of the work. Besides, the idea only "expressed" through the means of music might have enjoyed a wholly independent existence as an "idea" in and for itself, located beyond the realm of music. This is exactly how things were in Germany, in the 19th century. Under the guise of the mysterious unknown variable "x" placed in the musical equation, the external, "literary" content with religious, philosophical, historical, tragic, or any other elements, was thought to be found in the musical work, and was to determine the alleged "depth" or "spiritual value" of the given composition. Irrespective of the absolute value of this or another idea, which supposedly permeated the content of the musical work, such a critical approach attempted again to chain the work of art to the dramatic content of the historical epoch, and to trust its fate to the eternally shifting currents of reality. Contrary to the formal qualities of the musical work, the consideration of "music as expression" served only as a function of values which existed beyond the realm of music; music was only an idealized reflection of the fleeting reality.

Does not a great artist, instinctively following his deepest longings, aspire to create a solid, unmutable form which would transcend the eternally changeable current of life? Isn't the degree of intensity of his creative will expended to produce such a form, precisely the criterion for determining the quality of the work of art?

The separation of Chopin from the surrounding artistic atmosphere of the times helps to illuminate the fact that the "Romanticism" of his works does not exhaust their essential qualities. Thanks to his boundless creative energy and surprising objectivity when it came to the question of art, he was able to create

---

opposition to Hanslick's formalism. For an explanation of this theory in English see Friedrich von Hausegger, "A Popular Discussion of Music as Expression," trans. Michael Gilbert, in *German Essays on Music* (New York: Continuum, 1994), 99-105.

in his compositions positive values, which due to their un-
questionable "innovation," were well ahead of their time. These
values were so solid and enduring that the wealth of musical events
and all the musical experimentation of the nineteenth and the
beginning of the twentieth century were not able to overshadow their
brilliance. On the contrary, even the number of the "revolutionary"
changes in the kingdom of the art, so characteristic of the recent
years, only intensified the luster of his works, bearing evidence of
the inner vitality of Chopin's art. It is even more remarkable that
the monumental work of Wagner, which is closer to us in time [than
the music of Chopin's], is increasingly receding into the shadows of
the past - not as an unprecedented manifestation of the musical
genius, of course, but as a concrete stance in the debate over what
constitutes musical content.

Today's cultural phenomenon is the reaction of the art
world against its immediate past, against its "yesterday." This
reaction is a part of the continuously "emerging" reality around us
in which we all play too vital a part to be able to render an objective,
critical view of the changes. Yet, doubtlessly, this reaction is not
"revolutionary" - it will not bring about the beginning of the new era
in the arts. It remains too organically linked to that "yesterday"- if
only as a form of negation of the past. [Instead of bringing in a
revolution] it appears, rather, to be a "continuation," a part of the
ebb and flow - in harmony with the unyielding laws - of the great
breath of the ocean. This reaction is also - according to numerous
pessimists - a final limit, the tragic *Ultima Thule*[16] of the certain
cultural period threatened by the tidal surge which is never likely to
recede! However, such pessimism seems to be excessive and does
not essentially change our stance in this matter. Underneath the
abstract formalism of today's plastic arts, for instance, under the
ongoing intellectual effort to find the ultimate solution to the
problem of form, somewhere at the very bottom of the creative
emotions glimmers a hidden faith in the absolute, timeless value of
art (obviously, this belief is a paradox if one were to consider the

---

[16]Michałowski notes that "Ultima Thule" is in ancient geography the "end of the
world," i.e. an island located at the edge of the world; this term is taken from
Virgil. See Szymanowski, *Pisma muzyczne*, 100, note 11.

"futurism" as a peculiar, *sui generis,* "philosophy of life").[17] This faith has not been validated so far by the appearance of the quintessential works of art. Still, this state of affairs does not merit such a dark future outlook.

In the chaos of the contemporary art world, among many great and not-so-great ideas, make-believe controversies and disagreements, passions and calamities, there can certainly be detected a lively interest in the subject of art. Examined closely, this interest may give an indication of basic aspirations and the future direction of the arts. In the realm of music the direction of the future evolution is much more readily apparent because of the rhythm of the music's development which is subject to its own peculiar set of laws. From this vantage point it is clear how decisive was Chopin's role in the history of music and how important was the meaning of his work for the now-emerging "new" music. At the psychological roots of the "new" music lies an undeniable fact of its gradual liberation from the enchanted circle of the German influence [literally "niemieckość," i.e. "German-ness"].

Here, I do not mean to express a primitive disregard for the undoubtedly superb, aesthetic qualities of the German music. It is essential, however, to undo the legend of its "universality." It needs to be finally and unequivocally stated that music may originate from a different source than the ever more stifling ring of German "emotionality."[18] The emancipation of music from those influences must rest upon the recognition of its ethnic and national characteristics as the supreme artistic qualities. It is not only for the sake of the "formal" qualities of the musical work but also for the sake of its "spirit," its deepest meaning, that this liberation of music must take place. It has been already accomplished in both France and Russia. And how crucial a role Chopin's music played in bringing it about! A century before us he understood, beyond the shadow of a doubt, the whole depth and "organicism" of the problem of erecting the foundations for one's musical output on the

[17]This remark dates Szymanowski's text to its immediate context, i.e. the 1920s, when debates about the aesthetic ideals of "futurism" were as current as those focused on "postmodernism" have been in the 1980s and 1990s.

[18]Literally: "wzruszeniowość" - a neologism, without a proper English translation [e.g. "feeling-ness" or "moving-ness"].

basis of the rejection of the existing traditional, aesthetic canon, and the creation of one's own "canon" to replace it. This construction of the musical edifice began from a foundation that was naturally provided by Chopin's elemental relationship to the domain of music, a relationship rooted in his ethnic otherness [literally "rasowe odrębności," i.e. "racial distinguishing features" or "racial differences"].[19]

He was one of the greatest "revolutionaries" in music because, while bringing down formal and "spiritual" traditionalism, he opened the way for the freedom of musical expression. Still, his infallible instinct and sophistication led him to the practice of rigid "self-discipline." His supple imagination defined its own boundaries and its own principal directions. Within these self-imposed restraints he developed his *métier* - the most wonderful "craft" of formal perfection.

The "Polish character" [literally "polskość," i.e., "Polishness"] of Chopin's music is undeniable; yet, it does not consist in the fact that he composed polonaises and mazurkas (an example of falsely understood relationship between folk music and sources of the individual creative impulse!) to which alien ideological and literary meanings were often ascribed from **outside**. In the absolute "musicality" of his works he outgrew his times in a twofold sense: as an artist, he sought forms reaching beyond the dramatic and literary content of music, which were characteristic of Romanticism; as a Pole, he did not aim to reflect the tragic events in the **history of his nation,** but, instinctively, sought to express the **supra-historical** essence of his ethnicity [literally "rasa," i.e. "race"], which lies beyond national history. Chopin recognized that only by setting his art free from the dramatic and historical content he could ensure the preservation of its truly Polish character and endow it with the most lasting values. Such an approach to the question of "national music" - which in his own art proved to be a stroke of genius - made his compositions widely accessible far

[19]For a discussion of "racial" terminology in Szymanowski's essays see Zofia Helman's study in this volume. See also Maja Trochimczyk (Maria Anna Harley), "Chopin and the Polish Race: On Political Dimensions of Chopin Reception" ("The Age of Chopin: The Chopin Sesquicentenial Symposium" at Indiana University, Bloomington, 1999; proceedings forthcoming).

beyond Polish borders (in contrast to the music of Moniuszko)[20] and elevated his music to the category of universal art. His approach became a starting point of today's musical aspirations.

Here also lies the solution to the wondrous riddle of his undying contemporaneity. Today, perhaps, we may not experience with equal freshness his treatment of the musical material which was then so innovative. Yet, each singular element - a chord, modulation, melodic or rhythmic pattern - grown out of the untouched, virgin soil of his imagination - was the result of the most profound creative experiment. Chopin possessed an uncommon, objective and secure wisdom, which is a hallmark of those who fearlessly abandon the territories which had already been explored a thousand times over, realms which are predictable and not threatening with any revelations, lands where traditional "aestheticism" spreads like a bad habit and new ideas are quickly labeled as "fashionable trends." Only today - from the distance of almost a century - and while considering what had followed after him (on the one hand Romanticism, Post-romanticism, contemporary German music, and, on the other hand - and as an antithesis - the exuberant growth of the French and Russian music that owes so much to Chopin's art), only today it is possible to fully comprehend his extraordinary meaning in the evolution of universal music. We only wish that the widely adopted "transformation of values," that was initiated by Chopin a century ago, would, at last, become an accomplished fact in Poland as well.

We are far from advocating an indiscriminate reliance on what has, in his music, become - to a degree - the aesthetical tradition. What we are arguing for is the deepest understanding of his approach to Polish music in particular; we seek its release from the foreign bonds which were hampering its development, we search for the courage to "renounce," and for the will to create music from the individual impulse, based on its own foundations. Fryderyk Chopin's life's work serves as an everlasting example of what Polish music can be. It also stands as a prime symbol of Poland as a part of the **European** tradition - without relinquishing any part of its

---

[20]Stanisław Moniuszko (1819-1872) is the founder of Polish national opera (*Halka, The Haunted Manor*), and was the composer of many songs and religious pieces.

ethnic otherness [literally "rasowe odrębności," i.e. "racial differences"], yet, attaining the level of the highest European cultural achievement.[21]

Translated by Maria Piłatowicz

---

[21]At the end of the handwritten manuscript draft of this essay, Szymanowski includes a note about his motivation to express his profound beliefs about Chopin that led him to "leave the proper terrain of musical considerations" and become a "poacher" in the domains of "literature, history and philosophy of art." He then prays for forgiveness of such "boldness" for the sake of the benefit of doing "the right thing awkwardly, rather than not doing it at all" (Szymanowski, *Pisma muzyczne*, 100-101, note 12).

Fryderyk Chopin and Poland

by Stanisław Niewiadomski[1]

We must never forget that after the tragic catastrophe of the 1831 uprising, France extended her friendly hand to all Poles, welcoming every refugee with warmth, and enabling an existence for the rest of their lives; an existence which was then impossible for them in their home country. Furthermore, we must be grateful even more that among the refugees there were many of our nation's great individuals, who, like shining stars in Heaven, shone down their influence upon European culture and politics. The thoughts and actions of these great individuals could have only developed within circles outside of Poland at this time, and the results of their efforts upon those who remained oppressed and deprived of freedom produced a lasting and powerful effect.

Fryderyk Chopin was one of those great Poles who relied upon France's hospitality. Throughout the second half of his life he remained at Seine, and only from time to time did he ever journey outside France's borders. In France he also found companionship with an important French author, Ms. George Sand, and for ten years they shared a close relationship, which had obviously been a

---

[1]Stanisław Niewiadomski (1859-1936) was a composer and music critic of a conservative orientation (frequently attacking Szymanowski); author of a large number of romantic songs to texts by Polish poets, eg. Adam Asnyk, Adam Mickiewicz, Maria Konopnicka (incl. a version of the patriotic anthem *Rota*). He also published arrangements of folk songs and soldier's songs. In addition to many essays on Chopin, he wrote booklets on *Fryderyk Franciszek Szopen : największy muzyk polski* [F.F.Chopin - the greatest Polish musician] (Warszawa: Wydawnictwo Komitetu Dni Szopenowskich w Polsce, 1933) and *Stanisław Moniuszko* (Warszawa: Gebethner i Wolff, 1928). A member of his family, Eligiusz Niewiadomski (1869-1923) was a right-wing political activist associated with Endecja (National Democrats of Roman Dmowski); infamous for assasinating the newly-elected President of Poland, Gabriel Narutowicz (1922). The text of this essay is translated from "Fryderyk Szopen a Polska" in Mateusz Gliński, ed. *Szopen. Monografia zbiorowa* [Chopin. A Monograph by many authors], in the series "Monografie zbiorowe *Muzyki*" (Warszawa: Nakładem Miesięcznika *Muzyka*, 1932): 17-20. [This and all subsequent notes by the editor].

positive influence on his work in the last period of his life. French artists such as Berlioz, Franchomme, Delacroix, and Clésinger all played a very sympathetic role in his life, and they should be remembered with sincere gratitude.

Apart from these relationships, Chopin's whole life belonged to Poland. One half was completely Polish in terms of physical and spiritual identity; the second half, although socially linked with Paris, was more fundamentally connected with his homeland through the ties of love, longing, and his sense of duty. Poland, suffering, distant, and closed to him forever, assumed in his imagination a form so ideal, a shape so great, that he could not have loved it more. Certainly, he would not have loved Poland so intensely if he had stayed at home and had to live under those arduous circumstances, observing closely the humiliations affected through the strained relationships between the harassed Polish society and its Russian oppressors.

When Chopin came to Paris with a portfolio full of compositions, among which were such magnificent works as the two Concerti, Scherzo in B-minor, the etudes, and many other pieces, his creative maturity was already unquestionable. He did not need further tutelage, neither in the field of composition, nor in the field of performance. As a creator of music he followed only a desire to express his heart's sincere attachment to Poland. As a performer he was solely following his own genial taste - for a great deal of time had already passed since he finished his piano studies with Wojciech Żywny in Warsaw and he did not need to be taught any more. The differences that we may notice between the works that Chopin composed in Poland and the later ones written in France, do not so much result from the influences that Paris may have had on the young artist, but rather from those elements which reveal his intensely personal experiences. The times in Chopin's youth which he spent annually in the Polish countryside were the most carefree in his whole life, whereas the second half of his existence was filled with sorrow and depression, physical pain, and anxieties arising from living in a great city.

It is obvious that his sun-filled youth imprinted its features in all of his works up until op. 30; in other words, in those that he most likely brought with him to Paris. If we were eager to look for contemporary influences, without much effort we could find the traits of Hummel in his technically brilliant concerti, and certain features recalling the music of Field in the lyrical imagery of his nocturnes. Yet what a great difference exists between the creative powers of these composers and Chopin! How much richer is his ingenuity and how much more vivacious his imagination! The steps that he took both in harmony and chromaticism were so far reaching that they undoubtedly opened Liszt's and Wagner's eyes to a whole field of possibilities, as well as formed a new foundation for the subsequent development of piano technique and the basis for the piano literature in general.

While writing about himself in one of his youthful letters, Chopin described his ideal of "creating a distinct world for himself" that underlied the originality of his creative talent within which all the other phenomena resided. This originality encompassed primarily the Polish character [*polskość*][2] of his music which stemmed from the musical sources with which he satisfied the desires of his ear, his heart, and his imagination - when passing through a Polish village, its fields and woods, and listening to the tunes of a shepherd's pipe, to girls' songs, and to the rhythms of the *mazur*, *obertas*, and *krakowiak*.[3] Poland gave him the gift of music in the beginning of his life when, according to legend, village music[4] came to the manor-house of Żelazowa Wola with some act of homage and, accidentally, stumbled upon the very moment when, in a modest annex to that manor, the greatest musical genius of Poland was being born.

The Polish quality [*polskość*] of Chopin's music did not have any ready-made models in the history of our art, because earlier Polish composers of the 17th and 18th centuries - with the exception of Gomółka - never tried to introduce particular, national features into their compositions that belonged to the realm of

---

[2]The term *polskość*, "Polish-ness," may be translated as "Polish character," "quality," "traits," or "identity"- all these terms reflect its general meaning..

[3]For a different interpretation of the relative importance of these dances see the essay by Noskowski in the present volume.

[4]"Village music" or, literally, "wiejska muzyka" is the common name given to an ensemble of folk musicians, also known as a "kapela." Niewiadomski uses this term to emphasize that "music" visited the manor, not the musicians.

sacred music.[5] Moreover, composers active later, especially Kamieński, Stefani, Kurpiński, and Elsner, were not able to sufficiently enrich their melodies and dance rhythms with a creative imagination that could elevate their compositions to the heights of a truly Polish - but also truly universal - great art.[6] Indeed, this accomplishment requires the imagination of a genius. The rhythms of the polonaise, known to foreign composers of the past and of the present, expressed little in and of themselves. The triple meter, with its typical six eight-notes, and with the second of these eighth-notes halved into two sixteenth-notes, essentially did not differ from the rhythm of the Spanish bolero. Therefore, it was necessary to "polonize" this type of rhythm by breathing a new and distinct spirit into this conventional and representative dance that our ears had become much too accustomed to. Before Chopin, Ogiński achieved this to a certain extent in his lyric polonaises - and their melancholy strains resounded throughout Europe.[7] Chopin, however, endowed this lyricism with a foundation of great solemnity and majesty. His

[5]Mikołaj Gomółka (ca. 1535 - after 1591) was a composer of religious and secular choral music, including Polish Psalms (with dance rhythms) to texts by Jan Kochanowski, and a large number of other pieces. He was a member of the Royal Chapel in Kraków and a court musician for several Polish magnates.

[6]Maciej Kamieński (1734-1821) was the creator of Polish opera, active in Warsaw. His *Nędza uszczęśliwiona* [Poverty made happy] is the first opera with a Polish text; folk elements appear in music accompanying peasant characters. Jan Stefani (1748-1829) was a violinist, conductor and composer, director of the National Theatre in Warsaw, composer of the popular vaudeville *Cud mniemany czyli Krakowiacy i Górale*. Karol Kurpiński (1785-1857) was a composer and conductor, director of the Warsaw Opera (1824-1840) and professor of music. He composed over 20 operas, operettas, and melodramas, including *Zamek na Czorsztynie*[Castle on Czorsztyn], *Jadwiga, królowa Polski* [Jadwiga, the Queen of Poland], etc. Józef Elsner (1769-1854) was Poland's leading composer before Chopin, founder of a music school, director of the Warsaw Opera and Warsaw Conservatory, and professor at the University of Warsaw. Elsner composed symphonic, chamber and solo pieces, many operas, oratorios (including a *Passion*), and songs. His style blended features of Viennese classics with folk elements and conventional harmony.

[7]Michał Kleofas Ogiński (1765-1833) was a nobleman, Polish envoy to Italy, the Netherlands, and England; he was involved in politics during and after the partitions of Poland. His compositions are characterized by the sentimentality of *Emp-findsamer Stil* while his nostalgic polonaises are considered exemplars of national style before Chopin.

Polonaises in C-sharp minor, E-flat major, C minor, and F-sharp minor are not mere figures covered with a sentimental veil that whisper, "Les Adieux à la Patrie."[8] Instead they are magnificent spirits of revolt and complaint, clad in mournful robes that cover glittering silver armor and steel swords. In his book on Chopin, Liszt claims that the first person to give the polonaise a heroic character was Carl Maria von Weber. However, Weber's polonaises (in E major and E-flat major) sound foreign to the Polish ear, and thus they could never have been a model for Chopin. A work as Polish and original in every note as Chopin's Polonaise A major, could only have begun in the imagination of this great musician to whom the past, the present, and the future of Poland were not only sacred, but simply a part of his flesh and blood. Furthermore, we feel the same way about the mazurkas, in which he presents the complete spectrum of various moods and images. In cosmopolitan Paris, when this great artist and worldly man returned from the salons to his home and to his piano (his most trusted and faithful confidant) a Mazovian village emerged in his music, as if summoned from the infinite distance. The obedient instrument learned how to sing the village songs and how to resonate with the folk dance rhythms; Poland filled the foreign walls with life and nestled her beloved and faithful son in a heartfelt embrace.

In a way no less individual, he formulated other works that were free of Polish rhythms and melodies. There is no doubt that an attempt to recognize Polish elements in these works is far less easy. Nonetheless, it is beyond question that some of these pieces are overtly Polish in their themes and typical figures; moreover they intentionally conceal some national thoughts or traits that may have been prompted by the suggestions [literally "podszepty" i.e. "whispering"] of poetry, or by a certain memory, or even by news from his home country. Thus, not only his Scherzos, Ballades, Etudes, and Preludes, but even the Fantasy in F minor, Polonaise-Fantasy, and Barcarole bear profoundly national and prophetic features, in which almost every note repeats: "Poland, Poland, and Poland...."

From his father Mikołaj, Fryderyk Chopin inherited a

---

[8] Allusion to Ogiński's most famous Polonaise in A minor (1794), known in numerous versions, editions and arrangements.

creativity of mind, clear and intelligent judgment, and a kind of practical sense that even in spite of his predilection for salon life protected him from wasting away his talent, from distracting his mind in aimless activities, and from a lack of energy in his creative work. From his mother, whose Polish maiden name Krzyżanowska is widely known, he received his dreamy, delicate disposition full of subtlety and sweetness. He brought from Poland also a sophistication that was typically encountered in all Warsaw circles associated with the so-called high society. Later on, while living in Paris and belonging to similar yet more international circles as well as to the Polish émigré society, he was undoubtedly forced to pay his dues to the salons. For Chopin, this duty was not a burden. He was full of energy and elegance, polite and witty, highly sophisticated and, at the same time, attentive to the many humorous details of life. Also in his music he was capable of striking this elegant tone, frequently enriching his works with the typical, refined salon gestures. Only ordinariness, shallowness, or absence of expression were completely foreign to his music. Poland herself contributed to his twofold disposition by swinging back and forth between extreme political and social situations which were tragic at times, and a willful optimism which provided a glow of hope for the future. This aspect of Poland has found its faithful and most moving representation in Chopin's music. It should be no surprise then, that when this charming world of sounds created out of a love for Poland was directed toward her, it was reflected in every nerve of her physical organism, and in every part of her soul!

Robert Schumann's well-known saying about mazurkas being like cannons hidden among flowers, long considered only a rhetorical expression, has today reached its fulfillment.[9] These mazurkas have fought for the independence of Polish existence, and

---

[9]For Schumann's opinion's on Chopin see *Robert Schumann's Gesammelte Schriften über Musik und Musiker* [Robert Schumann's complete writings on music and musicians], 5th ed, 2 vols. (Leipzig, 1914) and Herman Erler, ed., *Robert Schumanns Leben aus seinen Briefen*, 2 vols. (Berlin, 1886), as well as several collections and selections of Schumann's writings. For a recent discussion of the relationship between Schumann and Chopin see Irena Poniatowska, ed., *Chopin w kręgu przyjaciół. Chopin im Umkreis seiner Freunde,* vol. 3, "Chopin - Schumann - Clara Wieck Schumann" (Warsaw: Polish Chopin Academy, 1997).

have done so in spite of the servitude and oppression which have gone on for so long, that this Nemesis in our history can not be crossed out from our memories. Therefore, are not Chopin's "cannons" a great symbol? They are a symbol of the only fight to which the cultural future of our nation would be entitled to wage.

Translated by Małgorzata Szyszkowska and Brian Harlan

Figure 1: Cover of Niewiadomski's Songs, Op. 40, *Słonko* [Little Sun], to texts by Adam Asnyk. Cover art anonymous. Collection of the Polish Music Center, Los Angeles.

Spelling Identity: Ch or Sz?

by Stanisław Niewiadomski[1]

Again I touch upon this subject that has been discussed many times, and even solved a few years ago through an inquiry by the periodical *Muzyka*, yet which is nevertheless still tottering.[2] This is not because of a matter of principle, rather it is more likely due to inattention, and here and there because of a slight obstinacy toward changing an old custom. At issue is the way of spelling a name, which despite its foreign sound, has for many years now been a synonym for something which for us is the dearest, and the most Polish in all of music. At issue is the spelling of the name of our most recognized musician:

Chopin or Szopen?[3]

There are more than a thousand occasions in which one may speak about the national meaning of the works of this Polish master. He never thought of himself as French, but rather took pride in his Polish nationality, such as in the fact that he managed to seek out, internalize, and master the Polish sound. He left in his works not only the most explicit testimony for his Polish-ness, but also some of the most powerful emblems of our culture, huge in the affection placed on them by the whole world, and crowned with immortal glory.

How we love his dear name, and how dear and sweet to our ears is the charm of the music linked to it forever! Yet when we speak about the "genuine" Polish-ness of this music, and when it

---

[1]This text is translated from Niewiadomski's essay "Ch czy Sz?" in Mateusz Gliński, ed., *Szopen. Monografia Zbiorowa* [Chopin. A Monograph by many authors], in the series "Monografie zbiorowe *Muzyki*" (Warszawa: Nakładem Miesięcznika *Muzyka*, 1932): 88-90. [This and all subsequent notes are by the editor, unless otherwise indicated].

[2]Discussions about the spelling of Chopin's last name began in the late 1870s. Several issues of *Echo Muzyczne* from 1879 and 1880 contain letters, editorials and comments about this matter. Dr. Barbara Zakrzewska-Nikiporczyk brought these references to our attention.

[3]The Polish spelling of "Szopen" reflects the customary pronunciation of the name "Shoh-pen," with an accent on the first syllable [translator's note].

comes to uniting the foreign sounding name of its composer with its national value, is there not something of a dissonance, ostensibly presenting a lie to the sincerity of both our attachment and our exaltation of him? But the flaw lies not in the sounding itself. For the Polish pronunciation has a specific accent, and his name has long ago lost its French-ness, which lies only in the spelling. It is indeed this spelling which clashes against our every day pronunciation, as well as against a world of ideas associated with the nationality of this artist.

Our writers and poets have best felt this. Typically, this case not withstanding, musicians more often follow their own personal prejudices toward the one that poses the positive claim rather than the merit of that claim. The hated Mr. X uses "sz," they think to themselves, then I will spell it with "ch." Other people use different spellings apathetically, giving the matter little - if any - thought.

There are also "rigorists" who take an attorney's stance rather than exploring the issue critically, and stubbornly repeat, "the son of Mikołaj set his name the same as his father did and we are not entitled to use a different spelling." Those same rigorists nevertheless forget all about the fact that they themselves change it at every step by pronouncing it completely in a Polish way. Who among Poles will say "Chopin" with an appropriate accent on the last syllable sounding as our "ę"? There would be absolutely no one. We all say: Szope*n*, Szope*na*, Szope*nowi* [Shop: en, ena, enovy] putting an accent accordingly to the nature of the Polish language on the second to last syllable. Is this harmful for the name of the great musician; does his worldwide, international significance suffer even a small bit from this?

Foreigners do not understand it in this every day pronunciation; they do not understand when we say Szopen, Szopenowski, Szopenek, Szopeniana, Szopenizm.[4] Yet if one of them coincidentally happens to live in Warsaw, on the street named Szopen, and they have been accordingly informed, they will certainly begin to understand and recognize that the point of this spelling is to

---

[4]These words mean: Chopin, Chopinian, Little Chopin, Chopiniana, Chopinism - and are, with the exception of the first two, neologisms, rather rare and unlikely to be used [translators' note].

celebrate the memory of a great man. For in spelling it this way, the people passing by who do not understand French could still pronounce it correctly, not as it is pronounced in Paris, but as it is pronounced in Warsaw and in the whole of Poland. Moreover, for whom do we write and discuss Szopen? Who reads the monographs of Hoesick, Opieński, Jachimecki, and others--foreigners or locals?[5] This is why we should have preserved the Polish spelling.

For the most part, the authors of these monographs explain themselves with historical exactness. Still, would it not be strange, or even wrong, for Przybyszewski to have entitled his enthusiastic literary work written in precise language, not *Szopen and Nation* as we read on the cover, but *Chopin and Nation* as rigorists would prefer?[6] Would Paderewski, in his famous and oft printed speech, be able to use the foreign spelling?[7] No. Indeed, he rightly knew that each use of "Chopin" would weaken the most important ideas of his thought, namely that Szopen's music is something as Polish as one can imagine. And was it not the same intention behind using

---

[5]Here, Niewiadomski uses the word "swoi" which literally means "ours" and is rendered as "locals." [translators' note]. See Ferdynand Hoesick (1867-1941), *Chopin. Życie i twórczość* (Warszawa: Nakładem księgarni W. Hoesicka, 1927); Zdzisław Jachimecki (1882-1953), *Fryderyk Chopin.* (Kraków, 1927); Henryk Opieński, *Chopin* (Lwów:: Książnica-Atlas, 1925). Notice that none of these titles use Niewiadomski's preferred spelling of "Szopen."

[6]Stanisław Przybyszewski, "Szopen a naród" [Chopin and nation] originally appeared in German, as "Chopin und Nation" in Przybyszewski's *Zur psychologie des individuum I. Chopin und Nietzsche* (Berlin, 1892). The Polish version of *Szopen a naród* was published in the 1910s (Kraków: Spółka Nakładowa Książka, n.d.).

[7]Paderewski, Ignacy Jan: "Mowa Ignacego Jana Paderewskiego" [Speech by I. J .P.], Speech of 23 October 1910, Lwów, *Obchód setnej rocznicy urodzin Fryderyka Chopina* (Lwów, 1912). Also published as *Chopin. A Discourse by I.J. Paderewski,* trans. Laurence Alma Tadema (London: W. Adlington, 1911). The whole speech was also published in Polish translation as *Chopin,* ed. Joanna Pasztaleniec-Jarzynska and Katarzyna Diehl (Warszawa: Stowarzyszenie Bibliotekarzy Polskich, 1991). A long excerpt, "Piewca polskiego narodu," appears in Mieczysław Tomaszewski, ed., *Kompozytorzy polscy o Fryderyku Chopinie. Antologia* (Kraków: PWM, 1980), 90-99.

the Polish spelling that governed Ujejski, Norwid, Konopnicka, Tetmajer and others?[8]

Experts on the Polish language such as the late Baudoin de Courtenay and Prof. Kryński clearly make a case for our civic rights to the Polish spelling.[9] This is not because of nationalist reasons, rather it is based upon the same ground by which we phonetically write all the names belonging to internationally known cultural figures, such as: Szekspir [Shakespeare], Wolter [Voltaire], Szyler [Schiller], Petrarka [Petrarca], and others.[10]

Should we not then at last bring ourselves to uniformity by shaking off the foreign spelling and gradually eradicating it even from the covers of catalogs and programs? Since so far in all of these cases the foreign spelling has been given priority, we should aspire to replace it with the appropriate spelling here as well.

The objection that a phonetic spelling might harm the memory of Szopen's personal beliefs and preferences has no ground at all. Szopen often read his name in *Kurier Warszawski* spelled in Polish as "Szopę," and never protested against it himself, nor did his father. He also never protested when his close friends, for example Stefan Witwicki, polonized his name. Legal, bureaucratic, or heraldic regards have never been at issue here. Miss Maria Wodzińska has been reported to say that instead of *tout court* "Chopin," she would prefer this name with the noble ending ski, as in Szopiński [Shopeensky] or Szopowski [Shopovsky]. But in this instance, there were certainly other regards at stake than simply those that have motivated the lovers of Szopen's genius.

---

[8]Kornel Ujejski (1823-1897), Cyprian Kamil Norwid (1821-1883), Maria Konopnicka (1842-1910) and Kazimerz Przerwa-Tetmajer (1865-1940) are famous Polish poets and writers, also active as literary critics.

[9]Here Niewiadomski refers to two eminent Polish linguists, Jan Baudouin de Courtenay (1845-1929), the author of numerous books on the grammar and history of the Polish language, studies in comparative linguistics, etc., and Adam Antoni Kryński (1844-1932) who penned a book on Polish grammar but was most active in the field of orthography. See Zenon Klemensiewicz: *Historia języka polskiego* [History of the Polish language] (Warsaw: PWN, 1981; first published in 3 vols 1961-1972), 676-677.

[10]Of the names mentioned here the polonized spelling of "Szekspir" and "Petrarka" remained in popular usage while the polonization of the names of Voltaire and Schiller was not accepted.

Furthermore, there is no evidence as to whether or not Szopen himself ever attached even the least of importance to the either French spelling, or to the origin of his name. He must have known quite well that his father's family was living in Lotaryngia, but he was not interested in this fact at all.

Therefore with a clear consciousness toward the memory of this immortal musician of ours, and with the deeply sincere desire to service our language the best way possible, let us write his dear name as we say it. In doing this we will avoid all the conceptual and linguistic oddities that came from the foreign spelling.

May expressions such as "Chopin's Polish-ness," "the familiar charm of the Chopin tune," "Chopiniana," "Chopinism," and so on, disappear from every literary and journalist production once and for all.

Translated by Małgorzata Szyszkowska and Brian Harlan

Figure 1: Cover of *Szopen. Monografia Zbiorowa* [Chopin: A monograph by many authors], Mateusz Gliński, ed. (Warszawa: Nakładem wydawnictwa Muzyki, 1932). Polish Music Center, USC, Los Angeles.

Is There a Chopin Tradition?

by Mateusz Gliński[1]

The music of Fryderyk Chopin is the most luxuriant, most wonderful flower that has sprung from the fertile soil of musical romanticism. It is a flower with new contours and shapes unknown to the music of the first half of the 19th century, a flower of a unique, indescribable, intoxicating fragrance. In the rich heritage of romanticism the work of Chopin holds a place of honor; nonetheless, it is not linked to romantic music in general by anything but loose connections of a formal nature. This may be attributed to the fact that Chopin's oeuvre is completely individual; it is unique to a degree that far exceeds the individuality of the pieces by other eminent musical romantics of the 19th century. Chopin's music mirrors the changing states of his soul; it is a reflection of his internal life. The subtle nature of Chopin, who was consumed by illness and artificially stimulated by the events of salon life, received impressions from everyday life in an over-sensitive manner, in the form of a kind of psychic resonance, at times violently scintillating, at other times fading away....

Therefore, the essence of Chopin's music, that was called by Przybyszewski "the music of a psychosis" may be found in its arhythmic nature.[2] This simple and blunt word was used by one of

---

[1] This text is translated from Gliński's essay "Czy istnieje tradycja Szopena?" in Mateusz Gliński, ed., *Szopen. Monografia Zbiorowa* [Chopin. A Monograph by many authors], in the series "Monografie zbiorowe *Muzyki*" (Warszawa: Nakładem Miesięcznika *Muzyka*, 1932): 78-81. Mateusz Gliński (1892-1976) was a musicologist, conductor and composer, author of several arrangements of Chopin's works. He worked as the editor of *Muzyka* (since founding the journal in 1924 until 1938) and published, among other works, an arrangment of a Chopin melody *Hymn to Poland* (Minneapolis, Minn.: Polanie Pub. Co, 1957), and *Chopin the Unknown* (Windsor, Canada: Assumption University of Windsor Press, 1963). Cf. Zofia Glińska, ed., *Testament Mateusza Glińskiego* [The Testament of Mateusz Gliński] (London: Oficyna Poetów i Malarzy, 1982). [This and all subsequent notes have been prepared by the editor].

[2] Exactly: "a-rhythm" i.e. "arytmja" in Polish. Stanisław Przybyszewski (1868-1927) wrote about Chopin in a number of essays, e.g. "Szopen a naród" [Chopin and the Nation] (Kraków: Spółka nakładowa "Książka," 1911). Maciej Zurowski, "Chopin et le Jeune Pologne: Chopin interprete par Przybyszewski,"

the greatest experts on Chopin's music - Paderewski.[3] In this aryth-
mic character, Paderewski sees the main proof of the idealized
kinship of Chopin with his homeland - Poland. Is not "the aryth-
mic" an innate feature of the Polish soul? This national trait was
expressed by Chopin in such a beautiful fashion that no other great
Polish prophet was able to surpass that because only music could
reflect this oscillation of our feelings, their reaching into infinity and
their concentration (transformed into heroism), their sudden fits of
frenzy that seem to crush rocks, and their powerlessness of doubt by
which the thought becomes darkened and the will to act dies out.
Only in this music, tender and tremulous, quiet and passionate,
sorrowful, strong and ominous, in music that willingly escapes the
discipline of the meter, that avoids the orderliness of the rhythm,
only in this music one can hear, feel and learn that our nation and
our land, that the whole Poland lives, feels and acts: "in tempo
rubato...."

This music, so changeable and so difficult to capture in its
subtle accents, this music that breaks away from the shackles of
metric discipline, was passed on by generations in a form which
usually does not give any key to the solution of numerous interpretative problems arising in practice, and at times, causes serious
doubts. There are several editions of Chopin's works; they differ
from each other not only in the marking of the tempi, in the interpretative remarks (agogics, dynamics) and the pedalization (according to Anton Rubinstein all the customary indications in this
domain are completely false!) - but even occasionally in individual
pitches. The differences are so large, that an intense dispute was
conducted a while ago (Kullak contra Mikuli) about the exact pitch

Revue de musicologie 75 no. 2 (1989): 185-189; Lukas Richter, "O poglądach
Stanisława Przybyszewskiego na muzykę" [About S. Przybyszewski's views on
music], *Muzyka* 24 no. 1 (1979): 3-27.

[3]Ignacy Jan Paderewski, *Chopin*, trans. by Alma Tadema and Paul Cazin, edited
by Katarzyna Diehl and Joanna Pasztaleniec-Jarzynska (Warszawa: Stowarzyszenie Bibliotekarzy Polskich, 1991). The booklet contains Paderewski's
speech delivered at the opening of the Chopin Centenary Festival in Lwów
(Lemberg in Austrian Poland, now Lviv in Ukraine), on October 23rd, 1910.
French translation: *Discours sur Chopin, prononcé le 23 octobre 1910 à Lvov,
à l'occasion du 100e anniversaire de la naissance de Frédéric Chopin* (Paris:
Association Paderewski, 1990).

played by Chopin in the Coda of the Second Ballade: was it D or D-sharp?[4] How many other, similar discussions are caused by all the various discrepancies among the different editions of Chopin's works!

Nonetheless, these imprecisions are of an external nature. The main obstacle to the unification of the interpretations of Chopin's works rests much deeper. It is hidden in the form itself that had to fix Chopin's work in notation. This form was conventional, stiff and completely insufficient for the extensive individualism of Chopin's style. Let us look at any of the piano pieces from Chopin's spiritual epigon, the Russian individualist, Skryabin. What Chopin left to the discretion of the interpretative intuition of the performers of his music, what he placed, as it was customary to put it, "between the lines," Skryabin fixed in writing, by introducing bold innovations in musical notation. Therefore he notated almost all the rhythmic oscillation, and by doing so he destroyed the symmetry in the construction of musical phrases that had been sanctified by tradition, and complicated the form of the work by introducing artificial, intricate rhythms.

Chopin's notation is only seemingly not complicated with regard to rhythm. It is this very relative primitivism that causes the understanding of hidden and not-fully-expressed creative intentions of our Prophet [*wieszcz*][5] to become increasingly difficult. With every year, this factor increases the plurality of languages in the large group of interpreters of Chopin's music. Therefore, in face of such interpretative difficulties a persistent "ideological rule" is very often put forward - it is the so-called **Chopin Tradition**. Alas, this nice-sounding concept is only, one should say, a fiction. For what

---

[4]Theodor Kullak (1818-1882) and Karol Mikuli (1819-1897) were Polish pianists and composers active in German-speaking countries. Kullak settled in Berlin, where he opened the Neue Akademie der Tonkunst which became the largest private school in Germany, with 100 teachers and over 1000 students, including Moritz Moszkowski, and Xavier and Philipp Scharwenka. Mikuli studied in Vienna and Paris (1844-1847; with Chopin), and later settled in Lwów where he directed the Galician Music Society and taught at the Conservatory.

[5]Traditionally the term "wieszcz" [prophet] is used only in reference to Poland's greatest romantic poets, Adam Mickiewicz, Juliusz Słowacki, Zygmunt Krasiński. Its usage by Gliński elevates Chopin to the rank of a national prophet. Niewiadomski and Noskowski use this term in the same way.

is tradition?

Busoni called tradition "a death mask" taken from life, a mask of which the features have been erased almost beyond recognition during the long years when the mask was used by an army of artisans [making their replicas of the artefact].[6] Perhaps this musical enthusiast [i.e. Busoni], inclined to exaggeration in his beautiful metaphor, did not show enough understanding for the laws of ideological continuity in the development of musical styles and laws that connect singular episodes in the history of music into a monumental whole.... Busoni nothwithstanding, what is the Chopin tradition? Where could it emerge? What paths could it have taken to reach our generation?

In order to answer these questions, recalling the course of Chopin's short life in a superficial way could suffice. The only source of Chopin tradition could be found in Chopin's productions in Paris, in the epoch of his great triumphs at the end of the first half of the 19th century. The only apostles of the music of this Prophet could be his disciples. "Chopin never had such talented pupils to mold as had Liszt" - wrote Chopin's eminent biographer, James Huneker, whose monograph, entitled *Chopin: The Man and His Music* was translated into Polish.[7] Huneker continues: "however, Chopin made some excellent piano artists. They all had, or have

---

[6]The quoted expression probably comes from Ferruccio Busoni, *Entwurf einer neuen Ästhetik der Tonkunst* [Scheme for a new aesthetic of music], reprinted in the series "Schriftenreihe zur Musik" (Hamburg: Wagner, 1973), originally published in 1911. English version, *Sketch of a New Aesthetic of Music,* transl. Dr. Th. Baker, in *Three Classics in the Aesthetics of Music* (New York: Dover Publications, 1962). See also Joseph Willimann, ed., "Magister und Scholarus-- Zwei Busoni-Texte von 1923: Das vergessene Zwiegespräch 'Später' und das vermeintliche Vermächtnis 'Zeitwelle'" [Magister and scholarus--Two Busoni texts from 1923: The forgotten dialogue and the alleged final legacy, "Zeitwelle"], *Schweizer Jahrbuch für Musikwissenschaft /Annales suisses de musicologie* no. 11 (1991): 139-168.

[7]James Huneker, *Chopin: The Man and His Music* (New York: C. Scribner's Sons, 1900), first American edition. Polish translation from the English edition (London, 1901) published in Lwów and Poznań in 1922. The passage is quoted according to James Huneker, *Chopin: The Man and His Music* (New York: Dover, 1966), reprint of the 1900 edition with a new introduction, footnotes, and index by Herbert Weinstock. In addition to editing Chopin's complete works for Scribner and writing on music history, Huneker also wrote fiction, e.g. *Painted Veils* (New York: Boni and Liveright,1920).

[inherited] his tradition but **exactly what the Chopin tradition is no man dare say**."

Even if it were accurate to compare a tradition to a death mask taken from the original, one should remember that the features of the original mien of Chopin's creative countenance in the domain of piano performance were completely ephemeral, variable, depending on a momentary disposition and on the state of his nerves and of his body. A series of historical testimonies proves with all certainty that Chopin often played the same piece in different ways, changing tempo, tone color and even nuances of the text.[8] About his performance habits, however, there has not been a fixed, definite opinion until today. Did not one of the greatest followers of his performative art - Karol Mikuli - in his introduction to the Leipzig edition of the works of the master, state that "Chopin the pianist remained almost completely unknown"?

The nature of Chopin's artistic activities, his separation from his native country (which could have been a more welcoming soil for the preservation of his tradition, than a hospitable, but still racially[9] foreign France), and his dislike of stage displays - these were the factors of the external nature, which, in connection to the extremely florid individualism of his music and his piano style, hindered the creation of a single piano tradition for the greatest Polish master of the piano. These factors resulted in the plurality of languages in Chopin interpretation. Already in the last century, the "royal scepter" in the domain of interpreting the music of this Prophet's music has passed from one hand to another, either connected to him through the powerful ties of a common race [*rasa*] that could not have been weakened by anything (Paderewski, Michałowski, Śliwiński), or not connected to the work of the Polish master by anything else besides the supra-national and supra-epoch interpretative intuition of a genius (Liszt, Rubinstein, Joseffy,

---

[8]References to this practice are found on p. 78 of the German translation of Huneker's book [Author's note]. Publication details of this version are not known.

[9]Similarly to Szymanowski the author uses the expression "racially foreign"[*obcy rasowo*] to denote national/ethnic difference.

Esipoff, Pachmann, Weiss).[10] All the great Chopin interpreters capture and enchant with their playing, drawing from the instrument the beauty of invention of this great poet of sound that had been hidden in the score. **But each of these masters plays differently**. Why? Because, as Huneker rightly stated, "in Chopin's music a multitude of pianists and styles is hidden and all the styles are acceptable if only they are logical, poetic, musical and are permeated with a sincerity and artistic truthfulness."

This offers an explanation why Chopin's work often awakens the same enthusiasm when being interpreted by artists of a completely different spiritual makeup. For some (e.g. .Michałowski) it is a work of an impeccable purity of line, of a hellenic distinctness of outlines, for others it is "the romanticism of the nerves" (Prof. A. Weissmann),[11] the confession of a heart weary with illness and "sorrow,"[12] but through each of these beautiful interpretations of Chopin the divine sun of genius shines and dazzles with its supernatural brilliance.

Translated by Maja Trochimczyk and Anne Desler

---

[10]Here we preserve some of the author's original spelling of the pianists' names. Aleksander Michałowski (1851-1938) was a Polish pianist and composer, who studied with Moscheles and Tausig, often played chamber music, avoided brilliance and virtuoso bravura in his interpretations, and taught Wanda Landowska, Harry Neuhaus, and others. Józef Śliwiński (1865-1930) was a Polish pianist and conductor, who studied with Rubinstein, and was known for his performances of Chopin and Schumann. The remaining pianists are Hungarian, Russian, Jewish and Ukrainian. Rafael Joseffy (1852-1915) was a Hungarian pianist, a student of Tausig and Liszt, who settled in the U.S. and edited Chopin's works in 15 volumes. "Esipoff" is probably Anna Esipova (1851-1914) a Russian pianist and teacher who studied with Leschetizky and was highly praised for the lightness of her touch and singing tone; her pupils included Prokofiev. Vladimir de Pachman (1848-1933), was a Ukrainian pianist known for his eccentricity. He studied at the Vienna Conservatory and focused on performing Chopin's works with a "superbly sensivite touch."

[11]Adolf Weissmann was a music critic active in Berlin in 1920s. There were many other musicians of the same last name.

[12]The Polish term for "sorrow" is *żal*, used by the author in quotation marks. This word is often used in reference to Chopin's music as an overriding aesthetic category that explains the prevailing mood of nostalgia in his music. For another instance in this volume see the essay by Zygmunt Noskowski.

Back to Chopin

by Witold Lutosławski

Chopin music stood - if one can say so - at the threshold of my life.[1] This is precisely *the* music which exerted the most powerful impression on me in my childhood; this impression could not be compared with anything else at that time. I listened to the Scherzo in B-flat minor, played by one of my teachers, while sitting underneath the table so that nobody could see how deeply moved I was.[2]

Later on, when I was "discovering" Bach, Beethoven and other great composers, and, in particular, when contemporary music - through Szymanowski's Symphony No. 3 - spoke to me with all of its enchanting force (and this happened when I was 11 years old) - for a short time Chopin moved into the background of my experiences.[3] However, he soon returned, but not in the same form that I knew from my childhood, not as the one whose music - experienced in the most intimate, though naïve way - moved me to tears that I so diligently tried to hide. Chopin returned to me in all of his power and beauty, as performed on the great stages of the

---

[1] The four-page undated manuscript of this essay may be found in the Witold Lutosławski Collection, Paul Sacher Foundation, Basel. The text was published as "Powroty: Chopin, nasz współczesny" [Returns: Chopin, our contemporary] *Polska* (9 (1970): 3-4, 20, 21); also published as "Chopin w moim życiu. Z archiwum Witolda Lutosławskiego," [Chopin in my life. From the archives of Witold Lutosławski] in a special issue of *Studio* (no. 1 (1 October 1995): 1-2) marking the occasion of the 13th International Chopin Piano Competition. [This and all subsequent notes by the editor].

[2] Lutosławski mentions this childhood fascination with Chopin in interviews with Irina Nikolska, *Conversations with Witold Lutosławski* (Stockholm: Melos, 1994), 74. In this book Chopin's name appears over twenty times - Lutosławski mentions him more often than either Beethoven or Brahms.

[3] The composer discusses this formative experience and his early fascination with Szymanowski's Symphony no. 3 in various interviews, most notably in Tadeusz Kaczyński, *Conversations with Witold Lutosławski. Revised and Expanded Version* (London: Chester Music, 1995; first published in 1972, first English edition 1984), 53-4; see also Irina Nikolska, op. cit., 74-75.

concert hall: it was the Chopin of Józef Hofmann, the Chopin of Brailowsky, Cortot, Orlow, and many others.[4]

At that same time a new image of Chopin appeared in my life when I was discovering his astounding features [*zdumiewające oblicze*] under my own fingers on the keyboard, during my studies at the Conservatory.[5] It happened precisely in this way - exactly "under the fingertips" and not solely through my ears and feelings - because this "keyboard-related" aspect of Chopin's music constitutes one of its most mysterious characteristics. In contrast to other compositions, I could practice works by Chopin without feeling any fatigue for long, long hours. It happened that way because (among other reasons) these works possess - in addition to their sonorous and spiritual aspects - their own, unusually highly-developed and one-of-a-kind characteristics, i.e. a purely physical, kinesthesic-tactile aspect that may be experienced by the performers. With no other composer in the whole history of music one could encounter the union of three elements that occurred with such an incomparable power and such an unbreakable cohesiveness: the elements of the hand, the keyboard, and the feeling of music through sound.

Nonetheless, this was not the only aspect of Chopin's music that allowed me to work on it for long hours and to listen to it with-

---

[4]Józef Hofmann (1876-1957) was a Polish - American pianist and composer, student of Moszkowski and Rubinstein. He was the founder of the Curtis Institute of Music. Alexander Brailowsky (1896-1976) was a French pianist of Russian descent who first performed Chopin's complete works in a series of recitals in Paris in 1924 and repeated this feat in 1960 for Chopin's 150th birth anniversary. Alfred Cortot (1877-1962) was a French pianist and conductor, the founder of École Normale de Musique in Paris who recorded numerous works by Chopin; Nicolai Orlow (1892-1964) was a Russian pianist known as an eminent interpreter of Chopin's music. Lutosławski probably heard these pianists in Warsaw during his studies at the Conservatory of Music in the 1930s. Biographical details of this period have not been researched yet.

[5]Lutosławski studied composition privately with Witold Maliszewski before becoming his student at the Warsaw Conservatory (1932 till 1937). His piano studies at the Warsaw Conservatory took place between 1927 and 1936 (with Artur Taube and Jerzy Lefeld). The program of the final piano recital included works by Chopin, Bach, Beethoven, Debussy, Liszt, Maliszewski, Mozart, Prokofiev, and Schumann. Cf. Tadeusz Kaczyński, *Lutosławski. Życie i muzyka* [Lutosławski: Life and music], vol. 9 in the series *Historia Muzyki Polskiej* (Warsaw: Sutkowski Edition, 1994), 22-23.

out the sense of fatigue [*znuźenie*]. I was convinced about this fact in the most forceful fashion much later, when for the only time in my life I was a member of the Jury of the International Chopin Piano Competition in Warsaw.[6] At that time I had to listen to Chopin's music for many hours every day, for several weeks on end. From my way of perceiving it [i.e. Chopin's music], this was virtually a trial by fire [*mordercza próba*].[7]   However, despite the performances of many participants of the first stage of the competition, who blundered their way through the music, "maiming" it in the process, and despite the necessity of listening to the same Sonata in B minor presented in very mediocre interpretations several times a day, despite my inability to do anything else during all that time - I still feel profoundly moved when I recall this period of an intense personal involvement [*obcowanie*] with Chopin's music.

Already before the war, I definitively gave up piano performance in order to dedicate myself exclusively to composition (here, I do not account for the duration of the war itself when playing the piano provided me with a basic source of income). This fact again created a distance between myself and Chopin, but our separation was not complete. Even today, I periodically return to his music.[8] From time to time I play through my favorite etudes,

---

[6]Unfortunately, the composer does not name the year and his "jury duty" is not mentioned in his biographies or interviews. Since the article first appeared in 1970 it could have happened in 1960 or 1955 (the programs of four competitions held between 1965-1985 do not list Lutosławski's name, cf. PMRC Collection).

[7]Lutosławski's expression means literally "murderous trial."

[8]The notion of returning to Chopin appears in an interview with Tadeusz Kaczyński (1972/1995), 171. When asked about what was of greatest value in the Polish music tradition to him, Lutosławski responded: "A truthful but extremely banal answer must be: Chopin. I go back to his music from time to time in various ways - I listen to it, or play it or study it. Even today - surprising, even absurd, though it may sound - I find in the course of my everyday work that his music refreshes my imagination in certain ways. But probably nobody would guess that Chopin's music had anything to do with the works which finally emerge from that relationship." Answering another question, about a particular Chopin work that he cherished as a "greatest revelation," the composer stated: "It is difficult to talk here about 'revelation,' since the word could be applied to so many things in Chopin which might not perhaps be ideally suited to illustrating my point. But there are certain pages or places in Chopin's

preludes, mazurkas, and larger works. I look through them and study them, continually discovering things that are new for me, things that are extraordinary. Above all, though, I always find in them something that remains unchangeably close to my heart, something that I love.[9]

These returns to Chopin have been particularly precious for me during difficult moments of my life.[10] At these times, they gave me a "dose" of a life-giving force by affirming my conviction about the existence of an ideal, better world - the world of artists and their creative imagination. The world brought to existence in Chopin's works is full of infinite enchantments and unfathomable riches that are, simultaneously, completely unusual. Despite its fantastic features, this world remains profoundly human: it is as deeply human as the intense, burning desire for the ideal.

Translated by Maja Trochimczyk

compositions which have a common origin though they differ in detail, theme or even texture. His *Prelude in D major* might be an example of this, or a phrase in the *Scherzo in E major*, the one with the dotted crotchets in the upper register. His *Etudes* contain a number of such passages."

[9]Irina Nikolska points out that Lutosławski's dramatic concept of form, with powerful culminations and an intricate flow of narration, revealing the true meaning of the musical developments only at the end of the work, is a result of his inspiration by Chopin. Cf. Irina Nikolska, "Dramaturgia i forma u Chopina a polska muzya XX wieku" [Dramaturgy and form in Chopin and Polish music of the 20th century] *Rocznik Chopinowski* 19 (part 1, 1987): 177-188, especially p. 184.

[10]The belief that music provides a form of "salvation" through its ideal beauty is a common thread in Lutosławski's interviews and statements. For a discussion of some of the tragic circumstances of his life and his ways of dealing with death in music see Maja Trochimczyk, "'Dans la nuit': The Themes of Night and Death in Lutosławski's Oeuvre," in *Lutosławski Studies*, Zbigniew Skowron, ed. (Oxford and London: Oxford University Press, forthcoming).

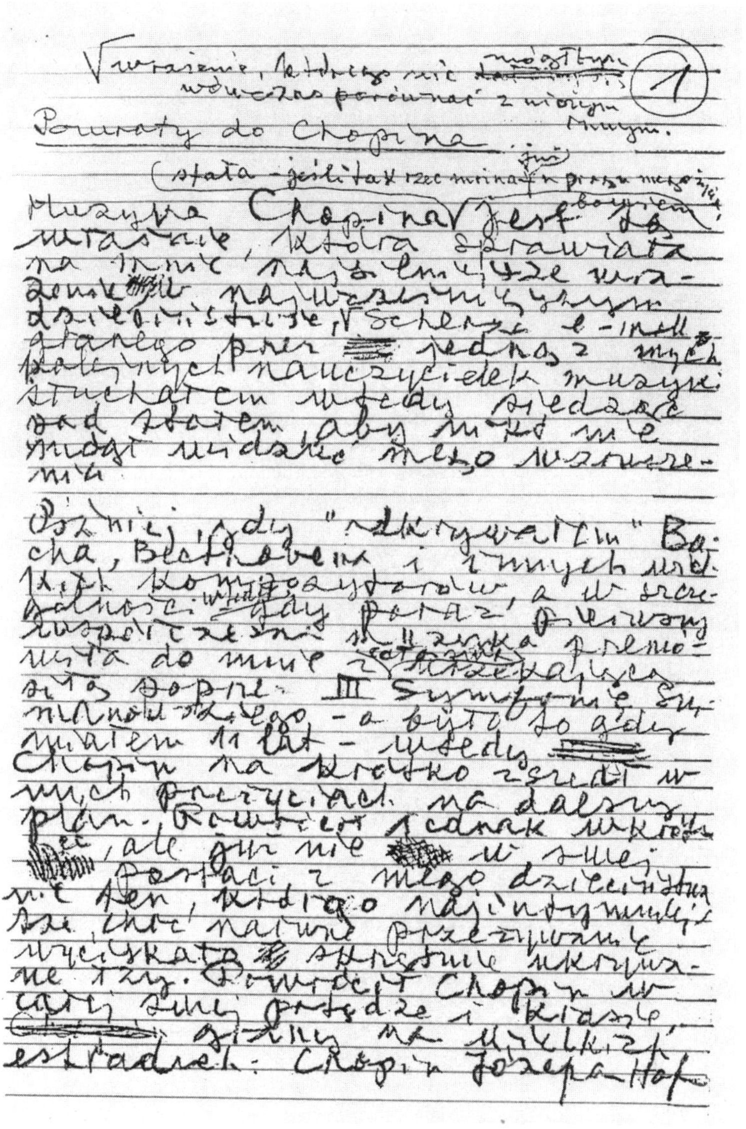

Figure 1: First page of Lutosławski's handwritten essay "Powroty do Chopina" translated here as *Back to Chopin*. Witold Lutosławski Collection. Paul Sacher Foundation, Basel, Switzerland. Used by permission.

Figure 1, cont.: Second page of Lutosławski's handwritten essay "Powroty do Chopina" translated here as *Back to Chopin*. Witold Lutosławski Collection. Paul Sacher Foundation, Basel, Switzerland. Used by permission.

PART II

ESSAYS IN POLISH MUSIC

(WILK PRIZES)

At Home with Phenomenology:
Ingarden's *Work of Music* Revisited

by Maja Trochimczyk[1]

Whereto?

What is "the work of music"? This question has spurred many answers, and is certain to stimulate many more: regardless of its definition, the "musical work" remains a paradigm of Western art music. What exactly is "Western art music," though? We will never get to Ingarden if we attempt to define it. Let us sweep this problem under the carpet, then, and focus on the notion of the work itself. In a recent excursus through the imaginary museum of musical works, Lydia Goehr argues that "the work" is an "open-concept" - a vessel which continuously changes form and content, so that we cannot say *what* the work is, we can only say *that* it is.[2] In Goehr's book, the name of Roman Ingarden, a Polish philosopher

[1]This paper is based on material from Chapter IV of my doctoral dissertation, entitled *Space and Spatialization in Contemporary Music: History and Analysis, Ideas and Implementations* (McGill University, 1994). A shorter version appeared in the *International Journal of Musicology* (vol. 6 (1998): 9-24; author listed as Maria Anna Harley) after being presented at the Annual Conference of the Canadian University Music Society, University of Calgary, June 1994. I wish to thank musicologists and music theorists (Zofia Helman, Bo Alphonce, Susan McClary, Alan Gillmor), philosophers (Philip Buckley and David Davies), and composers (Anna Zawadzka-Gołosz, James Harley) for helping me to improve this text by disputing my ideas and/or reading through the drafts.

[2]Open concepts (I) do not correspond to fixed or static essences, (II) do not admit absolutely precise definitions, (III) are intentionally incomplete so that unforeseen situations can lead to changes of definitions, and (IV) concepts are closed for certain purposes and open for others. See Lydia Goehr, *The Imaginary Museum of Musical Works: An Essay in the Philosophy of Music* (Oxford: Clarendon Press, 1992), 91. Goehr writes (p. 7): "I claim that the work-concept is an *open* concept with *original* and *derivative* employment; that it is correlated to the *ideals* of musical practice; that it is a *regulative* concept, that it is *projective*, and, finally, that it is an *emergent* concept."

of phenomenological orientation, appears only in the footnotes.[3] Does it mean that his phenomenological theory of the work of music, first formulated in 1928, and revised in 1957, is nothing but a historical footnote?[4] It must be more: why all the translations, why new editions?

Home, Sweet . . .

The preoccupation with the idea of the work of art is central to Ingarden's phenomenological aesthetics. In a lecture of 1970, for instance, Ingarden stated that "we should proceed in aesthetics not in an empirical-inductive way but work out an eidetic view of a general idea of a work of art and of the less general ideas of the works of the particular arts."[5] The notion of the "eidetic view" is very close to Husserl's "eidetic reduction," the fundamental concept of constituitive phenomenology: here, the Polish philosopher follows his teacher "back to the things themselves." The "thing" is the "work of art"- an intentional object which requires for its existence a material basis (i.e. the score, book, canvas), and a constitution in "the minds of the creator as well as the receptive experiences of the enjoyer of art."[6]

Ingarden's definition of *the work of music* crowns an

---

[3]Roman Ingarden (1893-1970) was a Polish philosopher of phenomenological orientation. After completing his studies with Edmund Husserl in Vienna, Ingarden was a university professor in Lwów (1925-1939) and Kraków (from 1945). His interests included onthology, epistemology, and aesthetics. References to his writings on music are included in subsequent notes.

[4]Roman Ingarden, *The Work of Music and the Problem of its Identity*. Trans. from the Polish by Adam Czerniawski (Berkeley: University of California Press, 1986). Orig. "Utwór muzyczny i sprawa jego tożsamości," in *Studia z Estetyki* [Studies in Aesthetics], vol. 2 (Warsaw: PWN, 1958), 163-299. The text was written in Paris, 1928, Lwów, 1933 and Kraków, 1958. The first versions was published as "O tożsamości dzieła muzycznego," in *Przegląd Filozoficzny* 26 (1933). Citations in this article are to Czarniawski's translation.

[5]Lecture in Amsterdam, 13 March 1970, quoted by Max Rieser in "Roman Ingarden and his Time," *The Journal of Aesthetics and Art Criticism* 39 no. 4 (summer 1971). Reprinted in Ingarden, *The Work of Music,* 159-173 (quoted from p. 159).

[6]Ingarden, *The Work of Music,* 160.

extensive discourse on the issue of its identity in a study that took its author 30 years to complete (1928-1958). The work is not the score, not the performance, not the perceptual experience, not the composer's idea; what is it, then? In the philosopher's words,[7]

> A musical work, understood as an artistic product of its composer, is first a schema designated by the score, second a determined multiplicity of possibilities designated by the areas of indeterminacy of the schematic product--each providing in realization one of the work's profiles. And each such profile may be realized within a certain class of identical, or at least similar, correct performances.

This definition articulates the co-constitution of the work by the imprecisely notated score and concrete performances. The "work itself remains like an ideal boundary at which the composer's intentional conjectures of creative acts and the listeners' acts of perception aim" (p. 119). It is one, "in contrast to the many concretions in specific performances."

Moreover - and Ingarden is very adamant about this point - the musical work "never attains the status of concrete sounds because these sounds are spatially and temporarily[8] individuated objects, whereas a musical work is a supraindividual and supratemporal structure, its individuality being purely qualitative."[9] In Ingarden's theory, the musical work is not ideal but intentional (p. 64). The work may not be experienced in itself, only in one of its profiles, articulated through a performance. The lacunae in notation allow for the introduction of ornaments, changes in instrumentation, tempo, etc. In Zygmunt Krauze's *Folk Music* (1972), for instance, the dynamic proportions between groups of musicians are left to the discretion of the conductor. The orchestra is subdivided into 21 small ensembles simultaneously performing authentic folk melodies (cf. Ex. 1, the seating plan and Ex. 2, an excerpt of the music). Through the course of the piece, the conductor selects instrumental groups to be momentarily highlighted by their higher dynamic level. Thus, individual melodies (or their pairs) briefly dominate the complex, spatially extended, continuous fabric of sound - a colorful, lively background from which the melodies arise and into which they

---

[7]Ingarden, *The Work of Music*, 150.   [9]Ingarden, *The Work of Music*, 120.

[8]This word is an erroneous translation of the Polish term "czasowo" which means "temporally" ("temporarily" means "tymczasowo").

dissolve. The fluidity of design expressed through lacunae in notation (the absence of dynamic signs in the score) cause each performance of *Folk Music* to be different. Yet, the work maintains its identity: its various interpretations are clearly recognizable as variants, or "profiles" of the same composition.

Ingarden's definition of the musical work may be applied equally well to Krauze's *Folk Music*, which specifies the positions of all instrumentalists on the stage and to Bach's *Kunst der Fuge* which does not have a "performing means structure" (term from Jerrold Levinson).[10] Only the areas of indeterminacy are different. Yet, Ingarden goes beyond separating the work and the performance; he notices that each performance may be "actualized" in many different ways by the members of the audience. He introduces a "differentiation between the work of music, its performance, and its concretion" (p. 20). The unrepeatable "concretion" of the performance occurs in a unique segment of lived time and depends on the listener's experience, knowledge, mood, attention, etc. (p. 66).[11] Ingarden models this idea of the "concretely experienced time" on Henri Bergson's concept of "duration" (*durée*).[12]

---

[10]Jerrold Levinson, "What a musical work is," *The Journal of Philosophy* 77 no. 1 (January 1980): 5-28.

[11]These perceptual images vary, even if, for instance, the same person repeatably listens to the same recording. The physical sound sequence is identical in each repetition, but the perception of it changes. For Ingarden, a recording is a full definition of a work, a real object, not an intentional object like the work itself (p. 116-119). The recording captures one of the multitude of possible performances, in which everything is "concretized" (p. 119).

[12]According to Bergson, duration is experienced in the flow of consciousness. See Henri Bergson, *Time and Free Will: An Essay on the Immediate Data of Consciousness,* trans. from the French by Frank L. Pogson (London: G. Allen & Unwin, 1950. Muirhead Library of Philosophy. 6th ed.; 1st ed. 1910). Original title: *Essai sur les données immédiates de la conscience* (1883-1887), published in 1889. Bergson explains: "pure duration is wholly qualitative. It cannot be measured unless symbolically represented in space" (p. 105). Pure duration, the unique, personal "time-as-experienced" is associated with intuition and the principle of life (*élan vital*). Ingarden mentions this theory as an inspiration for his analysis of the "concretely experienced time" in *The Literary Work of Art: An Investigation on the Borderlines of Ontology, Logic, and Theory of Literature,* transl. George G. Grabowicz (Evanston: Northwestern University Press, 1973). Orig. in German, 1st. ed. *Das Literarische Kunstwerk: Eine Untersuchung aus dem Grenzgebiet der Ontologie, Logik und Literaturwissenschaft*

According to the Polish philosopher, the work and the performance belong to two distinct ontological categories; the work is an object ("a purely intentional object," p. 117), the performance a process (p. 16). The performance occurs at a determined point in space and time (p. 11). In contrast, the "work of music possesses no defined spatial localization" (p. 18). It can be performed anywhere, at any time, but "no work is a *hic et nunc* developing acoustic phenomenon" (p. 19). Here, Ingarden clearly articulates the belief that "pure or disembodied sound" is the material of music.[13] In his theory, sounds as "processes or objects persisting and taking place here and now in real time and constituting the elements of specific performances do not belong to the musical work itself" (p. 42-43). "All the movements of the musical work itself exist together in a completed whole" while "each individual performance of a musical work spreads itself in time" (p. 16). Please note that Ingarden's ontology distinguishes three types of entities (in respect to their temporal permanence): *objects* subsisting in time (things), *processes* revealing the continuity of change, and *events* which occur instantaneously (temporal moments).

The supratemporality of the musical work does not preclude the existence of a unique, internal, temporal ordering within this work. Time in music is "structurally and qualitatively organized and the type and character of that organization depend on what sound structures fill out a particular movement or larger period of the work as a whole" (p. 76). Ingarden considers this "quasi-temporal structure" which "does not enter into the time-continuum of the real world" (p. 77) as an essential feature of each musical work. He explains that "both its supratemporality and its quasi-temporal structure remove the musical work from the real world and give it a self-contained character" (p. 79).

The fixed temporal form of the musical work may exist

(Halle an der Saalie: Max Niemeyer, 1931. 3rd. revised ed. Tübingen: Max Niemeyer, 1965). Polish trans. by Maria Turowicz, *O dziele literackim: Badania z pogranicza ontologii, teorii języka i filozofii literatury* (Warszawa: PWN, 1960).

[13]I borrow this expression from Don Ihde's phenomenological description of all auditory phenomena, including music. See Don Ihde, *Listening and Voice: A Phenomenology of Sound* (Athens, Ohio: Ohio University Press, 1976).

because of the work's articulation in the material basis of musical notation, defined as "a schematic construct with areas of indeterminateness" (p. 117).[14] The score is a sign system, an arrangement of symbols denoting pitch and rhythm, with additional information provided in verbal expressions (p. 39). The score designates the work and instructs on how to actualize it in performance. Yet, for Ingarden, the score is not a part of the work, which consists of sound constructs and non-sonic attributes of these constructs (I will discuss these terms later). Ingarden purges the work of music from texts, programs, images, evocations of feelings, etc. (pp. 50, 107). For him, all these elements merely *belong* to the work, they are not a *part* of it. Here, he reveals his allegiance to the formalist school of thought: he even cites Hanslick's *Vom Musikalisch-Schönen* (1854).[15] Since the notation is also extra-musical, only the bare structure of pure sounds remains. Having stripped music of all the "inessentials," the philosopher concludes that the musical work does not have a stratified structure and, thus, differs from works of the other arts. In his studies of the literary artwork, Ingarden proposed several conditions for a stratified structure: (1) the existence of diverse elements (in literature--sounds, meanings, objects); (2) homogeneous elements combining into a layer of a higher order, without (3) losing distinctiveness, and leading to (4) an organic totality of style emerging from the interaction of all these superimposed layers (p. 50). For Ingarden, the musical work does not satisfy these conditions.

---

[14]Here, I will follow Ingarden's usage of the term "the score" as a synonym of the notational definition of the work.

[15]See Eduard Hanslick, *On the Musically Beautiful* [Vom Musikalisch-Schönen,1854, trans. Gregory Payzant (Indianapolis, Indiana: Hackett Publishing Company, 1986). While Ingarden agrees with Hanslick and silently assumes the universal validity of absolute music, this idea has had many critics. Lydia Goehr points out the existence of the "separability principle" underlying the detachment of art from life (*The Imaginary Museum,* 158) while Carl Dahlhaus discusses "the principle of aesthetic autonomy" which frees music from its social functions and historical contexts. See Carl Dahlhaus, *The Idea of Absolute Music,* transl. from the German by Roger Lustig (Chicago and London: The University of Chicago Press, 1989). Originally published as *Die Idee der absoluten Musik* (Kassel: Bärenreiter Verlag, 1978).

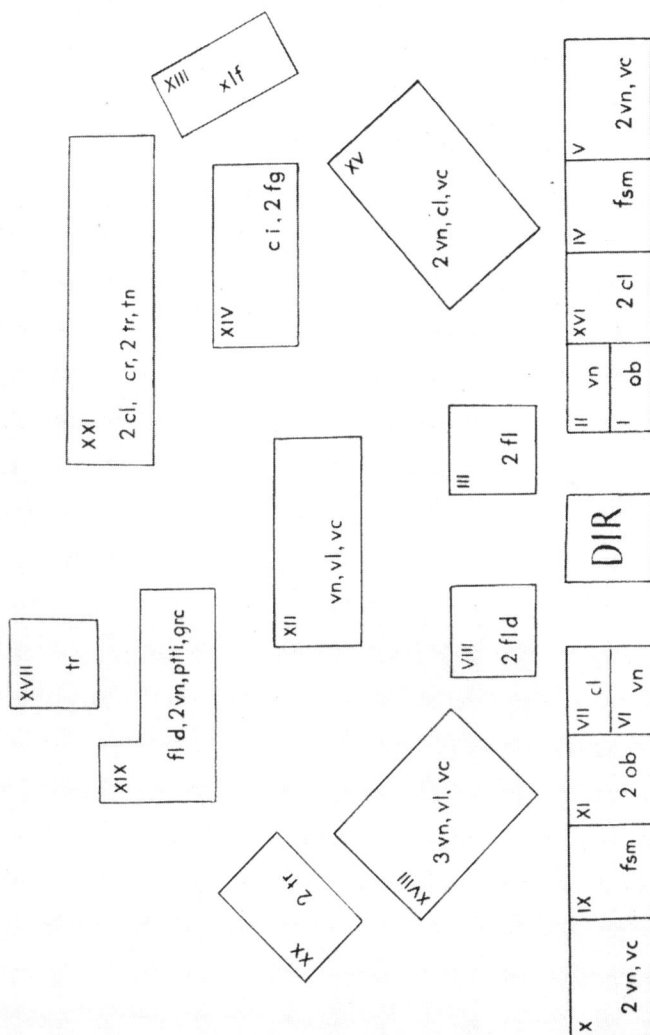

Example 1: Placement of 21 instrumental groups in Zygmunt Krauze's *Folk Music* for orchestra (1972). "DIR" indicates the location of the conductor. Zygmunt Krauze *FOLK MUSIC* (1973 by Universal Edition Vienna; Copyright by PWM-Edition, Kraków, Poland for Germany, the territories of the former Union of Soviet Socialist Republics and China). All Rights Reserved. Used by permission of European American Music Distributors Corporation, sole U.S. and Canadian agent for Universal Edition Vienna, and by permission of PWM.

Example 2: Collage of melodies in Krauze's *Folk Music,* p. 7.
Zygmunt Krauze *FOLK MUSIC* (Copyright 1973 by Universal Edition
Vienna; Copyright by PWM-Edition, Kraków, Poland for Germany, the
territories of the former Union of Soviet Socialist Republics and China).
All Rights Reserved. Used by permission of European American Music
Distributors Corporation, sole U.S. and Canadian agent for Universal
Edition Vienna, and by permission of PWM.

Example 3: Gesture of defiance in Witold Lutosławski's *Cello Concerto* (1969-1970), p. 44-45. *Cello Concerto* by Witold Roman Lutosławski. Copyright © 1971 by Chester Music Limited (PRS). All rights for U.S.A. & Canada controlled by G. Schirmer, Inc. (ASCAP). International Copyright Secured. All Rights Reserved. Reprinted by Permission.

. . . Home?

I would like to challenge Ingarden's rejection of musical imagery, texts and narratives from his definition of the "musical work" with a musical example from Witold Lutosławski's *Cello Concerto* (1969-70; p. 44-45, see Example 3). This work is appropriate because it ostensibly belongs to the domain of absolute music, among instrumental concerti by Chopin, Szymanowski or Bacewicz.[16] In Lutosławski's Concerto, however, the dramatic contrast between the two musical protagonists, that is, the solo cello and the orchestra led by the brass, appears to participate in a musical narrative which articulates the antinomy between the individual and the oppressive crowd. The orchestra repeatedly "shouts down" its sole opponent. At one moment in this struggle, the cellist makes a musical gesture of defiance, as if saying "just you wait and see!" Mstislav Rostropovich, to whom the *Concerto* is dedicated, knew of such situations from personal experience of life in the Soviet Union; he coined the "defiant" phrase quoted above during the rehearsals preceding the work's premiere. The programmatic narrative, however, originated with the composer himself. In one of the conversations with Tadeusz Kaczyński, Lutosławski described the *Cello Concerto* in dramatic terms, as the portrayal of the "conflict" between the soloist and the orchestra.[17] When, however, Kaczyński developed this general idea into a detailed plot, with gory details of "screams" and "beatings," the composer protested and asked to return to the terrain of absolute music. Notice that Lutosławski creates this vivid musical "drama" in the *Cello Concerto* purely in sound, without a text, without a programmatic title. Therefore, the apparently non-programmatic composition includes a hidden narrative based on

---

[16]Chopin wrote two Piano Concerti, Szymanowski two Violin Concerti, Grażyna Bacewicz (1909-1969), an accomplished violinist herself, was a composer of seven violin concerti and two with the cello as the solo instrument.

[17]See Tadeusz Kaczyński, *Rozmowy z Witoldem Lutosławskim* (Kraków: PWM Edition, 1972), 78-80; in English as *Conversations with Witold Lutosławski. Revised and Expanded Edition,* trans. by Yolanta May and Charles Bodman Rae (London: Chester Music, 1995).

non-musical gestures that are "coded" in instrumental sonorities. Although we know about the narrative schema of the *Cello Concerto* from the composer's interviews, the plot may be recognized without any extramusical props added on to the music. Here, the sound-constructs themselves and their homological relation to human gestures are carriers of meaning.

Ingarden would have had these elements banished to the sphere of "belonging" to the composition, not being a "part" of it. His work of music contains but a single stratum: sounds. Simultaneously, he does distinguish between the sonic and non-sonic components of the work.[18] In his theory, over and above the sonic components, that is, the layer of tone constructs, the musical work includes: (1) a quasi-temporal structure, (2) movement, (3) the intrinsic musical space in which the movement occurs, (4) emotional qualities, (5) aesthetically valuable qualities, (6) qualities of the values themselves (pp. 88-104). The philosopher borrows the notions of *movement* and *space* from Ernst Kurth's *Musikpsychologie* (1931).[19] *Movement* refers to the apparent motion of musical constructs, such as fast arpeggios or intertwined voices of a polyphonic composition seeming to move in a *musical space*, which "constitutes itself through the multiplicity of motions of the developing musical constructs" (p. 90-91). This space is related neither to the real space of performance nor to any imagined form of space associated with music. It is heard in motion and superimposed on the internal time of the musical work. Ingarden points out the plurality and hierarchical nature of musical *forms* which are the "shaping qualities" of sound constructs rather than forms in the

---

[18]Adam Czerniawski translates Ingarden's "dźwiękowe i nie-dźwiękowe składniki" (Ingarden 1958: 235) as "sounding and non-sounding elements" of the musical work. For several reasons, I prefer the more accurate translation of "sonic and non-sonic." In Polish, "dźwiękowy" refers to "sound" in itself, not to the physical actuality of the action of "sounding" which is expressed by the word "dźwięczacy." Ingarden does not use these terms in reference to concrete, physical processes.

[19]Ernst Kurth, *Musikpsychologie* (Berlin, 1931). Reprinted (Hildesheim, New York: Georg Olms Verlag, 1969). I discuss Kurth's ideas in the second chapter of *Space and Spatialization*. Related concepts of musical spatiality appear in Thomas Clifton, *Music as Heard: A Study in Applied Phenomenology* (New Haven, Conn.: Yale University Press, 1983).

strict sense (hence the italics). In music, various *forms* constitute recurring patterns, which, by virtue of their supratemporal nature and logical ordering introduce a "rational perspicuity" into the work (p. 96). Music without *emotional qualities* does not exist; yet these qualities differ from the particular feelings experienced by the performer or the listener. *Aesthetically valuable qualities* are revealed in both the sonic and the non-sonic elements of works (i.e the appeal of certain emotional qualities, the coherence of form, the correspondence of form and content, etc.). The *qualities of the values* are the most ambiguous; Ingarden does not clearly distinguish these qualities from values, and does not offer much beyond stating that each musical work is "designed to embody" a certain aesthetic value (p. 115).

The list of non-sonic components contains what Ingarden has already relegated to the domain of the "extramusical," for instance, the congruence between form and content, the beauty and ugliness of timbres, the qualities of lyricism or pathos, etc. This is just one of his inconsistencies. Actually, the whole differentiation into sonic and non-sonic components seems to contradict his belief that the musical work contains but a single sonorous stratum. Here, he is distinguishing at least two levels of this stratum by adding to music "extra-musical" elements ("qualities of values") that differ from imagery, texts, associations, and emotional content.

Where, What, Who?

Ingarden's theory locates music in the aesthetic domain of pure Art; this thesis has obvious socio-cultural limitations. The fullest critique of his stance has been offered by Zofia Lissa, a Polish musicologist of Marxist orientation, whose "Critical Remarks on Ingardenian Theory of the Musical Work" appeared in 1966 in Poland and in 1975 in Germany.[20] In this text, she referred mainly

---

[20]Zofia Lissa (1908-1980), "Einige kritische Bemerkungen zur Ingardenschen Theorie des musikalischen Werkes," in *Neue Aufsätze zur Musikästhetik* (Wilhemshaven: Heinrichshofen's Verlag, 1975), 172-207. Reprint from *International Review of the Aesthetics and Sociology of Music* 1 (1972): 75-95. Revision and German translation of "Uwagi o Ingardenowskiej teorii dzieła muzycznego" [Remarks about Ingarden's theory of the musical work] *Studia*

to the German translation of Ingarden's text, "Das Musikwerk," published in *Untersuchungen zur Ontologie der Kunst.*[21]

Lissa points out that Ingarden completely ignores the cultural aspects of musical works, such as their belonging to socially defined genres, their philosophical and cultural contexts, and the conditions of their reception (p. 173). She notices that Ingarden's range of examples is limited to the period from Johann Sebastian Bach to early Stravinsky, that is, from the age of Enlightenment to the beginning of the 20th century. Ingarden focuses on written music of European culture and ignores contemporary avant-garde (e.g. aleatoricism, electronic music, serialism) as well as the music of oral traditions, which, as Lissa reminds her readers, include highly developed non-European cultures and folk music of the Western world.

Considering the inconsistencies in Ingarden's theory of the stratification of the musical work reviewed earlier, it is not possible to unconditionally accept his definition of the musical work as the fundamental notion of Western music-making. However, it is equally impossible to completely reject his theory. Let us review some points of contention. For Ingarden, music has one layer, but it includes - by association, or extension - several different levels of non-sonic components. In addition, he claims that neither dance, nor music of religious ceremonies such as African drumming belong to music in the strict sense. Can we agree with that? Is there a concept of "music" - that we recognize and Ingarden strives to define - in African drumming? Ingarden writes about the dance (a distinct type of art, often co-existing with music): "The dance as ritual phenomenon or human expression should be classified with extra-artistic phenomena, birdsong and the like" (p. 46). Dance is dance, of course, and music is music - these are two different artistic domains. Does dance, though, belong with birdsong, a phenomenon of nature?

Estetyczne (1966): 95-113. English translation: "Some Remarks on the Ingardenian Theory of the Musical Work," in P. Graf and S. Krzemien-Ojak ,eds. and trans., *Roman Ingarden and Contemporary Polish Aesthetics* (Warsaw, PWN, 1975), 129-144. All references here are to the 1975 German edition.

[21]Roman Ingarden, "Das Musikwerk," in *Untersuchungen zur Ontologie der Kunst, Musik, Architektur, Film* (Tübingen: Niemeyer, 1962), 3-136.

In her essays, Lissa criticizes Ingarden's analysis of the relationships between the schematic notation and its different realizations in performance (she uses the example of electronic music to refute his thesis that notation is essential for a work's existence). Moreover, she does not share Ingarden's conviction that the quasi-temporal structure of the work implies a fixed ordering of the work's sections. Here she cites aleatoric compositions in open form, including pieces by Witold Lutosławski (*Jeux vénitiens*, 1961) and Kazimierz Serocki (*A piacere*, 1963), that do not have a stable temporal organization. Finally, the Polish musicologist notices the Ingardenian exclusion of vocal, vocal-instrumental and programmatic genres, limiting Ingarden's domain to "pure instrumental music" (p. 174-5). Thus, Lissa emphasizes the chronological, geographical, social and aesthetic boundaries of Ingarden's phenomenological theory.

While pointing out the contextual borders of Ingarden's "musical work," Lissa rightly scorns Ingarden's attempts at applying the "work-concept" to improvisation and folk music. The Arabic *maquam*, for instance, is not a work but a scale, a set of melodic formulas, and a formal type differently realized in each performance. This is an important point that recurs in later discussions of the "work-concept." According to Lydia Goehr, the disregard for conceptual differences between a work and an improvisation is a clear case of "conceptual imperialism."[22] Here, she rephrases Lissa's criticism of Ingarden's theory. It is obvious by now that many features of his conception limit its area of applicability to classical and romantic Western music.

Lissa's criticism goes further than pointing out the limitations of the domain of applicability of Ingarden's theory. In a later study of the ontology of musical works, Lissa attacks the idea itself as she argues that an all-embracing concept of the work cannot exist.[23] Each historical epoch brings a revision of the work's

---

[22]Goehr, *The Imaginary Museum*, 245.

[23]Zofia Lissa, "Über das Wesen des Musikwerkes." *Musikforschung* no. 2 (1968): 157-182. Reprinted in *Neue Aufsätze zur Musikästhetik* (Wilhemshaven: Heinrichshofen's Verlag, 1975), 1-54. German translation of "O istocie dzieła muzycznego" [On the essence of the musical work]. *Polish Musicological Quarterly. Muzyka* 13 no. 1 (1968): 3-30.

definition, which depends on shifting contexts and varying perspectives (e.g. ontological, technological, historical).[24] Therefore, the notion of the work is in constant flux. It is important to note that Ingarden's theory of the work of music and its critique by Lissa, especially in her second article, "Über das Wesen des Musikwerkes" (1975) inspired German discussions of the ontology of music, especially Carl Dahlhaus's concept of "music as text" (1979) and Hans Heinrich Eggebrecht's notion of "Opusmusik" (1975).[25] Both German scholars came to Ingarden's defense. Eggebrecht, for instance, strongly disagreed with Lissa's claim about the fluidity of the "essence of the musical work" and claimed that "the dissolution of the concept 'opus' would be identical with the dissolution of the principle of European music."

Yet, the "fluidity"of the musical work articulated in Lissa's texts clearly prefigured the idea of the openness of the "work-concept" presented by Lydia Goehr in *The Imaginary Museum of Musical Works* of 1992. Here, Goehr suggests that the existence of the work as separate from the score and from its performances is completely fictional.[26] She states that the object of music is found "through projection or hypostatization" (p. 174): "For each work composed we project into it 'object' existence" (p. 7). Thus, the notion of the musical work is projected onto the music and does not ontologically belong to it.

If this notion is "fictional," however, it is at least an intentional and intersubjective fiction. Ingarden's phenomenology describes the notion of the work as intentional, that is, as arising from intersubjective intentions which are shared by cultural communities and which change in historical time. He does not claim that music

---

[24]In "Über das Wesen des Musikwerkes" Lissa writes: "Eine jede Zeit stellt den bisherigen Begriff des Musikwerkes unter ein Frageziechen und modifiziert seinen Inhalt. Es gibt also keine absolute, unveränderliche Definition dieses Terminus. Er verändert seinen Sinn unter verschiedenen Gesichtspunkten: 1. dem ontologischen, 2. dem technologischen, 3. dem normativen, der aus dem vorigen hervogeht, und 4. dem historischen." (p. 52).

[25]Carl Dahlhaus, "Musik als Text," in *Dichtung und Musik. Kaleidoskop ihrer Beziehungen*, Günter Schnitzler, ed. (Stuttgart: Klett-Cotta Verlagsgemeinschaft, 1979), 11-28; Hans Heinrich Eggebrecht, "Opusmusik," *Revue musicale de Suisse romande* 115 no. 1 (January 1975): 2-11.

[26]Goehr, *The Imaginary Museum*, 106.

belongs to a transcendental world of pure ideas; on the contrary, he takes time and effort to characterize the limited changeability of the work that remains "identical" to itself despite the transience of its shifting profiles which arise from the work's "immersion in the world." The Polish philosopher subtly stratifies and contextualizes the musical work and he certainly does not think that what he describes is a fiction.

In a 1993 text, "History and the Ontology of the Musical Work," Leo Treitler again attempts to challenge the intentional status of the work on the grounds of its apparent non-historical nature.[27] Treitler equates Ingarden's "characterization of the musical work as an intentional object with a mode of existence like that of a unicorn" (p. 483). He cites Jeffrey Kallberg's fascinating study of Chopin's variants, which reveal the conceptual fluidity of design in several of his pieces including the *Nocturne* Op. 62, No. 1.[28] Treitler points out that the variability of this music resembles that of an oral tradition, and quotes from his research into the orality of Gregorian chant. At the end, he proclaims the openness and historical changeability of musical works as contradicting Ingarden's theory. But Ingarden was aware of this! That is why he introduced the notion of the "profile" into his definition of the musical work in the first place. In Ingarden's theory, the work's notational schema contains areas of indeterminacy which may be completed in a variety of ways, each giving rise to one particular profile of the work. The variants of Chopin's *Nocturne* are this work's different profiles, all endorsed by the composer. The musical work is not an "Urtext" - a fixed, completely unchangeable entity determined by the composer and reified by the editor of that composer's works.

---

[27]Leo Treitler, "History and the Ontology of the Musical Work," *The Journal of Aesthetics and Art Criticism* 51 no. 3 (Summer 1993): 483-497.

[28]Jeffrey Kallberg, "Are Variants a Problem? 'Composer's Intentions' in Editing Chopin," in *Chopin Studies*, Jim Samson, ed. (Cambridge: Cambridge University Press, 1990), 257-276.

At home? Absolutely!

The Polish philosopher's two-fold definition of the musical work has many advantages. He considers the schematic character of notation as a virtue: it allows for many different performances, which interpret and realize the same work in a multitude of ways. Ingarden does not identify the work with its notation and he does not reduce music to pitch-time relationships, while still acknowledging the primacy of melody, rhythm and harmony in structuring the music (p. 87). His notions of "quasi-temporal structure" and "sound-construct" are particularly rich in interpretative potential. Here, I will briefly discuss Ingarden's concept of the "sound-construct."

According to Ingarden's theory, every work of music consists of a chain of successive sound-constructs which "possess various properties of melody, rhythm, harmony, agogics, dynamics, and coloring" (p. 86). These complex entities pass one into another and form the "sound base" of the work (p. 83-4), the basic sonorous layer upon which "non-sonic" elements are superimposed. This idea of the "sound-construct" resembles the notions of "virtual image" or "auditory image" discussed in the psycho-acoustic theories of Stephen McAdams (1984) and Albert Bregman (1990).[29] Note that in current psycho-acoustic practice "sound" usually denotes the physical event, while "sound image," or "auditory event," or "auditory stream" describe its psycho-acoustic counter-part (Blauert used the second term in 1983; Bregman the third in 1990).[30] In accordance with the less precise musicological

---

[29]Stephen McAdams, *Spectral Fusion, Spectral Parsing and the Formation of Auditory Images* (Ph. D. Diss., Stanford: Stanford University, 1984). Albert S. Bregman, *Auditory Scene Analysis: The Perceptual Organization of Sound* (Cambridge, Mass.: Bradford Books, MIT Press, 1990). See also Maria Anna Harley, "Auditory Scene Analysis: Future Directions for Musicological Research," in *Musicology and Sister Disciplines*, David Greer, ed. (Oxford: Oxford University Press, forthcoming), 491-493.

[30]Jens Blauert, *Spatial Hearing.: The Psychophysics of Human Sound Localization,* transl. from the German by John S. Allen. (Cambridge: MIT Press, 1983). Orig. published as *Räumliches Hören.* (Stuttgart: S. Hirzel Verlag, 1974); Bregman, *Auditory Scene Analysis*.

parlance, "sound" in my text draws from both meanings; it refers to the idealized image envisioned by the composer and schematically notated in the score. This type of "sound" is, to use Ingarden's terminology, an "intentional object" and, as such, is not strictly perceptual. Musical notation designates the sound constructs imprecisely, while the performance realizes their concrete images by completing the notational schema in a particular way. Thus, the composers require the performers to produce a series of sounds (i.e. physical occurrences) in the hope of achieving a series of sound images (i.e. auditory events) as a result. They may, for example, superimpose sounds from several instruments of different timbres in order to create complex virtual sounds with a variety of "emergent properties" which do not belong to any of the elemental sounds. The famous opening chord of Igor Stravinsky's *Symphony of Psalms* (1931) is a notable example of this technique; many other instances may be found in the output of Oliver Messiaen, i. e. in his method of portraying birdsong in instrumental music by super-imposing several instruments that together articulate the timbral complexities of the portrayed natural sound. In compositions of the Polish school of sonorism, especially by Kazimierz Serocki, there is a marked tendency of juxtaposing several instrumental sounds to create larger sonic entities, particularly in works for percussion (*Continuum* for six percussionists, 1965-66).[31] Bregman comments that music tries to "fool the auditory system" into hearing fictions.[32] The existence of such "fictions" is one more indication that the musical works belong in the world of intentionality, beyond the real and the ideal.

Ingarden's limitation to purely instrumental, non-pro-grammatic music may also be seen in a positive light. As Don Ihde writes, "wordless music, in its sonorous incarnation, when com-pared to language is 'opaque,' as nothing is shown through the

---

[31]See Tadeusz Zieliński, *O twórczości Kazimierza Serockiego* [About the music of Kazimierz Serocki] (Kraków: PWM Edition, 1984). See also Maria Anna Harley, "The Polish School of Sonorism and its European Context," in *Crosscurrents and Counterpoints: Offerings in Honor of Bengt Hambraeus at 70*, Per F. Broman, Nora A. Engebretsen, and Bo Alphonce, eds. (Gothenburg, Sweden: University of Gothenburg, 1998), 62-77.

[32]Bregman, *Auditory Scene Analysis*, 457.

music. The music presents itself; it is a dense embodied presence."[33] The adoption of Ingarden's constraint reducing music to sound-constructs makes possible a description of the "embodied presence" of music without complications arising from its theatrical, narrative, or textual characteristics. It is important to remember, though, that this description does not capture the essence of music, but simply articulates one of its aspects.

Last but not least among the virtues of Ingarden's theory is the awareness of the mutability of the work of music in historical time. Ingarden notices that the work undergoes an apparent transformation as a result of changing opinions of the musical public (as expressed in writings and in performance practices). In a given country at a given time "a single intersubjective dominant aesthetic object" exists (p. 155). This object, that is, one of the work's profiles, may be modified because of the intentional nature of the work itself (which, however, does not change in the process).

Where Ingarden erred was in seeing all music in the light of his definition of the "work of music." The Polish philosopher also had a number of preconceptions about specific features of works, such as, for instance, the necessity for formal coherence. Ingarden claimed that internal, temporal discontinuity placed a composition at the "borderline between a musical work and a sequence of uncoordinated sounds" (p. 93). Contemporary music has seen many challenges to this belief, for example, in works by John Cage. Here, I do not mean *4'33"* - too often used as a symbol of the "emptiness" of modern music - but rather the *Freeman Etudes* for violin solo (1977-80/1989-90), which are notoriously discontinuous in perception. Yet, to all intents and purposes, they are works--with a fully notated score and a potential variability in performance. While Ingardenian notion of the "work of music" is applicable to Cage's compositions, I am not sure, if the philosopher would have been able to appreciate this work. In response to Lissa's attack, he clearly indicated that recent compositional "experimentation" did

[33]Don Ihde, *Listening and Voice: A Phenomenology of Sound* (Athens, Ohio: Ohio University Press, 1976), 158.

not interest him in the least.[34]

Home and Beyond

   Ingarden's theory, like all other products of human thought, is delimited by his knowledge, beliefs, silent assumptions, and cultural prejudices. It was created within a certain environment, a *Lebenswelt* of the Western-European intellectual tradition, a philosophical world of Husserl and Bergson, a musical world of Beethoven and Chopin, of Hanslick and Kurth. Within this Life-World, the "musical works" have a place of honor. Within this world, Ingarden's theory can be understood; here it functions. When taken beyond, to India or Africa, the phenomenology of musical works ceases to make sense. Music as a part of ritual, music in integral connection to dance, music linked to the whole universe through an elaborate symbolism of Indian theory is not the music that Ingarden knows, accepts, and explains. At home with the traditions of the Western culture, Ingarden concentrates on musical artefacts and suggests that these artefacts are totally dependent on human intentions. Musical works, like all other works of art, are created to be and to be contemplated. Let me conclude that, even with its limitations, Ingarden's phenomenological aesthetics guides well our peregrinations through "the imaginary museum of musical works" of the past and through new realms of works yet to be composed, performed, heard and reflected upon in the future.

---

[34]Roman Ingarden, "Uwagi do Uwag Zofii Lissy," [Remarks to remarks by Zofia Lissa], *Studia Estetyczne* vol. 3 (1966): 115-128. In German : "Bemerkungen zu den Bemerkungen von Professor Zofia Lissa." *Studia Filozoficzne* 4 (1970): 351-361.

Revitalizing Sonata Form: Structure and Climax in Szymanowski's Op.21

by Stephen C. Downes

Of the structures and designs found in instrumental music composed from the late eighteenth century onwards there is none more greatly privileged than sonata form. This status is based largely on the achievements of the Austro-German "Classical Masters" - Haydn, Mozart and, especially, Beethoven - a legacy that, as is well known, became a source of much anxiety for any nineteenth-century composer who dared to consider working with this form. It has often been said that nineteenth-century theory tended to fossilize a previously vital, varied form into dead rules and fixed schemes. Contemporary with this are the enlivening narratives supplied to sonata form movements by much literary, or poetic musical criticism:[1] in Romantic aesthetics the sonata became a drama, a heroic struggle to synthesize opposing forces into victorious apotheosis.[2] It was also seen as the most profound expression of the principles of evolution and becoming which were central to the idea of organic unity. In this essay theoretical and hermeneutic interpretations of sonata form from around the turn of the century will give a context for understanding the unusual design of Szymanowski's Second Piano Sonata in A major, Op. 21 (1911), which Alistair Wightman, one of Szymanowski's most productive apologists, has called "one of the very finest late-romantic transformations of sonata form."[3]

In his magisterial historical survey of the sonata, William S. Newman suggests that "one almost accepts as axiomatic the idea

---

[1]See Thomas Grey, "Metaphorical Modes in Nineteenth-Century Music Criticism: Image, Narrative, and Idea," in *Music and Text: Critical Inquiries,* Steven Paul Scher, ed. (Cambridge: Cambridge University Press, 1992), 93-117.

[2]On symphonic examples see Scott Burnham, *Beethoven Hero* (Princeton: Princeton University Press, 1995).

[3]Alistair Wightman, Preface to *Szymanowski Piano Works I,* Complete Edition, vol. B7 (Kraków: PWM Edition, 1983), xx.

that in the Romantic era a complete sonata must describe an over-all curve of force. It must, in other words, achieve a climax profile that takes in, and therefore unites, all of its movements."[4] In the nineteenth century the phenomenon of climax was imbued with special significance through its associations with the striving for the sublime or transcendent inherent in the notion of "becoming" - a central aspect of Romantic aesthetics.

"Romantic poetry is constantly developing," wrote Friedrich von Schlegel in 1798, "that is in fact its true nature: it can forever only become."[5] Leonard B. Meyer has proposed two types of climax in music, "syntactic" and "statistical," and argued that Romantic works characteristically exhibit an "emergent structure" which emphasizes "statistical processes" generated by the "secondary parameters" - texture, tessitura, dynamics, etc. - over the syntactic structure generated by the "primary parameters" - tonality, melody and rhythm.[6] Meyer's conclusion is that "the increasing importance of statistical form, coupled with the considerable growth in the size (length) of movements, leads to important changes in the structure of sonata-form movements."[7] At the vanguard of these changes, of course, was Beethoven. As Robert P. Morgan writes:[8]

> Although Beethoven did not abandon sonata form, his rethinking of it in more organic terms as a dynamically evolving process leading toward a moment of final culmination fundamentally affected both the structural and expressive features of his work.

---

[4]William S. Newman, *The Sonata Since Beethoven* (New York: W. W. Norton, 1983), 45-46.

[5]Friedrich von Schlegel, *Athenaeum,* translation from *Music and Aethetics in the Eighteenth and Early Nineteenth Century,* Peter le Huray and James Day, eds. (Cambridge: Cambridge University Press, 1981), 246.

[6]Leonard B. Meyer, *Style and Music: Theory, History and Ideology* (Philadelphia: University of Pennsylvania Press, 1989), 198.

[7]Meyer, *Style and Music,* 306.

[8]Robert P. Morgan, "Coda as Culmination: the First Movement of the *Eroica* Symphony" in *Artistic Theory and the Exploration of the Past,* Christopher Hatch and David W. Bernstein, eds. (Chicago: University of Chicago Press, 1993), 358.

Morgan describes the beginning of the *Eroica* as "a new kind of opening," and "a new, fundamentally developmental kind of 'first theme' which will require equally new treatment."[9] This notion, which seems to chime with Meyer's idea of "emergent structure," is far from new. At the beginning of this century Ernst Bloch argued that "unlike a theme of Mozart's or the theme of a fugue, the Beethovenian theme is itself an undeveloped one from the *Eroica* onwards" and that this became a model of procedure for Beethoven's successors - "Mahler, as the last, and often transparent, user of the old tonality, never pursued thematic development from an established beginning. And for this very reason, his *espressivo* does not derive from something but is moving towards something."[10] It was Adorno's opinion, too, that the most important thing about Beethoven's themes is that they "become." For Adorno, in fact, the "theme" and "outcome" in Beethoven's sonata forms is tonality and this, he argues, is why Schenker's theories provide a much more "fruitful" basis for analyzing the music of Beethoven than they do for that of Haydn or Mozart.[11]

　　Schenker's disdain for the emphasis on "surface" themes and melodies found in much nineteenth-century theory of sonata design is well known. Schenker's aim was to reveal the "concealed unity" which guaranteed the organic structure of sonata form masterworks and ultimately to demonstrate their derivation from a single, goal-directed Ursatz.[12] The aesthetics lying behind this theoretical view were widely held by composers of the late nineteenth century working with sonata form. As Peter Smith has noted, the idea of the sonata as an organically unified unfolding of

---

[9]Morgan,"Coda as Culmination," 363.

[10]Ernst Bloch, *Essays on the Philosophy of Music,* translated by Peter Palmer (Cambridge: Cambridge University Press, 1985), 231. This section comes from Bloch's *Das Prinzip Hoffnung* (1938).

[11]Theodor Adorno, "On the Problem of Musical Analysis," trans. Max Paddison, *Music Analysis* 1 (1982): 175.

[12]Heinrich Schenker, "Organic Structure in Sonata Form" in *The Masterwork in Music,* Vol. 2 (1926), trans. Orin Grossman, in *Readings in Schenker Analysis and Other Approaches,* Maury Yeston, ed. (New Haven: Yale University Press, 1977), 38-53.

developing material can be seen in both Schenker and Brahms's[13]

> attempts to reconcile the sharply articulated musical surfaces of
> the late eighteenth-century sonata style with the esthetics of the
> nineteenth century which, in contrast, favored continuous
> motion and highly evolutionary formal relationship. . . .
> Brahms and Schenker strove to subsume the elements of
> division and repetition within a continuous and dynamic
> unfolding.

In the first movement of Brahms' Piano Quartet in C minor
Op.60, for example, this continuous dynamism is generated by an
unstable first group which acts as an anacrusis to a structural
downbeat on a lyrical second subject. Smith points out how, in the
recapitulation Brahms "sustains" tension beyond this downbeat by
having the second subject in the dominant rather than the expected
tonic.[14]

A dynamic view of form was widely held by German
theorists in the early years of this century - just when the young
Szymanowski was immersing himself in all things Austro-German.
The lectures of August Halm at the Wickersdorf Freie Schul-
gemeinde emphasized the energetic properties of music. He analyzed Beethoven's *Waldstein* Sonata, for example, in terms of a
"dynamic-formal unfolding" or "dynamic curve."[15] The similarity
of these ideas to Ernst Kurth's "wave forms" - where music's kinetic
energy breaks down the articulations of Classical grouping structure
- is not surprising since Halm and Kurth met at Wickersdorf in
1911-12.[16] Both inherited and heightened the structural and

---

[13]Peter H. Smith, "Brahms and Schenker: A Mutual Response to Sonata Form,"
Music Theory Spectrum 16 (1994): 77.

[14]Smith, "Brahms and Schenker, 90.

[15]See Lee A. Rothfarb, "The 'New Education' and Music Theory, 1900-1925," in
Music Theory and the Exploration of the Past, Hatch and Bernstein, eds., 458-
62.

[16]See Ernst Kurth, *Selected Writings*, Lee A. Rothfarb, ed. (Cambridge: 1991),
12. Kurthian ideas strongly inform Józef Chomiński's lengthy (but now rather
old) discussion of Szymanowski's piano sonatas in *Studia nad twórczością
Karola Szymanowskiego* (Kraków: PWM Edition, 1969). Amongst other topics,
Chomiński consideres ways in which Classical schemata are transformed by

aesthetic importance given to climax by nineteenth-century romanticism and praised Bruckner's symphonies in particular as some
of the finest examples of this principle. In the 1927 revision of his
1911 *Musical Form*, Hugo Leichtentritt includes diagrammatic
"curves of intensity" for part of Bruckner's Eighth Symphony
(1885), as well as the last movement of Beethoven's *Hammerklavier*
Sonata and Wagner's Prelude to Act I of *Tristan and Isolde*.[17]

For Brahms, as Siegfried Kross has suggested, the model of
structure and climax suggested by the sonata form movements of
Beethoven's middle period was something of a problem:[18]

> The creation of a symphonic form which would become
> constantly more intense, reaching a climax only in its finale,
> had become such a problem for Brahms that he drew the
> conclusion that "if one dares to compose symphonies after
> Beethoven, they must look completely different.

According to Kross, this ultimately led Brahms to break
with the Beethovenian model of apotheosis. Indeed, the curious
dissolution of the "heroic" opening of Brahms's Third Symphony
(1883) into a rather resigned closure has been be taken by Susan
McClary to reveal "tonality and sonata in narrative crisis."[19] Smith
argues that in this movement Brahms keeps the tonal tension going
right through the recapitulation by withholding the structural
dominant until the coda. This is certainly a climactic moment but
the rhetorical shape of the movement as a whole undermines the
narrative paradigm of a continuous struggle to resolution (even the

---

energetic processes. My analysis which was carried out before I was able to
consult Chomiński's essay, shares this concern but gives it a much broader
context.

[17]Hugo Leichtentritt, *Musical Form* (Cambridge, Mass.: Harvard University
Press, 1951). The Beethoven reference is on page 339, the Wagner on 357, the
Bruckner on 385 and 417.

[18]Siegfried Kross, "Thematic Structure and Formal Processes in Brahms's Sonata
Movements," in *Brahms Studies: Analytical and Historical Perspectives,* George
Bozarth, ed. (Oxford: Clarendon Press, 1990), 426.

[19]Susan McClary, "Narrative Agendas in 'Absolute Music:' Identity and Difference in Brahms's Third Symphony," in *Musicology and Difference,* Ruth Solie,
ed. (Berkeley: University of California Press, 1993), 330.

finale's more intense struggle ends in similar resignation). It could be argued that one of the main differences between Brahms and Bruckner lies in their solutions (or otherwise) to the problematic relationship of structure and climax in sonata form. This relationship, which appears to be an almost universal source of concern to nineteenth-century composers, was what subsequent, early twentieth-century Austro-German theorists like Halm, Kurth and Leichtentritt took as a central principle.

For the young Szymanowski, whose music circa 1906-1912 combines the chromatic tonal musical idiom of contemporaneous German works with a characteristic "Young Poland" enthusiasm for Nietzsche's concept of the "Dionysian" and the Schopenhauerian "Will," a solution to this issue was paramount. For Szymanowski, climax must somehow retain its power to express and confirm the principle of romantic becoming. Brahms's apparent failure, or unwillingness, to deliver the climactic apotheosis is unthinkable for Szymanowski, and he never pulls his punches in the struggle. His Second Piano Sonata in A major, Op.21, written between spring 1910 and summer 1911, is a fascinating example of the rethinking of sonata structure in the light of these concerns.

Szymanowski composed the sonata for his great friend, Artur Rubinstein. In September 1911 the composer wrote:[20]

> I just finished my Second Piano Sonata before Artur's departure - at first I did not attach any great importance to it, but after detailed scrutiny and Artur's playing of it, all of its "concealed qualities" came to light with the result that Ficio [the conductor Grzegorz Fitelberg] and Artur are highly taken with it, rating it almost more highly than the Second Symphony.

In order to reveal those "concealed qualities" it seems appropriate to employ analytical techniques derived from Schenker, for whom the power of "organic" sonata form lies in "concealed unity" rather than "superficial, surface themes and modulations." To indulge Schenker's nationalism a while, Szymanowski's letter suggests that he had succeeded where previous "Italian" composers

---

[20]Teresa Chylińska, *Karol Szymanowski: His Life and Works,* Polish Music History Series, vol. 5 (Los Angeles: Friends of Polish Music at USC, 1993), 57.

characteristically failed, for[21]

> instead of organic works of art, they created works whose parts
> are comparable to raisins placed in dough - even in a baked cake
> the raisins are clearly distinguishable. The sonata, however, is
> no cake; it is a tonal mass formed from a unitary material in
> which the raisins are not distinguishable.

By his own admission it seems that Szymanowski's ripest "raisins" lie concealed within the work's structure. That he held this work in high regard is confirmed by an extended description of the piece in a letter to the musicologist Zdzisław Jachimecki. It was very rare for Szymanowski to discuss technical details of his work. In this description he conceives the whole work as being in two parts and rather curiously describes the first as "a regular sonata form."[22] It is, in truth, far from "regular." Rather, it exploits an unusual dynamic relationship between the first and second subject areas, a reformulation of functions of exposition, development and recapitulation, and a unique solution to the problem of the balance between the first movement and the rest of a multi-movement work. I will examine these three areas- thematic character and contrast, first movement structure, and the form of the whole piece - in turn.

Thematic Character

In the first movement the dynamism which drives the structure and the climactic closures which articulate it, are not merely products of the rhetoric of what Meyer calls "secondary parameters," they are also generated by a carefully-paced progression from "vagrant" chromatic symmetries to "home" diatonic tonality. The contrasting character of the two principle "themes" is essential to this progression. In fact, it is arguable that "thematic" is hardly the right way to describe the opening section at all. It is a perfect example of Ernst Bloch's notion of the "undeveloped" opening. The turbulent, unstable rhythm and harmonic ambiguity

---

[21]Schenker, "Organic Structure," 52.

[22]A translation of this description is in Chylińska, *Szymanowski*, 57-61.

suggest the as yet unformed, as if the piece is emerging from some
primeval chaos to gradually "become." The initial upward surging
phrases are like uncertain, embryonic versions of the characteristic
"rocket" gestures of the heroic sonata. Again, this can be interpreted as a post-Beethovenian gesture. As McClary has said, beginning with the *Eroica*, Beethoven "began to make it seem that the
protagonist [the first subject] was inventing itself and determining
from its own quirks its own tailor-made succession of narrative
events, while still holding on to the norms of tonality and sonata that
guaranteed intelligibility."[23] Now, it is how tonality and the principles of sonata are regained that make Szymanowski's movement
so dynamic.

The principal controlling harmony of the opening section is
the diminished seventh. Jim Samson has identified measure 16 as
the first "structural downbeat" but does not fully explain why this
is heard as such.[24] As Ex. 1 shows, this is a significant point of
arrival because it is here that a system of the three transpositions of
diminished seventh harmony is completed. The right hand in
measures 1-8 appears to consist of three chromatically embellished
statements of diminished seventh I (B - D - F - G-sharp); measures
9-15 are controlled by diminished seventh II (G - B flat - C-sharp -
E). The appearance in measure 16 of the third diminished seventh
III (A - C - E-flat - G-flat) completes the twelve-note aggregate
within this system. Its structural importance is signaled or highlighted by the new chordal texture and elaboration by neighboring
harmonies (including other diminished sevenths) as the top voice
outlines the controlling chord.

Procedures such as this are merely an extension of
nineteenth-century practice. To further pursue the Beethovenian
legacy one could cite the "counter-structure" of diminished sevenths
that operates in the slow movement of the Piano Sonata Op. 10, No.
3.[25] In Beethoven, of course, this remains subsidiary to the diatonic
structure. In later nineteenth-century chromatic style the position
becomes more ambiguous. In the Prelude to Act III of Wagner's

---

[23]McClary, "Narrative Agendas," 336.

[24]Jim Samson, *The Music of Szymanowski* (London: Kahn & Averill, 1980), 56.

[25]See Christopher Wintle, "Kontra-Schenker: *Largo e Mesto* from Beethoven's
Op. 10 no.3," *Music Analysis* 4 (1985): 145-182.

Parsifal, for example, a diminished seventh system appears to be the controlling principle of harmonic structure: the triads on the musical surface being merely momentary products of voice-leading between more fundamental diminished chords.[26]

Similarly, the opening section of Szymanowski's sonata contains brief triadic clarifications within the prevailing diminished seventh environment. The "G-sharp - E" third outlined by the chromatic bass descent, accompanying the initial presentation of diminished seventh I (B - D - F - G-sharp), gives these measures a strong dominant quality. The start of the second statement of this diminished seventh is accompanied by a similar bass descent from G-sharp. This time, however, it stops at F and this pitch is treated as the local dominant to B-flat, the bass motion of a fourth being coincident with the upper voice arrival on D (measure 6). This initiates a pattern which suggests triads on B-flat, A, D-flat and C. The ambiguity of this passage (measures 5-9) is generated not through lack of tonal references but, rather, by their super-abundance. The upper line can be heard as maintaining the diminished seventh I up to the A-flat of measure 9 which, in fact, turns out to be a passing note within the first statement of diminished seventh 11. The triadic resolutions, meanwhile, suggest that the upper line outlines a sixth (C - A-flat) in F major-minor. The metric irregularities and placing of accents create further ambiguity in this line by hinting at the potential significance of C - D-sharp - F-sharp, alien members of diminished seventh III. (One might also point out the introduction of whole-tone sonorities.) What is clear is that the passage is transitional between more stable statements of diminished sevenths I and II. But the triadic refe-rences within this transition are significant in that they adumbrate the future tonal argument. When the model is sequentially repeated a semitone lower (measures 12-15) the clearest tonal reference is now to E. Thus a relationship between F and E is emerging. F returns as the bass note supporting diminished seventh III, and this finally resolves, via B-flat, to an A-major triad at the end of measure 20. The passage which follows, continues the preoccupation with diminished sevenths, leading to momentary clarification of A-minor (measure 35- suggesting a

---

[26]Robert P. Morgan, "Dissonant Prolongation: Theoretical and Compositional Precedents," *Journal of Music Theory* 20 (1976): 62-72.

modally mixed tonality). This is quickly brushed aside, but the tonal
relationship of F and E to A, though as yet incompletely formed, is
suggested.

The first clear, cadential progression does not occur until
measures 40-44. This is the moment which Szymanowski described
as a *Höhepunkt* - a recourse to German terminology which confirms
his debt to German Romantic aesthetics and, in particular, to dynamic conceptions of form.[27] The "home" diminished seventh type I
moves into a climactic clarification of E-flat. The tritonal relationship of this to the previously emergent A tonality suggests symmetrical organization of the work's harmonic structure.   But the
succeeding "linking theme," to use Szymanowski's description,
reveals the E-flat to be the first chord in a functional II-V7 preparation of D-flat, the key of the second subject area (Ex. 2). Significantly, though, this diatonic progression is colored by the re-
introduction of diminished seventh type III (D-sharp - F-sharp - A -
B-sharp). The pitch A is the only member of type III that is not also
part of V7/D-flat. The significance of this dissonant pitch as the
dominant seventh harmony is heightened by descending chromatic
motions in inner parts spanning a D-flat/C-sharp - A-major third.
Thus A persists in lurking, only partially revealed, in the
"background."

The transition was markedly contrasted from the opening
section by clear cadential articulation. This characteristic persists
in the theme which follows. Indeed, the opening measures of the
second subject area make pointed references to cadential 4-3
suspensions and its phrases function like a "classical" sentence - a
short, 2-measure idea is repeated and followed by a longer,
balancing but more developmental phrase (Ex. 3). The introduction
of this type of stable thematic construction is a vital stage in the
ongoing process of emergent structure. As Adorno might say, in
this piece the "tectonic" and the "dynamic" are one.[28]

---

[27]Chylińska's translation, (*Szymanowski,* 58) does not refer to this single use of
German in a description otherwise entirely in Polish. On the importance of
"highpoints" in Romantic music see Kofi Agawu,   "Structural Highpoints in
Schumann's *Dichterliebe,*" *Allisic Analysis* 3 (1984): 159-180.

[28]Theodor Adorno, *Mahler: A Musical Physiognomy,* translated by Edmund
Jephcott (Chicago: University of Chicago Press, 1992), 93.

Diminished Sevenths

Example 1: Tonal structures in mm. 1–20 of Szymanowski's Piano sonata op. 21. 1a: Diminished sevenths.

1b: Analysis of tonal structures.

Example 2: Transition to Second Subject (mm. 44–53). Szymanowski's Piano Sonata Op. 21. From Karol Szymanowski, *Dzieła* [Works], vol. 14, *Utwory fortepianowe* [Piano Works], Władysław Kędra, ed. (Kraków: PWM Edition and Vienna: Universal Edition, 1968). Used by permission.

This differentiation of material contrasts with another Polish sonata of the time, Paderewski's Piano Sonata in E flat minor Op.21 (1903) whose "continuous drive," in Newman's description, "becomes essential partly to mask the late-Romantic composer's increasingly inability or hesitation to commit himself to frank, clear-cut themes. Yet without such themes the drive sacrifices its main structural landmarks."[29]

The stability of this passage is, however, only relative. Under the "cadential" 4-3 melodic motions the A-flat fifth of the local tonic is chromatically altered to A-natural, the pitch whose shadowy presence persisted through the previous section. Indeed, the stronger diatonic and thematic character serves to highlight chromatic inflexion. The shift from A-flat to A-natural introduces a significant surface augmented triad (D-flat - F - A-natural) and initiates a process in which eventually all seven pitches of the A major diatonic collection, and a climactic resolution on V/A, appear within a period which opens and closes in D-flat. Szymanowski is exploiting the common tone D-flat/C-sharp to fluctuate between two keys a third apart, creating what William Benjamin has called "interlocking diatonic collections."[30]

The second subject area as a whole outlines a developmental wave form which peaks at a climactic return of the theme (measure 91) where reharmonization and enharmonic "respelling" makes the previously latent A major manifest. This is part of a process leading to a *precipitando* arrival on the dominant of A which marks, in Classical tonal fashion, the end of the exposition of material (Ex. 4). This dominant ends an exposition that had eschewed outright

---

[29]Newman, *The Sonata Since Beethoven,* 689.

[30]William Benjamin, "Interlocking Diatonic Collections as a Source of Chromaticism in Late Nineteenth-Century Music," *In Theory Only* 1 (1976): 11-12 & 31-52. This feature of the harmonic organisation of the phrase is reflected in a larger dimension. At measure 78, the midpoint of the second subject area, there is again a resolution onto the dominant of A. This, in turn, moves by semitonal part movement to the dominant of D-flat, a progression which is then treated sequentially to generate a resolution onto a C triad, thus completing a pattern of three triadic resolutions at distances of a major third. The first two triads are easily understood as dominants in the prevailing D-flat/A major context, so, similarly, the C triad is heard as a dominant allusion to F major - the key center which completes the D-flat - A - F augmented triad relationship.

diatonic affirmation of its tonic. In the first subject area A major-minor was suggested as one of several tonal allusions subsidiary to progression within a system of diminished sevenths, the position of A at the top of a latent hierarchy of tonal centers being conveyed by the dominant quality of the opening and the "cadences" (if that is the right word) of measures 18 and 35. The second subject area alludes to A as a source of chromaticism within a D-flat tonal area. Momentary resolution onto the dominant of A is emphasized by its position at the central, climactic point of the phrase (measure 60), but the thoroughly emphatic dominant that signals the end of the exposition shows that Szymanowski is still concerned with shaping the large structure by diatonic articulation at major formal junctures. It is at these moments that the "background" of tonal expectations emerges on the musical surface.

First Movement: Tonal and Rhetorical Structure

Having examined the character of the two main contrasting sections of the exposition I will now go on to explore the design of the first movement as a whole, in particular the way in which Szymanowski reinterprets the functions of development, reca-pitulation and coda. Several parallels can be drawn between this movement and Berg's Piano Sonata, written just two years earlier (1908). In both works progression through a system of symmetrical chords plays a highly significant role in harmonic structure. In the first part of its exposition Berg's work exploits augmented triads in a manner similar to the way Szymanowski uses diminished sevenths in the opening section of his sonata - establishing a means of harmonic progression towards completion of the total chromatic. Berg uses this system as a crucial agent in the move to recapitulation. The "home" B - E-flat - G triad which characterizes the opening theme is meticulously avoided during the bulk of the development, gradually emerging only in the retransition as a sign of return. This allows Berg to dispense with diatonic articulation at this structural juncture.[31] The opening material thus returns as part

---

[31]Wintle, in "Kontra-Schenker," points out the importance of augmented triads in Berg's Sonata.

of a continuously developing argument.

Szymanowski, too, is concerned with reshaping the dynamics of conventional sonata design - in particular by re-inventing the nature of recapitulation and enriching tonal resources with symmetrical harmonies of structural import. The emphatic elaborations of V/A that ended the exposition are followed by a return to diminished seventh harmonies and the fluid turbulence of the opening material. Szymanowski does not control the appearance of diminished sevenths as Berg controls augmented triads. The "home" diminished seventh type I returns just four measures into the new section (though most of the harmony is of type III). This, along with the unstable, open-ended phrases, undermines any sense of recapitulation when the opening theme and diminished seventh I return 33 measures later (measure 140) - it is a moment undifferentiated from the material which precedes it. Before we know it, exact transposition of material from the exposition has led to climactic articulation of the preparation of the "modulation" (from nowhere?) to the recapitulation of the second subject. The conventional structural downbeat at the moment of recapitulation is absent.

Wagner's criticism of Beethoven's use of traditional re-capitulation in the *Leonore Overtüre* No.3 is to the point here:[32]

> Whoever has eyes to see will recognize precisely in this great overture how detrimental it was for the master to retain the traditional form. For can anyone capable of understanding such a work not admit that I am right in identifying its weakness as the repetition of the first part following the middle section, which distorts the idea of the work to the point of incomprehensibility; and all the more since in all other parts, and especially at the end, the dramatic development can be recognized as the master's sole determinant? Whoever is sufficiently unbiased and has the sense to realize this will have to admit that it could only have been avoided by completely

---

[32]Wagner, "Über Franz Liszts symphonische Dichtungen," trans. Morgan, in "Coda as Culmination," 375. Schenker, in turn, in a discussion of recapitulation in sonata form, criticizes Wagner for focusing on the demands of a supposed program rather than "the drama of the fundamental structure," *Der Freie Satz* [Free Composition], vol. 3 of *New Musical Theories and Fantasies* (New York: Schirmer Books, 1979), 137 n.

giving up the recapitulation... and that from this would have
come the point of departure for the construction of a new form.

As Adorno said, recapitulation "revokes what, since
Beethoven, had been the decisive element, the dynamic of
development."[33] The Romantic generation after Beethoven did not
give up recapitulation but, as Charles Rosen has suggested,
"preferred to place the climax, the point of extreme tension, very
near the end of a work ... what they reject, in most cases, is the sense
of climax and resolution at the end of the development and the
beginning of the recapitulation."[34] In a later work which engages
with sonata form - the last movement of Mahler's Sixth Symphony
(1903)- Adorno sees recapitulation "not separated from what went
before, the musical flow passing unnoticed into it."[35] This is very
similar to what happens in Szymanowski's sonata. But the principle
of recapitulation - the restatement of previous themes and resolution
of tonal dissonances not dissolved or disregarded, it is merely
displaced to later in the structure. As Samson says in a discussion
of Schoenberg's early experiments in sonata form, the First String
Quartet- which appears to have been modeled in some way on the
first movement of the *Eroica*, and the Chamber Symphony - "while
a contrast between tonally stable and tonally unstable passages
remained essential to the sonata dialectic in the nineteenth century,
there was [at the turn of century] a much more flexible attitude
towards the placing of such passages."[36] Szymanowski's development section is mainly based on material from the characteristically
unstable first subject area. This leaves the second subject free to
function as the agent of tonal resolution. Replaying the dynamics of
the opening section allows Szymanowski to build another climax to
the movement's first emphatic statement of the home, goal tonality
and to do so without interrupting the flow by an articulated
restatement of a first subject.

---

[33]Adorno, *Mahler*, 94.

[34]Charles Rosen, *Sonata Forms*, revised edition (New York: W.W. Norton,
1988), 393.

[35]Adorno, *Mahler*, 93.

[36]Jim Samson, *Music in Transition* (London: Dent, 1977), 96.

The transition to the second subject is transposed down a major third, so that A major rather than D-flat is the diatonic goal. Samson sees this as "preserving an important aspect of sonata dialectic" in its statement of material previously exposed outside the home key.[37] Although there is a remnant of this function I am not so sure that it is as straightforwardly traditional as that. Up to this point, the tonic has only been implied by passing clarifications or dominant assertion: this restatement of the movement's only clearly articulated theme is where the tonic A first emerges clearly as part of a single trajectory of becoming. As the development section dissolves the obligation to recapitulate a first subject area, the structure resembles a two-part AA" design, with the first part moving from "chaos" to the dominant via the mediant, and the second from renewed "chaos" to final confirmation of the tonic. Again there is a remnant of traditional sonata process in the "interruption" caused by the dominant area leading not to tonic but to renewed "chaos" in the development. In this respect Szymanowski's design retains some similarity to Schenker's model of sonata structure with an "interruption" of the descent of the fundamental line at the end of the exposition.[38] We can recall McClary's idea that Beethoven attempted "to make it seem that the protagonist was inventing itself and determining from its own quirks its own tailor-made succession of narrative events, while still holding on to the notions of tonality and sonata that guaranteed intelligibility." Szymanowski, of course, is stretching the norms of sonata design further than (or at least, very differently from) Beethoven in an attempt, as my title suggests, to revitalize the form. The structure which results blurs and reinvents traditional articulations and functions. Example 5 attempts to draw together some of these aspects of overall design in the movement.

---

[37]Samson, *The Music of Szymanowski*, 57.

[38]Problems associated with accommodating the transposed second subject structure within a single *Ursatz* are discussed by Smith in "Brahms and Schenker."

Example 3: Diagram of tonal structure in the second subject of Szymanowski's Piano Sonata op. 21.

Example 4: Move to Structural Dominant at the close of the exposition in Szymanowski's Piano Sonata op. 21, mm. 91-97. Copyright 1912 by Universal Edition A.G., Wien, Copyright renewed 1940. Copyright of the revised version 1968 by Universal Edition, A.G., Wien. All rights reserved. Used by permission of European American Music Distributors Corporation, sole U.S. and Canadian agent for Universal Edition A.G., Wien.

Example 5: First movement. Design, tonal structure and "intensity curve."

Example 6: Coda of the first movement of Szymanowski's Piano Sonata Op. 21, mm. 231-343. Karol Szymanowski, Piano Sonata in A major, op. 21. Copyright 1912 by Universal Edition A.G., Wien, Copyright renewed 1940. Copyright of the revised version 1968 by Universal Editon A.G., Wien. All rights reserved. Used by permission of European American Music Distributors Corporation, sole U.S. and Canadian agent for Universal Edition A.G., Wien.

Example 5 is carefully drawn to reflect the durational proportions of a recently recorded performance by Martin Roscoe.[39] An informally sketched, Leichtentrittian, "curve of intensity" locates the main climaxes.

The example also shows how transposition to A guarantees another important aspect of harmonic structure. The transition to the second subject now becomes informed by the "home" dimi- nished seventh type I rather than type III. As in the corresponding passage in the exposition, the one pitch member of the diminished seventh which is dissonant with the associated dominant seventh is retained and emphasized. In the recapitulation this pitch is F-natural. By exploiting keys a major third apart Szymanowski has ensured that the same augmented triad emerges in the foreground chromaticisms of both statements of the second subject. In the exposition A-natural was introduced as a chromatic inflection of the D-flat triad; here, F-natural is introduced in identical fashion as an inflection of the A major triad. The same process of fluctuating tonality is pursued in the recapitulated second subject as that demonstrated in Ex. 3, so that now the F major diatonic collection interacts with the prevailing A major, with a resolution on the dominant of F at the mid-(and highest) point of the phrase. This suggests the possibility of extending the relationship of keys a third apart from D-flat to A to F - completing at a middleground level the augmented triad that informs the chromatic surface.

The climactic end of the second subject area is altered to facilitate resolution onto E as dominant of A. The coda which follows is short by late nineteenth/early-twentieth-century standards (it is only 13 measures longer than the codetta to the exposition) but it serves a vital function within the single tonal trajectory of the movement for it is here that F begins to emerge as an important source within the controlling A major (Ex. 6). The rhetoric of the coda is certainly emphatic, but its brevity is significant. The possibility of F as the third member of an augmented triad of tonalities remains largely unfulfilled. Significantly, A major remains the tonal center of the second part of the sonata.

---

[39]Martin Roscoe, pianist, *Second Piano Sonata in A major, Op. 21* by Karol Szymanowski, in vol. 1 of *Szymanowski Piano Works*, Naxos CD 8.553016 (1995).

Szymanowski's decision to employ a mono-tonal scheme for the whole work is not simply, as Samson has suggested, "in recognition of the tonal instability of his basic material,"[40] it is a decision more strongly motivated by a concern to create a single, evolving tonal structure which unites the whole work in a single, dynamic impulse. The coda to the first movement looks beyond its own close towards the tonal preoccupations of the second part of the sonata.

The Structure of the Work as a Whole

The second part of the sonata consists of a theme and nine variations which contain within them the functions of intermezzo, scherzo, slow movement, and fugal finale. Example 7 sets out the design and the main tonalities. Szymanowski's idea of subsuming several functions within one continuous movement is, of course, far from new (four-movements-in-one pieces by Liszt and Schoenberg come immediately to mind) but it brilliantly serves the purpose of creating one grand sweep to a final apotheosis and offers a solution to the "problem" of the finale - about which more later. Each variation plays a role within a goal-directed trajectory, allowing Szymanowski to include dance movements (a minuet and a sarabande) without losing the "kinetic clarity and lucidity of gradation" which Boris Asafiev (displaying his debt to Kurth) saw as the advantage of the sonata cycle over the suite (where minuets and sarabandes might be more expected).[41]

The theme is given in Example 8. Its first chromatic element is the semitonal motion from C-sharp to B-sharp, enharmonically sounding like a mixture of major and minor. This is a reinterpretation of the chromatic dyad which would be the main element in a resolution of an augmented triad F - A - C-sharp to an F triad to complete the symmetrical system implied by the first movement (recall Ex. 5). Here it initiates a chromatic process in

---

[40]Samson, *The Music of Szymanowski,* 60.

[41]Boris Asafiev, *Musical Form as a Process* (1930), trans. in *Russian Theoretical Thought in Music,* Gordon D. McQuere, ed. (Ann Arbor: UMI Research Press, 1983), 233. Asafiev edited and wrote an introduction for the Russian translation of Kurth's study of counterpoint in 1931.

which elements of F major interact with the prevailing A major (see the analysis below Ex. 8). This signals that the unfinished business of the first movement expanding the relationship of F within an A major tonality- will be the main concern of the first part of the second movement, as Example 7b, which outlines the tonal structure of the whole of the second part of the sonata, demonstrates. Variations 7-9 confirm the A major tonality by movement from I to V via the submediant - recalling the importance of that tonal area in the emergence of A in the structure of the first part- as preparation for the final synthesis.

The set of variations, and indeed the whole sonata, works towards the synthesis and apotheosis of the fugal finale. Szymanowski describes the music from variation five as "apparently tending toward some ultimately decided expression."[42] This final goal is preceded by a glimpse of the turbulent instability of the first part of the sonata, a reminder of chaos before the coming of order - as, in Szymanowski's words, "a series of nearly disordered chords . . . ushers in a violent change of mood" after the sixth variation (minuet). The variation which follows he describes as a "frenzied movement" in which there are "a few fragments of new themes which immediately disappear without trace." This leads to a cyclic return of the theme of the opening of the sonata, specifically linking this section to the works inchoate origins, before "this entire chaos suddenly lessens and sinks into nothingness."

The theme from the opening of the sonata returns once more in the closing climax of the fugal finale as part of the last variation's act of monumental synthesis. Fugue was a favorite device of Szymanowski's to bring large-scale works to a close (he also used it in the First Piano Sonata and the Second Symphony). As we have seen, finales became notorious stumbling blocks for composers after Beethoven. Wagner once said to Cosima that "last movements are the precipices; I shall take good care to write only single movement symphonies."[43] The conflation of intermezzo, dance, cyclic return and slow movement leading to final fugue within the continuous second part of Szymanowski's sonata is designed to solve this problem.

---

[42]Chylińska, *Szymanowski*, 59.

[43]Quoted in Grey, "Metaphorical Modes," 102.

Example 7: Second Part: Overall design and tonal structure

Mm	Title	Key	Tempo indications; Description
1	Theme	A	*Allegretto tranquillo*
17	Variation 1	A	*Poco piu Vivace*
33	Variation 2	A	*Poco meno (Andante tranquillo)*
49	Variation 3	F	*L'istesso tempo*
62	Variation 4	B-flat	*Allegretto scherzando e capriccioso*
93	Variation 5	f-sharp	*Tempo di Sarabande*
130	Variation 6	E	*Tempo di minuetto*
183	Variation 7	A	*Largo*
238	Variation 8	c-sharp	*Allegro molto impetuoso*
276	Variation 9	A	*Allegro Moderato (poco scherz.) (Fugue)+Coda-Poco meno Allegro; Grandioso ed imposante.*

Example 7a: Overall design.

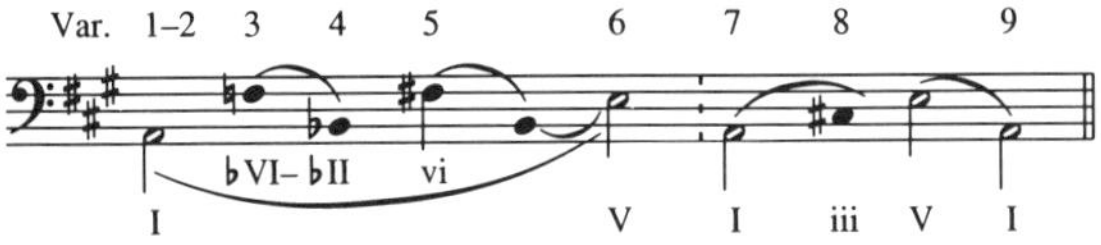

Example 7b: Tonal structure.

Example 8: Theme of the Second Movement in Szymanowski's Piano Sonata Op. 21, mm. 1–16. From Karol Szymanowski, *Dzieła* [Works], vol. 14, *Utwory fortepianowe* [Piano Works], Władysław Kędra, ed. (Kraków: PWM Edition and Vienna: Universal Edition, 1968). Used by permission.

But why end with a fugue? We can usefully explore the differing characterizations of fugue and sonata form to understand Szymanowski's decision. Asafiev, describing what he calls the "psychological role" of the symphonic finale wrote:[44]

> it seems to me that it would be most correct . . . to characterize the meaning and development of the finale's formation as a wave-like intensification of unified feeling, or as an ascent, in opposition to the dramatic formation of the first movement of the symphony which is characterized by conflict, by the overcoming of contradictions.

By the time of the final fugal variation the "drama" of the tonal conflict opened up, and only partially resolved, by the first movement of Szymanowski's sonata has been worked out. Fugue seems to be the ideal vehicle for the expression of Asafiev's "intensification of unified feeling." Both Bloch and Halm viewed fugue as lacking the dynamic tension of sonata form, but the latter saw the richer harmony of the nineteenth century as the means to climaxes not found in Bacchanal fugue, enabling "the more expansively formed fugue" which "had to manifest more distinct high points and climactic curves."[45] Halm also highlighted the continuity which fugal writing assured:[46]

> The fugue theme . . . must demand extension- its melody is indeed spun out when the next voice announces the theme, and the voice that first had the theme is here in particular not permitted to discontinue either externally or internally caesuras must simply be avoided, since not all the sounding voices may have a caesura at the same time. "Infinite melody" rules in the fugue.

The young Szymanowski would have loved the Wagnerian terminology which Halm employs here. The idea of continuity

---

[44]Asafiev, *Musical Form,* 233.

[45]August Halm, "On Fugal Form, Its Nature, and Its Relation to Sonata Form" (1913), trans. Edward Lippman, in *German Essays on Music,* Jost Hermand and Michael Gilbert, eds. (New York: Continuum, 1994), 122.

[46]Halm, "On Fugal Form," 124.

which Halm ascribes to fugue has a long tradition. Marpurg, in the mid-eighteenth century, highlighted this too, and furthermore, linked this aspect to a characteristic process of culmination toward the end. Again, comparison with sonata form is instructive, particularly with regard to return or recapitulation of material. David A. Sheldon has written:[47]

> In a . . . sonata . . . a tonic return represents a return to the material of the very beginning (albeit with new associative meaning) and a lessening of the tension created by the preceding development. In a fugue, on the other hand, Baroque theorists such as Marpurg and Scheibe stress that the developmental process should continue. The effect of this tonic return is expected to be one of culmination, not one of resolution. It is by means of momentum and energy that a fugue closes, not recapitulation and repose.

We have already seen how Szymanowski ensures continuity of tension in the sonata design of the first movement by employing a new approach to recapitulation, so it is not surprising that the momentum of fugal writing should attract him. The main issue, though, is Sheldon's last sentence concerning the way a fugue closes. With virtuoso contrapuntal technique and rhetorical control Szymanowski builds up wave upon wave towards the final climax of the last pages. Here Szymanowski exploits almost every conceivable device - broadening tempo, massive textures over long pedal points, contrapuntal combinations including cyclic return of the sonata's opening theme, and a *precipitando* rush to the final cadence - in the attempt to produce one last culmination in synthesis. The music (and the pianist) is straining at every seam, and it is hard to deny an element of bombast (Ex. 9).

It is easy to see in Szymanowski's closing passages an imminent crisis in how large pieces end. It was a crisis felt by many of his contemporaries - composers, aestheticians and theorists alike. As Bloch said, "by its very nature the end is a very difficult chapter, even for Beethoven." [48] For Beethoven's successors, Bloch

---

[47]David A. Sheldon, "The Stretto Principle: Some Thoughts on Fugue as Form," *Journal of Musicology* 8 (1990): 566.

[48]Bloch, *Essays,* 40-41.

argues, "climax and resolution are necessary but very often this results in the exaltation having the appearance of being simply a neat arrangement." For Bloch it was Bruckner who eventually was able to "disinfect the symphonic organism . . . rid it of all extrinsic fever -heat mounting only in accordance with the will and not in accordance with the work." Whether one agrees with Bloch's verdict on Bruckner (hero, too, of Kurth and Halm), the point is justly made. A work like Skriabin's Fifth Piano Sonata (1908), where, as Samson notes, "formal tensions result . . . from a conflict between the cumulative momentum of the music . . . and the formal constraints of the tripartite model,"[49] ends, not in climactic apotheosis (as did his previous, and very similarly structured, Fourth Piano Sonata) but in a violent, almost destructive gesture of tonal ambiguity. The end of Szymanowski's *King Roger*, "curiously premature and inconclusive" as Samson calls it,[50] has been compared to the end of Skriabin's *Prometheus* - in both an end seems to be imposed upon material that suggests continuous, endless, transformation.[51]

In an assessment of Henry James, Joseph Conrad wrote, "the desire for finality is one for which our hearts yearn, with a longing greater than the longing for the loaves and fishes of this earth." Conrad continues, however, by suggesting that "one is never set at rest by Mr. Henry James' novels. You remain with a sense of life going on. It is eminently satisfying, but it is not final." [52] As the nineteenth century ended and a new "modem" era seemed to be opening up, the "problem of the happy end" as Bloch put it, became acute. "All new music," suggests Adorno, "is tormented by the question of how it can close, not merely end," and while Adorno

---

[49]Samson, *Music in Transition*, 169.

[50]Samson, *The Music of Szymanowski*, 151.

[51]On the poetic/psychological resonances in the curious ending of *King Roger* see my "Themes of Duality and Transformation in Szymanowski's *King Roger*, " *Music Analysis* 14 (1995): 257-313.

[52]Quoted in David Lodge, "Ambiguously Ever After: Problematic Endings in English Fiction" in *Working With Structuralism* (London, New York: Routledge, 1986), 151. On narrative closure in relation to Szymanowski's Op. 24 see my *Szymanowski as Post-Wagnerian: "The Love Songs of Hafiz" Op. 24* (New York: Garland Publishing, 1994), 190-223.

believes that the "intensification of expansive power" of the finale of Mahler's Sixth Symphony "needs to be complemented by a capacity for imposing order."[53] Robert Samuel's cites Sponhauer's view of the movement as ultimately a negation of closure and rejection of the Utopian goal of the sonata ideal.[54] As in so much modem fiction, the archetypal romantic (heroic) narrative plot is discarded as illusory. One might here cite Sibelius's Fourth Symphony, exactly contemporary with Szymanowski's sonata, which, in Eero Tarasti's semiotic reading, contains reversals of the "chaos-order" narrative program and negations of kinetic properties of the "Will."[55]

The relationship of climax and form remained a central compositional and aesthetic concern throughout Szymanowski's artistic life. This project sometimes generated entirely new formal solutions. For example, Samson compares and contrasts Szymanowski's First Violin Concerto with Skriabin's *Poem of Ecstasy* - in both there is a "single long progression towards the final climax" but in Szymanowski's piece, unlike Skriabin's this "gradually unfolding structure . . . is achieved entirely without the support of a sonata form background."[56] In his exotic scores (the Third Symphony, for example) Szymanowski brings climactic progression into a dialogue with Oriental stasis, the result of which is entirely individual. But Szymanowski continued to turn to sonata designs and fugal finales in several later works (the two String Quartets, 1917 and 1928, and the Third Piano Sonata 1918). Joseph Straus has written that "it is no longer possible in this century . . . to write a sonata form that arises organically, spontaneously, and seamlessly from the musical relationships . . . twentieth-century composers inevitably approach the sonata self-consciously and often . . . with

[53]Adorno, *Mahler*, 96-97.

[54]Robert Samuels, *Mahler's Sixth Symphony: A Study in Musical Semiotics* (Cambridge, New York: Cambridge University Press, 1995), 80.

[55]Eero Tarasti, *A Theory of Musical Semiotics* (Bloomington: Indiana University Press, 1994), 242-65.

[56]Samson, *Music in Transition*, 170.

malice aforethought."[57] This is not so in Szymanowski. As Zofia Helman has said, the deliberate gulf or "distance" between old forms and new techniques in Neoclassicism is hardly felt in Szymanowski:[58]

> what Szymanowski did was to transform and develop the older ideas of form by adapting them to more modern tonal means. The classisizing tendencies in his later works stemmed not so much from the current trends in French and Italian music as from a continuity with tradition which can be seen in his first compositions.

In this Szymanowski reveals himself as a composer of fundamentally Romantic temperament (in spite of his public proclamations to the contrary in the 1920s). The final pages of the Second Piano Sonata might sound like an end to end all like endings. In truth, it was just a beginning.

---

[57]Joseph Straus, *Remaking the Past: Musical Modernism and the Influence of the Tonal Tradition* (Cambridge, Massachusetts: Harvard University Press, 1990), 132.

[58]Zofia Helman, Preface to *Szymanowski Instrumental Works: String Quartets*. Complete Edition, vol. B6 (Kraków: PWM Edition, 1978), viii.

Example 9: The ending of Szymanowski's Piano Sonata Op. 21, mm. 586-597. Karol Szymanowski, Piano Sonata in A major, Op. 21. Copyright 1912 by Universal Edition A.G., Wien, Copyright renewed 1940. Copyright of the revised version 1968 by Universal Edition A.G., Wien. All rights reserved. Used by permission of European American Music, Distributors Corporation, sole U.S. and Canadian agent for Universal Edition A.G., Wien.

APPENDIX
Chronology of Works Cited

1883   Johannes Brahms: Symphony No. 3
1885   Anton Brucker: Symphony No. 8

1903   Gustav Mahler: Symphony No. 6
        Ignacy Jan Paderewski: Piano Sonata in E-flat
        Alexandre Skryabin: Piano Sonata No. 4

1905   Arnold Schoenberg: String Quartet No. 1

1908   Alban Berg: Piano Sonata
        Arnold Schoenberg: Chamber Symphony No. 1
        Alexandre Skryabin: Piano Sonata No. 5
        Alexandre Skryabin: *The Poem of Ecstasy*

1911   Karol Szymanowski: Piano Sonata No. 2
        Jan Sibelius: Symphony No. 4
        Hugo Leichtentritt: *Musikalische Formelehre*

1913   August Halm: *Von Zwei Kulturen der Musik*
        August Halm: *Die Symphonie Anton Bruckners*

1915-17 Ernst Bloch: *Geist der Utopie*

1916   Karol Szymanowski: *Violin Concerto No. 1*

1917   Ernst Kurth: *Grundlagen des linearen Kontrapunkts*
1920   Ernst Kurth: *Romantische Harmonik*
1925   Ernst Kurth: *Bruckner*

1926   Heinrich Schenker: *Organic Structure in Sonata Form*

1930   Boris Asafiev: *Musical Form as Process*

1938   Ernst Bloch: *Das Prinzip Hoffnung*

Figure 1: Portrait of Karol Szymanowski by Stanisław Ignacy
       Witkiewicz (friend of the composer); dated August 1930.

Sources and Materials of Szymanowski's *Stabat Mater*

by Richard Zielinski

Origins of Szymanowski's *Stabat Mater*

While in Paris in 1924, Szymanowski was commissioned by the Princess de Polignac (1890-1927) to compose a choral work with orchestra. Although the practical aspects of the commission are obscure, the Princess was evidently very specific about the "nature of the work, requiring a piece for soloists, choir, orchestra (perhaps with Polish text) - a kind of Polish requiem."[1] According to Teresa Chylińska, "Szymanowski's original scheme was a kind of 'peasant requiem' - something peasant and ecclesiastical, naively devotional, a sort of prayer for souls - a mixture of simple-minded religion, paganism, and a certain austere peasant realism."[2] During 1924 however, Szymanowski and the Princess "gradually lost touch with one another,"[3] and the "peasant requiem" never materialized.

The idea "was revived at the end of 1924, when Szymanowski was commissioned by Dr. Bronisław Krystall, a Warsaw industrialist, to write a work in memory of his wife, Izabela Krystallowa."[4] In January 1925, work on Krystall's commission was - as Jim Samson writes - "interrupted for several months after the death of Szymanowski's niece, Alusia Bartoszewiczówna (the daughter of his sister, Stanisława)." Having spent months consoling his grieving sister after the loss of her young and only child, Szymanowski decided to use as text the sequence *Stabat Mater dolorosa* instead of the *Requiem* when he returned to work on

---

[1]Jim Samson, *The Music of Szymanowski* (New York: Taplinger Publishing, 1981), 180.

[2]Teresa Chylińska, *Szymanowski*, trans. A. T. Jordan (New York: Twayne Publishers & The Kosciuszko Foundation, 1973), 130.

[3]Samson, *The Music of Szymanowski*, 188.

[4]Alistair Wightman, *The Music of Karol Szymanowski* (Ph.D. dissertation, University of York, 1972), 230.

Krystall's commission. The composer explains:[5]

> A whole series of motives induced me in my resolve to write the
> religious work, *Stabat Mater*, from inner, personal compulsions,
> right down to external circumstances of life that resulted last
> winter in my lying aside other already started "secular" works,
> and dedicating myself exclusively to work on the *Stabat Mater*.

The external circumstances to which Szymanowski refers
range from the practical to the personal. Szymanowski's financial
situation was not good, and he was no doubt strongly attracted by
a commission which could greatly help him and his family. The
Russians had destroyed Tymoszówka, together with most of Szymanowski's treasures; he and his family were living an unfamiliar
life in a small apartment in Warsaw. Finally, as already noted, the
entire family was mourning the death of Alusia Bartoszewiczówna
(Szymanowski's favorite niece). One can easily imagine that all
these circumstances, but especially the last, contributed to Szymanowski's decision to set a poem, which depicted the Holy Mother
grieving at her Son's death. In the *Stabat Mater*, he combined old
and new elements of Polish music within a religious framework;
moreover, rather than the Latin text, Szymanowski used a modern
Polish translation by Józef Jankowski.

The Latin Text and its Polish Translation

Appendix I contains the entire *Stabat Mater* poem in both
the original Latin and Jankowski's Polish translation, with English
translations of both. It is the Polish translation, not the Latin, which
is central to Szymanowski's *Stabat Mater*. I will begin its discussion with a profile of its author. A poet, writer and philosopher,
Józef Jankowski (1865-1935) began his career as a journalist and
literary critic and from 1896-1900 was co-editor of a humorous

---

[5]Kornel Michałowski, *Katalog Tematyczny Dzieł i Bibliografia* [Thematic
catalogue of works and bibliography] (Kraków: PWM, 1967), 195; quoted in
Wightman, *The Music of Karol Szymanowski*, 230.

weekly *Kurier Świąteczny* [Holiday Courier]. Several collections of his poetry were published: *Staccato* (1892), a humorous long poem *Lalka* [*Doll*, 1895], *Rytmy i rymy* [*Rhythms and rhymes*, 1897], *Zwrotki* [*Stanzas*, 1903] and a few small dramatic pieces for the stage. Jankowski's writings, which were initially very light with humorous or satirical overtones, later focused on the subjects of religion and ethics, especially in the publication *Poezje. Seria Liryczna* [*Poems, Lyric Series*] which was edited in 1910.[6] Jankowski was also a prolific translator. Among the classical works he translated were *Z Psalmów Dawidowych* [*From the Psalms of David*, 1916]; *Z Poezji Chińskiej* [*From Chinese Poetry*, 1902]; Heine's *Niemcy* [*The Germans*, 1911]; *Winter Tales* [*The Winter Tales*, 1911]; and *Pieśni ofiarne* [*Sacrificial Songs*, 1918] by Indian poet Rabindranath Tagore. In 1915, paralysis of the legs made Jankowski immobile and unable to travel. It was at this time that an interest in religion emerged; the Polish translation of the *Stabat mater dolorosa* poem probably dates from this period of his life.

According to Kornel Michałowski, what captivated Szymanowski's interest in Jankowski's rendering of the *Stabat mater dolorosa* was "the unusually primitive, almost 'folk-like' simplicity and naivety of the translation."[7] Michałowski finds that the Polish "translation preserves the metrical and rhyme scheme of the Latin, but its imagery is more vivid and intense."[8] Compared to the original Franciscan poem, Jankowski's modern Polish version is simultaneously much more violent and realistic. In an interview given to Mateusz Gliński and printed in 1926 in the periodical *Muzyka* (No. 11/12), Szymanowski explains his reasons for wanting to compose religious music in the vernacular:[9]

---

[6]Mieczysław Horoch and Paweł Jarosinski, "Józef Jankowski," in *Polski Słownik Biograficzny*, Roman Tborski, ed., translated by Jan Adamczyk (Kraków: Zakład Narodowy Imiena Ossolińskich, Wydawnictwo Polskiej Akademii Nauk, 1962-64), 543.

[7]Michałowski, *Katalog,* 231.

[8]Ibid.

[9]Szymanowski's interview with Mateusz Gliński, *Muzyka* no. 11/12 (1926), transl. by Alistair Wightman, cited in Wightman, 597-599.

For many years now I have been thinking about Polish religious music (but not liturgical, where certain formal canons are obligatory). I have certain opinions, too many to mention, on this matter. But in my view, it ought to be about, above all, directly emotional action, and so of course one based on a universally comprehensible text, on the, so to say, organic fusing of the emotional content of the words with its musical equivalent. Perhaps I am mistaken, but I have the impression that for even those who know Latin best, this language - because it has lost direct contact with life - has become an elevated, naturally, but congealed form, not open to further development. It has lost its emotional content, retaining only a conceptual one. This does not apply to Roman (classical) literature, which in the nature of things uses a language which at the time of writing was still alive, capable of expressing directly the emotional content of the then-contemporary concepts of life.

Jankowski's text in stanza (8b), "Let me accept death from the executioner," is more personal and graphic than the Latin "Grant that I may bear Christ's death." Moreover, since the Polish version recounts an execution instead of Christ's death, it may well be that Szymanowski related the Polish version to the killing and suffering endured by the people of Poland through years of foreign occupation, war and revolution. Alistair Wightman has argued that Jankowski's poem paints a truer picture of the "troubled religious consciousness of Polish Catholicism than the elegantly turned Franciscan original."[10] Szymanowski himself indicated how important the Polish text was to him: "when singing in a country church of *Święy Boże* [Holy God; see Example 1a] or my favorite *Gorzkie żale* [Bitter Sorrows; see Example 1b], every word of which is poetically a living organism for me, it always rouses the religious instinct in me a hundred times more powerfully than the most artistic Latin mass."[11] It seems clear that the direct, explicit character of Jankowski's poem was fundamentally important to Szymanowski, quite possibly having political as well as religious and personal connotations.

---

[10]Wightman, *The Music of Karol Szymanowski,* 232.

[11]Interview with Mateusz Gliński, *Muzyka* no. 11/12 (1926), quoted in Wightman, 597-599.

Szymanowski's Study of Early Music

The request in 1924 from Princess de Polignac for a "Polish Requiem" encouraged Szymanowski to research earlier choral works. During 1924 Szymanowski conducted a study of "pre-Palestrinian and Palestrinian periods together with old-Polish religious music."[12] Szymanowski explains, "for the first time I feel a flickering of interest in musicology, having heard the various Perotin's and Anonymous's of the 13th and 14th centuries in the Hofkapelle. I must study a little."[13] One work which Szymanowski studied carefully and which "pleased him greatly"[14] was the *Gloria* from a *Mass* (circa 1420-1430) of the Polish fifteenth-century composer Mikołaj of Radom (Nicolaus of Radom). In this *Gloria* many characteristics of early vocal music can be seen: parallel movement between voices, modal pitch organization, and strongly patterned rhythms. Szymanowski borrowed many of these and other early music techniques and reapplied them in composing the *Stabat Mater*.

In most sacred works from the thirteenth and fourteenth centuries plainsong was an important source for the material used throughout a composition. One might guess then, that while following the early-music models Szymanowski would use the *Stabat Mater* plainsong (Example 2) as a cantus firmus or, at least, as motivic material for his composition. The plainsong itself is a very simple melody consisting of twenty-three notes, arranged entirely in ascending and descending step-wise passages with the exception of a minor third interval between the fifth and sixth notes and a perfect fifth between the sixteenth and seventeenth notes (see Example 2).

Analysis reveals that four motives constitute the essential material of the *Stabat Mater dolorosa* plainsong (Example 3).

---

[12]Samson, *The Music of Szymanowski*, 189.

[13]Zofia Helman, ed., *The Works of Karol Szymanowski*, vol. 7, quoted in Wightman, *The Music of Karol Szymanowski*, 235.

[14]Ibid.

Example 1a: *Święty Boże* (Holy God). From Jan Siedlecki, ed.,
Śpiewnik Kościelny (Kraków: Instytut Wydawniczy Księży
Misjonarzy, 1987), p. 434.

Example 1b: *Gorzkie żale* (Lenten Psalm). From Jan Siedlecki;
op. cit., 417–418.

Example 2: *Stabat Mater* plainchant, first stanza.

Motive [P]:   (notes 1–4) A turn on *G*; in order, the lower neighboring note, principal note, upper neighboring note and principal note.

[PI]:   (notes 11–14) Inversion of motive [P]. A turn on *E*; in order, the upper neighboring note, principal note, lower neighboring note, and principal note.

[PR]:   (notes 19–22) Retrograde of motive [P]. A turn on *G*; in order, the principal note, upper neighboring note, principal note, and lower neighboring note.

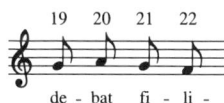

[PRI]:   (notes 17–20) Retrograde inversion of motive [P]. A turn on *G*; in order, the principal note, lower neighboring note, principal note, and upper neighboring note.

Example 3: Motivic material from *Stabat Mater dolorosa* plainsong.

Motive [DS]:   (notes 6–16) A descending scale, octave span, from
                C to *C*.

Motive [U3]:   (notes 4–7) An upward third, approached and left by
                step from below.

Motive [U5]:   (notes 15–18) An upward leap of a fifth approached
                and left by step from within the interval.

Example 3, cont.: Motivic material from *Stabat Mater*, continued.

Example 4a: Szymanowski, *Stabat Mater*, No. 2, *Quis est homo - I któż widząc*, mm. 11–15.

Example 4b: Szymanowski, *Stabat Mater*, No. 2, *Quis est homo - I któż widząc*, mm. 11–16.

Example 4c: *Stabat Mater dolorosa* plainsong, first two phrases.

These four motives [P, DS, U3 and U5] (together with [PI, PR and PRI], which are versions of [P]), all play an important part in Szymanowski's *Stabat Mater*. In a few instances, Szymanowski apparently used the entire *Stabat Mater dolorosa* plainsong as a model for melodic material. When the bass voice of the chorus in No. 2, mm. 11-16 (Example 4a) is transposed down a minor third to F Aeolian from the original modality G-sharp Aeolian, its close similarity to the *Stabat Mater* plainsong becomes particularly apparent (Example 4b - 4c). Szymanowski's melody contains only the first two phrases, omitting the final two notes but interpolating an additional pair of notes (bracketed in Example 4b) into each phrase; the mode is also changed from Hypolydian (which sounds major to modern ears) to Aeolian (minor).

Szymanowski incorporated into the *Stabat Mater* melodic elements found in the two Polish hymns cited earlier in this chapter, *Święty Boże* [Holy God] and *Gorzkie żale* [Bitter Sorrows]. In each case, Szymanowski quotes the opening phrase; he uses the descending scale which can also be found in the *Stabat Mater* (plainsong). The opening of *Gorzkie żale* is quoted at the very beginning of Szymanowski's *Stabat Mater*, in the flute in No. 1, m. 1. The flute's opening three pitches (A - G-sharp - B), a descending half-step followed by an upward leap of a minor third, are an exact transposition of the opening pitches (B-flat - A - C) of the *Gorzkie żale* (Example 5). Moreover, the second measure of *Gorzkie żale*, a stepwise descent of a fourth, is implied though not stated explicitly in the flute's descending fourth (B to F-sharp).

Parallel motion is another early music characteristic that Szymanowski employs with great consistency throughout the *Stabat Mater*. Although Mikołaj of Radom's *Gloria* is not quoted directly, it provides a good example of such writing in mm. 9-11. In Szymanowski's *Stabat Mater*, parallelism occurs most frequently at the interval of a third, as in movements No. 1, mm. 8-11 (clarinets), No. 2, mm. 11-16 (chorus and horns), and No. 6, mm. 1-16 (clarinets, see Example 6).

Examples of parallel motion at the fourth or fifth are not as frequent as parallel motion at the third. Nevertheless, Szymanowski does sometimes use the sound of parallel open fifths to produce an "archaic" quality. Indeed, the very first cadence, in mm. 3-4 of No. 1, is characterized by this sound (Example 7).

Example 5: Szymanowski, Stabat Mater, No. 1 *Stabat Mater – Stała Matka*, flute I, m. 1 (left), and *Gorzkie żale* (Lenten Psalm), mm. 1–2 (right).

Example 6: Szymanowski, Stabat Mater, No. 6 *Christe, cum sit – Chrytus niech mi*, clarinet I, II mm. 1–4.

Example 7: Szymanowski, Stabat Mater, No 1 *Stabat Mater – Stała Matka*, flute and clarinet, mm. 3–4.

Example 8: Szymanowski, Stabat Mater, No. 1 *Stabat Mater - Stała Matka*, women's chorus, mm. 39–41.

Example 9: Szymanowski, Stabat Mater, No. 1 *Stabat Mater - Stała Matka*, mm. 14–18.

Parallel chords which create a texture reminiscent of faux-bourdon can be found in the same movement in the women's chorus, mm. 39-48 (Example 8). Long pedal tones and the extensive use of modes are other important techniques linked to early music. Both can be seen in No. 1, mm. 14-19 (Example 9). Here the soprano solo, moving over a sustained pedal tone or drone in the contrabass, creates oblique motion akin to that found in early organum. The soprano solo also illustrates Szymanowski's use of modes. The opening phrases divide into three parts; although the "tonic" remains *A* throughout, the scale content changes from Aeolian (natural minor) in m. 14 to Ionian (major) in mm. 15-17 to Lydian in mm. 15-17.

These examples could easily be supplemented by other references to early music in Szymanowski's *Stabat Mater*. Was the use of such "archaic" techniques designed to appeal to Polish listeners and to enable Szymanowski to rekindle interest in a truly Polish music? Certainly they would have been familiar to the people of Poland and combined with materials taken directly from folk sources would have constituted an idiom that was both accessible and innovative.

Elements of Folk Music in the *Stabat Mater*

In 1925, Szymanowski wrote a brief article entitled "Béla Bartók and Folk Music" which revealed much about his own views of folk music. In this essay, Szymanowski praises Bartók's "untiring efforts in developing a musical culture in his own country and his endless research and collecting of Hungarian and Romanian folk music."[15] He notes that Bartók "hopes to establish a Hungarian school that will equal the great musical cultures of Germany, France

---

[15]Karol Szymanowski, "Zagadnienie 'ludowości' w stosunku do muzyki współ-czesnej (Na marginesie artykułu Béli Bartóka 'U źródeł muzyki ludowej')" [The issue of 'folk quality' in reference to contemporary music (on the margins of Bela Bartók's article "At the sources of folk music")], *Muzyka*, no. 1 (1925), reprinted in *Karol Szymanowski: Pisma*, vol. 1, *Pisma muzyczne* [Music writings], Kornel Michałowski, ed., (Kraków: PWM Edition, 1984), 168-175 [editor's note]. The quotation comes from a translation included in B. M. Maciejewski and Felix Aprahamian, *Karol Szymanowski and Jan Smeterlin: Correspondence & Essays* (London: Allegro Press, 1969), 97.

and Russia,)" and he observes that "our aim in Poland is a very similar one . . . ."[16]

Earlier, in 1924, Szymanowski had written a profile for a Warsaw journal, *Warszawianka,* in which, according to Jim Samson, "he hailed Stravinsky as the greatest living composer, a master coming at a crucial turning point in the ideology of art to give concrete expression to the mood and anxieties of the masses."[17] At this time in Poland, "where critics seem still to apply the Beethoven-Wagner yardstick of artistic judgement,"[18] Szymanowski was determined to pursue folk music from his own land, in part because of his admiration for Bartók and Stravinsky. The Polish composer later explained: "Each man must go back to the earth from which he derives. Today I have developed into a national composer not only subconsciously but with a thorough conviction using the melodic treasures of Polish folk."[19]

Szymanowski focused his new musical interests on the Zakopane region, especially the *górale* culture,[20] which became a very important source for his compositions and helped him build a language with which he could communicate to his fellow compatriots. Musicologist Adolf Chybiński thus described Szymanowski's

----

[16]Ibid., 98.

[17]Samson, *The Music of Szymanowski,* 182.

[18]Szymanowski, "Zagadnienie," op. cit., quoted from Maciejewski and Apra-hamian, 98.

[19]*International Encyclopedia,* s.v. "Karol Szymanowski," by Felix Łabuński, quoted in Michael Piasek-Wański, *Karol Szymanowski's Philosophy of Music Education* (Doctoral dissertation, University of the Pacific, 1981), 87.

[20]The term "górale" is used here in the original Polish version of the masculine plural form of the word "góral" - meaning literally "a man from the mountains" and referring to the inhabitants of the Podhale area surrounding the rocky Tatras. English translations of this term include "highlanders" and "mountaineers," but the original is perferable in current scholary practice [editor's note].

experiences in Zakopane:[21]

> Ever since 1922 Szymanowski joined those who "could not live
> without Zakopane". . . . the splendid Museum of the Tatras was
> growing under the devoted and sensitive care of Juliusz
> Zborowski, the dedicated regionalist, who was the first man in
> Poland to record on phonographic cylinders (since 1914) the
> dialect and the music of the highlanders. He soon became a
> close friend of Szymanowski's. The future author of *Harnasie*
> was a frequent guest at the Tatra Museum . . . . The "custodian
> of the treasures of the mountain folk" often hummed for
> Szymanowski *górale* songs, which he had collected by the
> hundred.

One might reasonably expect to find that Szymanowski's
interest in folk music significantly influenced his composition of the
Stabat Mater. To understand the folk music Szymanowski encountered during his visits to the Tatra region, one might do well to
examine musical examples drawn from this area, specifically *górale*
folk music. In the early part of this century Polish "musicologists
Adolf Chybiński, Helena Windakiewicz, Lucian Kamieński, Marian
Sobieski and his wife Jadwiga began recording folk music from this
region on the gramophone."[22] Later, in the 1930's "archives of
recordings were built in the southern city of Poznań under
Kamieński and in Warsaw under the direction of Julian Pułkowski,
containing a total of 25,000 recordings."[23] These recordings would
have provided a direct access to folk elements used in Szyma-

---

[21]Adolf Chybiński, *Szymanowski a Podhale* [Szymanowski and the Podhale
region] (reprinted: Kraków: PWM Edition, 1974); quoted in Teresa Chylińska,
Szymanowski, trans. A. T. Jordan (New York: Twayne Publishers Inc. & The
Kosciuszko Foundation, 1973), 122. See also Teresa Chylińska, *Zakopiańskie
dni Karola Szymanowskiego* [Zakopane days of Karol Szymanowski] (Kraków:
PWM Edition, 1986).

[22]*The New Grove Dictionary of Music and Musicians*, Stanley Sadie, ed., s.v.
"Poland, Folk music, Function and Content" by Jan Stęszewski (London:
Macmillan, 1980), 30. For a discussion of the role of scholars and outsiders in
the shaping of folk music of the Tatra mountains see the article by Timothy
Cooley in the present volume.

[23]Ibid.

158 Zielinski: *Szymanowski's Stabat Mater*

nowski's *Stabat Mater* had they survived; unfortunately all of these collections were destroyed during World War II. Therefore, we are not able to form any definite conclusions about the direct influence of *górale* folk music on Szymanowski's *Stabat Mater*, as well as his *Słopiewnie*, op. 46b (1921), and *Twenty Mazurkas*, op. 50 (1924-1925). Nonetheless, there is much indirect evidence that will guide the following overview of possible citations and references. In a letter to Zdzisław Jachimecki concerning the publication of the first biography of Szymanowski, the composer wrote:[24]

> I am concerned with one evolutionary point with which I would like to acquaint you, namely the "Lechitic," ancestral Polish character which you discerned in the *Słopiewnie*. It was indeed a turning point, starting a development continuing through the Mazurkas (of which you know only 8), the *Stabat Mater* and a new ballet on which I am now working. I believe this to be a point which should be stressed and analyzed in depth. I am concerned, myself, with crystallizing elements of tribal heritage.

British musicologist Jim Samson described some of the "elements of tribal heritage" in the first English language analysis of Szymanowski's music.[25] Samson gave the following general account of the *górale* music as including:[26]

> Various kinds of polyphonic singing for high men's and deep women's voices, including distended parallelism, by use of pedal points either of open fifths or of jarring minor seconds, and a remarkable heterophony of two fiddles over a simple bass on three stringed instruments, and finally a tendency for Lydian patterns and descending shapes to predominate.

---

[24]Szymanowski to Z. Jachimecki, 2 February 1927, *Zakopane*, quoted in Chylinska, *Szymanowski*, 118.

[25]See Adolf Chybiński, *Karol Szymanowski a Podhale* (Kraków: PWM Edition, 1974); Jerzy Rytard, ed., *Wspomnienia o Karolu Szymanowskim* [Memories of Karol Szymanowski], (Kraków: PWM Edition, 1982).

[26]Samson, *The Music of Szymanowski*, 167.

Example 10a: Szymanowski, *Słopiewnie*, No. 2 ("Zielone słowa"), mm. 1–4.

Example 10b: Szymanowski, *Mazurka*, op. 50, No. 1, mm. 1–4.

Example 10c: Szymanowski, *Mazurka*, op. 50, No. 18, mm. 1–6.

Example 11a: No. 5, *Virgo virginum – Panno słodka racz*, mm. 45–49.

Example 11b: No. 2, *Quis est homo – I któż widząc*, mm. 1–4.

Example 12: *"Sabała" folk tune.*

Many of these elements (modal patterns, ornamentation, pedal tones, and choral passages in parallel movement) are present in *Słopiewnie*, the twenty *Mazurkas*, and the *Stabat Mater*. An open-fifth pedal point supporting a modal melody is clearly seen in *Słopiewnie*, No. 2, "Zielone słowa" [Green words; see Example 10a]. The first Mazurka from Opus 50 (Example 10b) features an open-fifth pedal tone, ornamented melody, and an accompaniment characterized by parallel motion. Szymanowski's use of "jarring minor seconds" can be seen in the *Mazurka*, Op. 50, No. 18 (Example 10c). In the *Stabat Mater*, open fifths, parallel motion, and ornamented, modal melodies are central to the first movement, as has already been shown (Examples 10a, 7-10). Seconds are used to enrich the harmonies of No. 5, mm. 45-49 (violin I and II; see Example 11a); and, expanded to the interval of a ninth, they anchor the accompaniment of No. 2, mm. 1-4 (celli and double bass; see Example 11b).

We know that as part of his research in 1920-24, Szymanowski "began to keep a notebook in which he sketched numerous highlanders' melodies."[27] In 1944, however, this notebook was destroyed during the Warsaw Uprising, eliminating any possibility of directly linking his collection of folk melodies to his music, especially the *Stabat Mater*. Nevertheless, indirect evidence suggests that Szymanowski's melodic materials during this period were influenced by a very popular folk tune from the Tatra region, the "Sabałowa" tune (Example 12).[28] This melody can be "traced back at least as far as Jan Krzeptowski Sabała, a storyteller, hunter and according to legend, a highland robber of the mid-nineteenth century."[29] From the *Sabałowa* tune Szymanowski evidently borrowed at least the scale, i.e. "the ancient Polish folk mode called the Podhalean mode characterized by a raised-fourth scale degree and a lowered-seventh scale degree."[30]

The Podhalean scale with the sharp (Lydian) fourth and the

---

[27]Ibid., 168.

[28]Chybiński, *Karol Szymanowski a Podhale*, 14.

[29]Samson, *The Music of Szymanowski*, 167.

[30]Ann K. McNamee, "Bitonality, Mode, and Interval in the Music of Karol Szymanowski," *Journal of Music Theory* 29 no. 1 (Spring 1985), 64.

descending melodic contour are present in the opening four measures of Szymanowski's *Słopiewnie*, No. 3, "Św. Franciszek" [St. Francis] (Example 13a). In the *Stabat Mater*, the same elements are also present, though not so obvious. For example, in No. 5, mm. 1-3, Szymanowski uses the sharpened fourth in the celli and double bass melody (Example 13b), which may even loosely paraphrase the last two bars of *Sabałowa*; meanwhile, a descending motive in the violins m.39ff (Example 13c) may be distantly linked to the folksong's opening measures.Numerous sources, then, ranging from secondary research, through letters, to the music itself, indicates that Szymanowski "stylized a variety of folk music elements from the Tatra region"[31] throughout the *Stabat Mater*. In a chapter of *Polish Music*, edited by Stefan Jarociński, Zofia Lissa thus summarizes these influences: "Through the use of archaic formulas and folk idiom, he composed a work purely Polish in character. [The *Stabat Mater*] is Szymanowski's most inspired work, reaching out for the religious traditions of the Polish peasants."[32] Szymanowski's treatment of these folk idioms, however, was by no means "archaic;" rather, he employed distinctly new and innovative compositional practices, influenced especially by Debussy and Stravinsky.

Contemporary Influences on the *Stabat Mater*

Szymanowski employed a variety of contemporary techniques in creating a musical context for the references to early music and folk traditions in the *Stabat Mater*. Though these techniques range widely, it suffices here to concentrate on four: (1) sound planes (parallel motion in all voices), (2) linear cadences, (3) added-tone chords, and (4) ostinato patterns. We know that Szymanowski was familiar with Debussy's music and had been especially impressed by *Pelléas et Mélisande*. In Debussy's music Szymanowski may have discovered two important techniques: the use of sound planes and linear cadences.

---

[31]Telephone interview with Wanda Wilk, Director of the Polish Music Reference Center, University of Southern California, Los Angeles, California, 14 May 1991.

[32] Zofia Lissa, "Karol Szymanowski," in *Polish Music*, Jarociński, Stefan, ed. (Warszawa: Polish Scientific Publishers, 1965), 163.

Example 13a: Szymanowski, *Słopiewnie*, No. 3, "Św. Franciszek" (St. Francis), mm. 1–4.

Example 13b: Szymanowski, *Stabat Mater*, No. 5 *Virgo virginum – Pano słodka racz*, celli/contrabass, mm. 1–3.

Example 13c: Szymanowski, *Stabat Mater*, No. 5 *Virgo virginum – Pano słodka racz*, violins, mm. 39–42.

Example 14: No. 5, *Virgo virginum* –- *Panno słodka racz.* mm. 60–65.

Example 15: No. 1 *Stabat Mater – Stała Matka*, mm. 22–24.

Example 16: No. 1 *Stabat Mater – Stała Matka*, m. 4. (left)
Example 17: No. 2 *Quis est homo – I któż widząc*, mm. 11–12. (right)

In the *Stabat Mater*, planning can be seen in *No. 2. Quis est homo - I któż widząc*, mm. 1921 (strings and woodwinds) and in *No. 5. Virgo virginum - Panno słodka racz*, mm. 21-31 (violins, violas and woodwinds).

An even more striking example occurs in No. 5, mm. 60-65 (Example 14), where two separate planes are presented in counterpoint. The woodwinds and strings, in parallel seventh chords, present a two-measure descending ostinato; meanwhile, the chorus, doubled by the horns and organ, moves in parallel sixths against the motion in the woodwinds. A third, static layer is provided by the percussion and by the pedal point on C.

Linear cadences are sometimes associated with layering of sound planes; in No. 1 such cadential figures occur in mm. 8-9, mm. 11-13, mm. 22-24 (Example 15), mm. 34-36 and mm. 61-63. Bichordal passages and chords with added tones also occur at important moments in the Stabat Mater. The first cadence in the work, at measure 4, beat 3, of No. 1, can be analyzed as two superimposed chords, G-sharp - D-sharp in the harp and horn I, and C-sharp - A (Example 16) in horns II and III. The resulting dissonance between G-sharp minor and A major creates a gong-like effect. Szymanowski also added dissonant tones, usually in seconds, to more conventional chords. In No. 2, *Quis est homo - I któż widząc*, this technique is employed throughout. It is especially clear in mm. 12-18, where the chorus, flutes, clarinets, horns III and IV, trumpets, violin I and celli move in parallel thirds defining harmonies in G-sharp Dorian, while the remaining instruments insert a dissonant major second G-sharp and F-sharp on beats two and four. The added-tone procedure is outlined in violins I and II, mm. 11-12 (Example 17).

A considerably more prevalent device, utilized by Bartók, Stravinsky and many contemporary composers as well as by Szymanowski in the *Stabat Mater*, is ostinato, defined as "a clearly defined melodic phrase which is persistently repeated, usually in the same voice part and at the same pitch."[33] Two particularly important ostinatos occur in the harp, viola, and celli of *No. 1 Stabat Mater - Stała Matka*, mm. 37-39 (Ex. 18a), and in the harp and double bass, through much of *No. 2. Quis est homo – I któż widząc* (Ex. 18b).

---

[33]*The Harvard Brief Dictionary of Music*, 2nd ed., s.v. "ostinato."

Example 18a: No. 1 *Stabat Mater – Stała Matka*, mm. 37–39.

Example 18b: No. 2 *Quis est homo – I któż widząc*, mm. 1–3.

In conclusion, the *Stabat Mater*, op. 53, can be seen as the culmination of the musical style of Karol Szymanowski's final, national period. In works such as the *Stabat Mater*, Szymanowski consolidated all of his past experiences in an effort to create a musical idiom that would communicate directly with his fellow compatriots and promote a truly contemporary Polish music. He combined his study of early music with his research into folk culture, placing both of these in the context of new techniques introduced by his contemporaries, such as Debussy and Stravinsky. His efforts were not lost on the audiences and, in closure, it will be useful to examine the response of the press to the premiere of this magnificent work.

Polish Reception of the *Stabat Mater*

The newspaper review of Szymanowski's *Stabat Mater* premiere appeared one day after the concert in Warsaw's *Kurjer Poranny* [Morning Courier], Thursday, January 10, 1929. The reviewer's comments reflect many of the distinctive features of the *Stabat Mater:*[34]

> [At] Yesterday's concert, the symphony orchestra of the Warsaw Philharmonic performed for the first time the *Stabat Mater* by Karol Szymanowski. The work belongs among the most current compositions of Szymanowski and is extremely characteristic of his entire bulk of creation during recent years. The main characteristics of the *Stabat Mater* are the simplicity and extreme finesse. The simplicity of the means is combined, however, with an extreme richness of sound and orchestral colors which have a very original character.

The author continues with a brief explanation of Szymanowski's use of the Polish text and concludes his review with a survey of the entire work:

---

[34] "*Stabat Mater* by Szymanowski with Philharmonic," *Kurjer Poranny*, 10 January 1929, trans. Jan Adamczyk.

> As a type of religious music the *Stabat Mater* of   Mr.
> Szymanowski is something completely new. It is composed to
> Polish texts, so it will be easier for the average listener to
> understand. It is characterized by extreme humanistic qualities
> and therefore is removed from the usual type of oratorio . . . .
> It has an extremely pastoral character which doesn't exclude
> places of extreme strength and power of expression. The *Stabat
> Mater* consists of six numbers [each of] which has a rounded
> and a cohesive entity within itself. Almost every one of these
> fragments uses a different vocal ensemble, thanks to which the
> composer has achieved great variety in his music. Because of
> this one will listen to the Stabat Mater of Szymanowski with
> extreme attention, since out of one work different types of music
> speak to the listener depending on the moment.

From this review of the premiere it is evident that the critic
both understood Szymanowski's previous works and recognized the
new directions embodied in the *Stabat Mater*. The reviewer enume-
rated many of the features which have been discussed in the course
of this paper: the importance of the Polish text, the music's simplicity coequal with an extreme richness of sound and orchestral color,
and the great variety of "types of music" brought together in a
single work. At least from the perspective of one reviewer, Szymanowski's effort to integrate several national and historical styles into
a new and distinctly Polish musical language appears to have been
successful.

The strength of Szymanowski's integration of early, folk,
and contemporary stylistic elements lies in his skillful use of techniques that are shared and commonly utilized in each of the three
styles. For example, parallel motion is a feature shared by early
music, by folk harmonizations of traditional melodies, and by the
modern technique of sound layering. Similarly, each stylistic source
stresses modalism rather than tonality. Modern ostinatos resemble
the repetitive phrases and rhythms of folk music as well as the
rhythmic modes and isorhythmic techniques of early music. Clearly,
Szymanowski carefully selected musical devices that would be
consistent with each of his stylistic sources. The *Stabat Mater*
manifested Szymanowski's hopes of reinvigorating Poland's
national musical traditions. His expectations proved to be justified;
the critical   reception   of   the   first   performance   confirmed

Szymanowski's status as a leader of Polish music.

Between the two World Wars Szymanowski's music and his theoretical writings attempted to guide Polish musicians, both young and old, to the ideals established by Chopin; at the same time he encouraged exploration of the innovative musical styles of contemporary Russian and French composers. Szymanowski warned Polish composers not to imitate his own music and to avoid German influences. Many of the older Polish professors and performers shunned Szymanowski's advice and openly criticized his vision. Although Szymanowski suffered greatly under these personal attacks, the seeds of Szymanowski's message, to reestablish a national style on the basis of close links with the international avant-garde, were firmly planted in the minds of young Polish composers. Many later Polish composers have been influenced by Szymanowski and his works, although it is difficult to trace specific stylistic traits because of the diversity inherent in Szymanowski's music. The influence of Szymanowski's ideals may be seen, for example, in post-war works based on folk music, especially of the Tatra mountains (e.g. the ballet-cantata *Wierchy* [The Mountain Tops] by Artur Malawski). Composers Grażyna Bacewicz and Henryk Mikołaj Górecki openly acknowledged Szymanowski's influence, as did Witold Lutosławski.[35] Karol Szymanowski's foresight and determination to break Poland out of its musical deadlock created a structure on which Polish contemporary music could be built.

---

[35]In the 1930s, Bacewicz often performed both of Szymanowski's Violin Concerti as a soloist, but she preferred to draw from the folklore of the Mazovian plains in her music (in addition, she avoided religious themes). Górecki has shared Szymanowski's passion for the Podhale area near the Tatra mountains, both as a source of musical inspirations and a place of residence, as well as his interests in early Polish music. For Lutosławski, Szymanowski's Symphony No. 3, and not the pieces in national style, provided the formative influence and the stimulus to become a composer [editor's note].

APPENDIX
Stabat Mater in Latin and Polish
with English Translations

Latin *English translation* Monks of Solesmes, *Chants of the Church* (Belgium: Desclee & Company, 1953), 140-141.	Polish *English translation* Literal translation of Polish text by Jan Adamczyk. [words added by Szymanowski are in brackets].
No. 1. Stabat Mater	**No. 1. Stała Matka**
1a. Stabat Mater dolorosa *There stood (the) Mother sorrowful,* juxta crucem lacrimosa, *beside (the) cross in tears,* dum pendebat Filius. *while hanging (on it) was her son.*	1a. Stała Matka bolejąca *Stood mother in pain* koło krzyża łzy lejąca *by the cross her tears pouring out* gdy na krzyżu wisiał Syn. *when on the cross the Son was hanging.*
1b. Cujus animam gementem *Whose soul sighing,* contristatam et dolentem *saddened and grieving,* pertransivit gladius. *the sword pierced.*	1b. A jej duszę potyraną, *And on her trampled soul,* rozpłakaną, poszarpaną *that was crying, was torn* miecz przeszywał ludzkich win. *pierced by the sword of human faults.*
2a. O quam tristis et afflicta *O how sad and afflicted* fuit illa benedicta *was that blessed* Mater Unigeniti! *Mother of the only begotten!*	2a. O, jak smutna, jak podcięta *Oh, how sad, how afflicted* była Matka Boża święta, *the holy Mother of God was,* cicha w załamaniu rąk! *quietly clasping her hands in horror*
2b. Quae moerebat et dolebat, *She was mourning and grieving,* pia Mater, dum videbat *(the) tender mother, while she saw* nati poenas incliti. *her Son's pains, (her) noble (Son).*	2b. O, jak drżała o truchlała, *Oh, how she cringed with fear,* I bolała, gdy patrzała *and grieved, while she looked* na synowskich tyle mąk.*at her Son's so many sufferings.*

No. 2. Quis est homo	No. 2. I któz widząc
3a. Quis est homo qui non fieret, *Who is (the) man who would not* *weep* Matrem Christi si videret *(the)* *Mother of Christ if he saw* in tanto supplicio? *in such suffering*	3a. I któż, widząc tak cierpiącą, *And who, seeing her so suffering.* łzą nie zaćmił się gorącą,*Did not* *cloud himself with a hot tear* nie drgnie, taki czując nóż? *will not shudder, feeling such a* *knife?*
3b. Quis non posset contristari, *Who (would) not be able to grieve* Christi Matrem contemplari, *Christ's mother to contemplate* dolentem cum Filio? *(as she was) grieving with her son?*	3b. I kto serca nie ubroczy, *And who will not have his heart* *bleed,* widząc, jak do krzyża oczy wzbiła, *see how she raised her eyes to the* *cross* oczy, z bólu drętwa już. *eyes, already numb with pain.*
4a. Pro peccatis suae gentis *For (the) sins of His own nation* vidit Jesum in tormentis [ah!] *she saw Jesus in torments, ah!* et flagellis subditum. *and by scourges beaten down.*	4a. [Ach,] Za ludzkiego rodu winy *For the trespasses of mankind* jak katowan był jedyny,[ach!] *how her only one was beaten, ah!* męki każdy niosła dział. *she bore each part of his suffering.*
4b. Vidit suum dulcem natum *She saw her own dear child* moriendo desolatum, *dying (and) forsaken,* dum emisit spiritum. *while He breathed forth (His)* *Spirit.*	4b. I widziała, jak rodzony *And saw how her only begotten* jej umierał opuszczony, *Son was dying abandoned,* zanim Bogu duszę dał. *before he gave his soul to the Lord.*
No. 3. O Eia, Mater	**No. 3. O Matko, źródło**
5a. [O] Eia Mater, fons amoris, *O (dear) Mother, fount of love* me sentire vim doloris *(let) me feel (the) weight of sorrow*	5a. O Matko, źródło wszechmiłości,, *Oh, Mother, source of all love,* daj mi uczuć moc żałości, *let me feel the power of sadness,*

5a, cont. fac, ut tecum lugeam. *grant that with Thee I may weep*	5a, cont. niechaj z Tobą dźwignę ból. *with you I can bear the pain.*
5b. Fac, ut ardeat cor meum *Grant that fervent be (the) heart of* *me.* in amando Christum Deum. *in loving Christ (my) God* ut sibi complaceam. *that to Him I may be pleasing.*	5b. Chrystusowe ukochanie *Let the precious love of Christ* niech w mym sercu ogniem stanie, *in my heart become a fire,* Krzyża dzieje we mnie wtul. *press close into me the deeds of the* *cross.*
6a. Sancta Mater, istud agas, *Holy Mother this do (for me),* crucifixi fige plagas *of the Crucified fix deep (the)* *wounds* cordi meo valide. *in the heart of me indelibly.*	6a. Matko, Matko, miłosiernie *Mother, Mother, look* wejrzyj, Syna Twego ciernie *with pity, your Son's thorns* w serce moje wraź jak w cel. *in my heart stick into it like a* *target*
6b. Tui nati vulnerati, *Of thy Son (so) wounded,* tam dignati pro me pati, *so gracious (as) for me to suffer,* poenas mecum divide. *His pains with me do thou divide.*	6b. Rodzonego, męczonego, *The one you bore, the tortured one,* Syna Twego ofiarnego, *your Son, share with me* Kaźń owocną ze mną dziel. *the fruitful execution of the* *sacrificed one.*
No. 4. Fac me tecum	**No. 4. Spraw, niech płaczę**
7a. Fac me tecum pie flere, *Make me with thee lovingly to* *weep,* Crucifixo condolere, *with the Crucified to sympathize* donec ego vixero. *as long as I shall live.*	7a. **Spraw**, niech płaczę z Tobą razem, *Cause me to cry with you,* krzyża zamknę się obrazem *I will lock myself with the image of* *the cross* aż po mój ostatni dech. *until my last breath.*
7b. Juxta crucem tecum stare *Beside the cross with thee to stand* et me tibi sociare. *and myself with thee to join.*	7b. Niechaj pod nim razem stoję, *Let me stand underneath him* *together,* dzielą Twoje krwawe znoje. *and sharing your bloody toils.*

7b, cont.	7b, cont.
in planctu desidero. *in sorrow I desire.* [juxta crucem, juxta crucem] beside the cross [tecum stare, desidero.] *With thee to stand, I desire.*	Twą boleścią zmywam grzech. *With your pain I wash away the* *sins.* [z Tobą razem, aż po mój, *with you together, until my* ostatni dech.] *last breath.*
No. 5. Virgo virginum praeclara	**No. 5. Panno słodka, racz**
8a. Virgo virginum praeclara *Virgins of virgins, noble Lady* mihi jam non sis amara, *to me now (do) not be bitter* fac me tecum plangere. *make me with thee to mourn.*	8a. Panno słodka, racz, mozołem *Sweet Maiden, rather, with much* *effort* niech me serce z Tobą społem *may my heart together with you* na golgocki idzie [szczyt], skłon. *to Golgotha go to the slope top.*
8b. Fac, ut portem Christi mortem, *Grant that I may bear Christ's* *death,* passionis fac consortem, *of His Passion make (me) sharer,* et plagas recolere. *and of His wounds a worshipper.*	8b. Niech śmierć przyjmę z katów ręki, *Let me accept death from the* *executioner,* uczestnikiem będę męki, *I will be the participant in the* *torture,* razów krwawych zbiorę plon. *I shall gather a harvest of bloody* *blows*
9a. Fac me plagis vulnerari, *Make me with His wounds wounded* fac me cruce inebriari, *make me of His cross enamored,* et cruore Filii. *and of the blood of thy Son.*	9a. Niechaj broczy ciało moje, *May my body bleed;* krzyżem niechaj się upoję, *May I be totally filled with the* *cross;* niech z miłosnych żyję tchnień! *May I live on the breaths of love!*
9b. Flammis ne urar succensus, *With flames lest I burned* *consumed,* per te, Virgo, sim defensus *by thee, O Virgin, May I be* *defended*	9b. W morzu ognia zapalony, *In the sea of fire,* z Twojej ręki niech osłony *from your hand let me take the* *protective*

9b, cont. in die judicii. *in (the) day of judgement.*	9b, cont. puklerz wezmę w sądu dzień! *breastplate in the day of judgement!*
No. 6 Christe, cum sit hinc exire	**No. 6 Chrystus niech mi bedzie**
10a. Christe, cum sit hinc exire, *Christ, when it is time hence to* *part,* da per Matrem me venire *grant (that) through (Thy) Mother I* *may come* ad palmam victoriae. *to (the) palm of victory.*	10a. Chrystus niech mi będzie grodem, *Christ let me be a walled city,* krzyż niech będzie mym przewodem, *let the cross be my guide* łaską pokrop, życie daj, życie daj, *sprinkle me with grace, give me* *life,*
10b. Quando corpus morietur, *When (my) body shall die,* fac, ut animae donetur *grant that to my soul be given* paradisi gloria. *of paradise (the) glory.*	10b. Kiedy ciało me się skruszy, *When my body will crumble,* oczyszczonej w ogniu duszy *for the soul purified in the heart* glorię zgotuj, niebo, raj. *prepare glory, heaven, paradise.*

Figure 1: The first page of Szymanowski's manuscript of *Stabat Mater*, with the dedication to Ms. Izabella Kristallowa. Collection of the National Library, Warsaw, Poland. Used by permission.

Lutosławski's *Partita* for Violin and Piano: A New Perspective on His Late Music

by Michael L. Klein

Shortly after the death of Witold Lutosławski, the *New York Times* published this sketch of the Polish composer's life:[1]

> Although his career seemed to follow a familiar arch - early days working in the shadow of Béla Bartók, a formative encounter with Cage's techniques of indeterminacy in the 1950's, participation in the East European avant-garde of the 1960's and 70's, a period of consolidation and simplification in the 80's - he met the systems and fashions of the time and conquered them, adapting each to his unfalteringly distinctive voice.

We may respond with approval to this sketch, describing Lutosławski's career as a "familiar arch," because it resonates with notions of a musical meta-history in which all composers begin their careers in the shadow of an established master and find their voice by progressing from imitation to elaboration to simplification. We can find evidence of such a progression in Lutosławski's music by comparing works from the 1950s, 60s, and 80s. In the second movement of his 5 *Bukoliki* (1952), Lutosławski combines a simple diatonic melody with an octatonic accompaniment in a manner that is reminiscent of early Bartók or Stravinsky. In *Jeux vénitiens* (1961) there is an explosion of complexity in rhythm, pitch material, and texture, which denies the conceptualization of music as a melody with accompaniment, and highlights the layering of timbral blocks of sound. Turning to the *Piano Concerto* (1987), we find that melody and accompaniment come to the fore again. In the cantilena for solo piano, which opens the third movement of this concerto, clear references to whole-tone and octatonic collections seem to suggest a return to a simpler style of composition.

Although the image of a familiar arch seems to describe accurately both musical meta-history and Lutosławski's compo-

---

[1]Alex Ross, *New York Times*, 6 March 1994, 33 (H).

sitional history, it does not lighten the burden of discovering what circumstances led him to favor simpler textures and smaller pitch collections in his music after 1980. Clues to this question appear in a published interview, in which Lutosławski talks about the thinner textures that characterize his late music:[2]

> One of the important steps here was to invent a method of writing thinner textures; I just reached it only a few years ago. Please notice that in the sixties my pieces employed large masses of sounds almost exclusively, as in the *Symphony no. 2*, and to a smaller extent in *Livre pour orchestre, Trois poèmes d'Henri Michaux, Jeux vénitiens*, etc. It was so not because I delighted in sound masess [sic] - I simply lacked suitable tools for writing in a thinner texture.

At this point the interviewer, Gregorz Michalski, suggests that *Partita* for violin and piano (1984) is the composition in which Lutosławski realized the solution to writing thinner textures. Lutosławski replies:[3]

> *Partita* is really a piece of primary order, it belongs with my most important compositions. . . . So I have found a certain "path" that could even be described as rules which simply revealed themselves to me. I have always imagined that large masses should only constitute a certain percentage of the music of a work, though out of necessity I have worked just with them. . . . Meanwhile, thin textures, with a smaller number of simultaneous sounds, were still a question for me. This issue, as I say, clarified itself late, but luckily it did. And only then I could set about such pieces as the *Concerto for Oboe and Harp*, or now the *Piano Concerto*.

In this brief passage, Lutosławski practically defines his late style, while simultaneously hinting at a problem in his earlier music. He tells us that the sound masses that characterized his music of the 1960s in such works as *Trois poèmes d'Henri Michaux* and the

---

[2]Statement quoted from Grzegorz Michalski, "An Interview with Witold Lutosławski," *Polish Music* 23, no. 2-3 (1988): 13.

[3]Ibid.

Symphony no. 2 could not sustain a repertoire of large-scale compositions. From this perspective, we might view Lutosławski's music of the 1980s and '90s as a response to the problem of composing solely with large sound masses. This response entailed the development of a method for writing thinner textures, and in order to examine the nature of these textures, we can do no better than to look closely at one of the works that Lutosławski mentions as an important example of his late style, *Partita* for violin and piano (1984).

* * *

In order to reveal more fully the nature of the compositional changes that we find in a late work like *Partita*, I will outline Lutosławski's method of composition in earlier works. In the *Five Songs* (1957) on texts by Kazimiera Iłłakowiczówna, Lutosławski introduces a background saturated with ***harmonic aggregates***, ordered pitch collections containing all twelve pitch-classes in which each of the pitch-classes is fixed in a single register. Example 1 shows the first harmonic aggregate that structures the piano part of the first song in this collection, "Morze" (The Sea). Lutosławski tells us that, when comparing harmonic aggregates, he considers primarily the intervals between pitches that are adjacent in register, and he does not consider the total interval-class content nor the total interval content.[4] We can represent this thinking numerically as a string of integers representing the number of semitones upward in pitch space from the lowest note in the harmonic aggregate to the highest note. Thus, the numerical representation of the harmonic aggregate in Example 1 is 7-1-3-3-1-3-3-1-3-3-1. In order to show the twelve distinct pitch-classes in each harmonic aggregate, we can also represent them as a set of integers (C=0) separated by commas between brackets < >. An arrow to the left of the brackets indicates that the pitches are ordered in pitch space from lowest to highest. A number to the left of the arrow indicates the octave in which the lowest pitch of the harmonic aggregate appears. I will often present both of these numerical representations together as in Example 1.

---

[4]Cf. Ove Nordwall, *Lutosławski*, Christopher Gibbs, trans. (Stockholm: Edition Wilhelm Hansen, 1968), 109-112.

3 ↑   <6,   1,   2,   5,   8,   9,   0,   3,   4,   7,   T,   E>
        7 - 1 - 3 - 3 - 1 - 3 - 3 - 1 - 3 - 3 - 1

Example 1: Harmonic Aggregate from "Morze".

Example 2: Mirror — Symmetric   Example 3: Parallel—Symmetric
          Harmonic Aggregate   Harmonic Aggregate

Example 4: Witold Lutosławski, *Concerto for Piano and Orchestra*,
1987, rehearsals no. 3–4, frg. Copyright © 1991 by Chester Music
Limited (PRS) All rights for USA & Canada controlled by
G. Schirmer, Inc. (ASCAP) International Copyright Secured.
All Rights Reserved. Reprinted by Permission.

Lutosławski favors harmonic aggregates that exhibit some type of symmetry.[5] Theorists are accustomed to considering transpositional or inversional symmetry when examining *pitch-class* space, but in this case I refer to symmetry in *pitch* space. Following Jonathan Bernard's work on the music of Edgard Varèse, I will divide symmetrical pitch formations into the two categories of Parallel Symmetry and Mirror Symmetry.[6] In *Mirror Symmetry* the order of the intervals in the interval string from bottom to top is the same as that from top to bottom. Example 2 shows the second harmonic aggregate in "Dzwony cerkiewne" (Church Bells), the fifth of the *Five Songs*. The interval string for this harmonic aggregate is the same from bottom to top as from top to bottom, and an arrow in the example shows the center interval of the mirror symmetry. In *Parallel Symmetry* the harmonic aggregate can be divided into a number of subsets, each of which contains the same interval string from bottom to top. Example 3 shows a harmonic aggregate from "Wiatr" (Wind), the second of the *Five Songs*. In this example brackets reveal the successive subsets, each having an identical interval string, showing that this harmonic aggregate has the property of parallel symmetry.

In *Jeux vénitiens* (1961) Lutosławski expanded the rhythmic possibilities of his compositional style with the use of limited aleatory techniques.[7] The term *limited* refers to the fact that with

[5]I examine Lutosławski's use of harmonic aggregates more formally and with more detail in *A Theoretical Study of the Late Music of Witold Lutosławski: New Interactions of Pitch, Rhythm, and Form* (Ph.D. dissertation, State University of New York at Buffalo, 1995).

[6]Jonathan W. Bernard's work on Varèse appears in its most comprehensive form in *The Music of Edgard Varèse* (New Haven: Yale University Press, 1987). An examination of symmetry in pitch space is included in his "Pitch/Register in the Music of Edgard Varèse," *Music Theory Spectrum* 3 (1981): 1-25. Both publications are based on his dissertation, *A Theory of Pitch and Register for the Music of Edgard Varèse* (Ph.D. dissertation, Yale University, 1977). Those familiar with Bernard's work will notice similarities between Varèse's and Lutosławski's use of symmetrical pitch formations and their implications for the use of register.

[7]Other terms used to describe Lutosławski's use of chance elements are *limited aleatory, controlled aleatoricism, aleatoric counterpoint, aleatorism of texture, collective ad libitum,* and *ad lib technique.* Lutosławski is not consistent in his use of terms for limited aleatory sections. In writings and conversations

few exceptions Lutosławski restricts his use of aleatory to the rhythmic coordination of the various parts in an ensemble. Lutosławski employs these aleatory techniques in *ad libitum* sections in which he not only notates the pitches, rhythms, articulations, and dynamics, but also shows clearly the entrances of the various instruments; hence, only the manner of coordinating the various parts is left to the performers. *Ad libitum* sections generally lack a common meter. In describing a performance practice for these sections, Lutosławski requests that the performers play their parts with the same expressive freedom of a solo or a cadenza. During such sections the conductor ceases beating time and uses the baton either to indicate cues or to show the beginning of a new section. The notational consequences of an *ad libitum* section are that all accidentals apply only to the pitch that immediately follows, and that any visual coordination of parts in the score does not reflect a rhythmic coordination that Lutosławski might prefer.

Steven Stucky has demonstrated that Lutosławski often uses simple arithmetic procedures to insure a rhythmically complex performance of an *ad libitum* section.[8] Example 4 reproduces the *ad libitum* section of rehearsal numbers 3 - 4 in the first movement of the *Piano Concerto*. Each of the three flute parts contains a grouping of sixteenth notes separated by a sixteenth rest (note that Flute 3 performs only one pitch class, A-flat). The number of sixteenth notes in each grouping follows a simple arithmetic progression: Flute 1 contains groupings of 4 sixteenths followed by a rest, and Flute 2 contains groupings of 5 sixteenths followed by a rest. The process continues at rehearsal number 4 where Flute 3 begins groupings of 6 sixteenths. The different number of sixteenth notes in the three flute parts insures that repetitions among parts will not

---

Lutosławski claimed to prefer the term "limited aleatory," however he often referred to such portions of his music simply as *"ad libs."* This term is unfortunate since it can imply either that the performer may choose to skip a passage, or that the performer can choose pitches and/or rhythms; neither of these implications ever applies to Lutosławski's music. Despite the difficulties implicit in this array of terms for Lutosławski's rhythmic technique, I will continue to use them interchangeably but will attempt to confine usage to the terms "limited aleatory" and *"ad libitum."*

[8]Steven Stucky, *Lutosławski and His Music* (New York: Cambridge University Press, 1981), 107-132.

coincide. Lutosławski is quite open about his method of presenting pitch material in an *ad libitum* section:[9]

> Within an aleatoric section, pitch can be strictly fixed. This is the simplest way of organising pitch within an aleatoric section. We compose a . . . . chord, which serves as the basis of that section. The instruments only play the notes belonging to that chord. It may occur that the chord never actually sounds in its entirety--it is supplemented by our memory and imagination.

Only one harmonic aggregate unfolds within each *ad libitum* section, and because of this ratio of one harmony per ad libitum we can understand better Lutosławski's practice of using pitches that are fixed in register.

Harmonic aggregates and their presentation in *ad libitum* sections are the major elements of Lutosławski's style from the 1960s until the early 1980s. To see how these elements change in his late music, I shall turn to the first ad libitum section from *Partita*. This work was the subject of several conversations that I had with Lutosławski months before his death. During these conversations, Lutosławski claimed that the *ad libitum* sections of *Partita* were extraordinary in his output, and that in the first ad libitum section, which makes up the entire second movement, his method for creating the material in the violin part differed from his method for creating the material in the piano part. This second point seemed so contrary to the evidence in the first *ad libitum*, that I suspected at first that Lutosławski was allowing some personal agenda to direct me to a path leading to an analytic dead-end. But, after reconsidering the ad libitum sections of the *Partita*, I have found evidence that not only confirms Lutosławski's characterizations but also provides clues to uncovering compositional procedures that he used throughout his career.

In no other work by Lutosławski does a single *ad libitum* govern an entire movement. In earlier works the static effect of ad libitum sections seems to negate the possibility of creating large-scale structures from a single *ad libitum* section. Already we

---

[9]Bálint András Varga, *Lutosławski Profile: Witold Lutosławski in Conversation with Bálint András Varga,* Stephen Walsh, trans. (London: J. & W. Chester/ Edition Wilhelm Hansen London Limited, 1976), 24.

have a characteristic that individuates this *ad libitum* in *Partita* from those of earlier works. In order to show how Lutosławski avoids the problem of stasis in this *ad libitum* section, I shall investigate both its rhythmic and pitch construction.

In notating the first *ad libitum* from *Partita,* Lutosławski places the parts of both the piano and violin in separate boxes in order to insure that the performers will not allow visual cues to influence any rhythmic coordination of the music. Nonetheless, the two parts share rhythmic patterns, and on the basis of these patterns we can attempt to align the parts in a single score. Example 5 presents one attempt to accomplish such an alignment. Two points of rhythmic coordination are evident in the score. The first is at the beginning of the movement in which gestures of thirty-second notes with intervening rests characterize both the violin and piano parts. The second appears midway through the movement in which both parts begin with a half note proceeding to a dotted-quarter followed by two quarters, three eighths, and so on. At both of these points we can align the piano and violin parts with some success, suggesting that this *ad libitum* has a two-part form.

At the opening of the movement, I have allowed the rests with fermatas in both the violin and piano parts to create a series of echoes between the two instruments. After two repetitions of this rhythmic material, the echo effect becomes difficult to maintain, since the piano simply has too many notes in relation to the violin. Turning to the second point of coordination in this movement, we find that once again the piano has too many notes to achieve a perfect alignment of the two instruments. Although both instruments begin with the same rhythmic patterns, the piano has seven more sixteenths in the course of its pattern than the violin. This same problem reappears at successive repetitions of this rhythmic pattern through the end of the movement.

Despite the fact that Lutosławski avoids using precisely the same rhythmic patterns in the parts of the violin and the piano, we find no obvious evidence of the simple arithmetic progressions that characterize the rhythmic patterns in the *ad libitum* sections of his earlier compositions. A single exception might be that the violin performs the rhythmic material of the second part of the *ad libitum* four times, while the piano performs this material only three times.

Example 5: Alignment of violin and piano parts in *Ad Libitum* from
Partita for Violin and Piano by Witold Roman Lutosławski.
Copyright © 1986 by Chester Music Limited (PRS)
All rights for USA & Canada controlled by G. Schirmer, Inc. (ASCAP)
International Copyright Secured. All Rights Reserved.
Reprinted by Permission

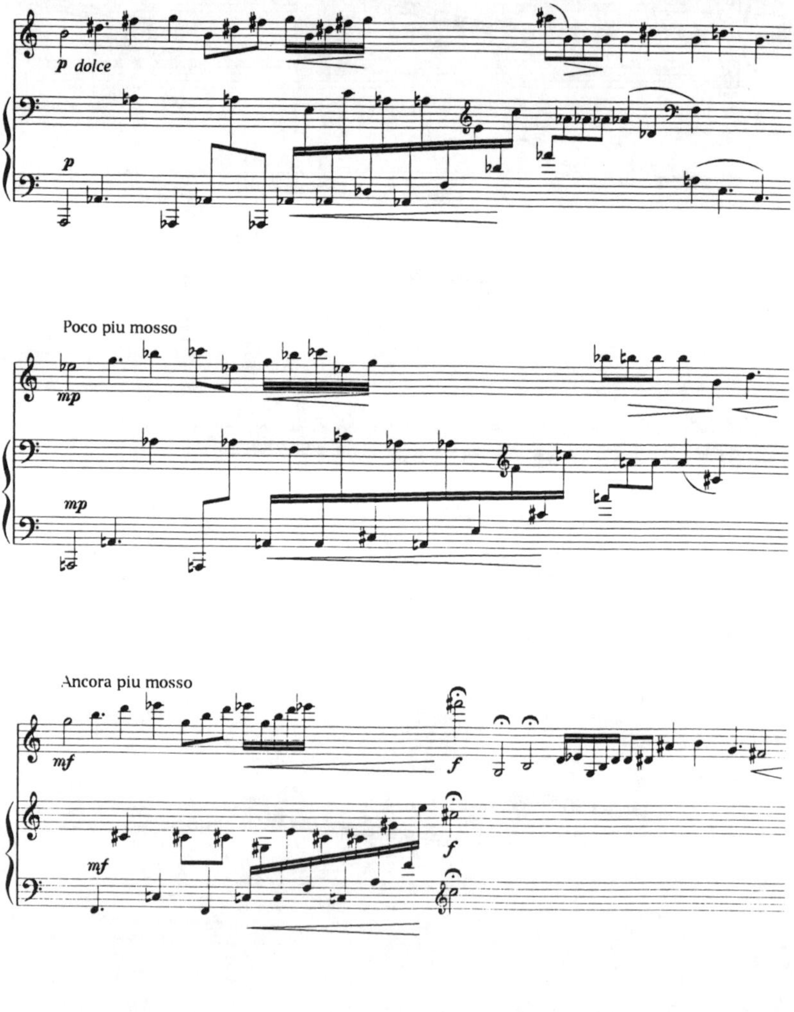

Example 5: *Ad Libitum* from *Partita,* continued.

However, the use of extra notes in the piano part does seem consistent with his practice of insuring that any performance will render a rhythmically complex surface. Certainly the similarity in the rhythmic patterns of the two instruments suggests that Lutosławski was not referring to rhythm when he claimed that his method of composing the violin part was different from his method of composing the piano part. To understand his claims, therefore, I will turn to the pitch organization in the second movement.

In each of the three *ad libitum* sections of the *Partita*, Lutosławski unfolds pitch-class aggregates, not harmonic aggre-gates. This transformation from pitch space to pitch-class space is immediately apparent in the piano part of the first ad libitum section, where a gesture of 7 notes appears in four different registers throughout the first half of the movement. Lutosławski creates the aggregates in the *Partita* by assigning hexachords to both the piano and the violin. In the first *ad libitum*, pitch-class set {2, 3, 6, 7, T, E}, belonging to set-class (014589), generates all of the pitch material of the violin part while the literal complement of these pitch-classes {0, 1, 4, 5, 8, 9}, belonging to the same set-class, generates all of the pitch material of the piano part.

Set-class (014589) is one of the all-combinatorial hexachords, and Lutosławski uses two other all-combinatorial hexachords, (012345) and (012678), in the remaining *ad libitum* sections of the *Partita*. In the case of the first *ad libitum*, the appearance of the same hexachord in both instruments along with the rhythmic similarity between their two parts led me to the conclusion that Lutosławski created the material for the two instruments by similar means.

In light of Lutosławski's comments contradicting my original conclusion, I have reevaluated my analysis of the pitch material in this *ad libitum*. By assigning the label (014589) to the two hexachords, I treated the pitch material as a static entity, and I ignored the generative processes that create these hexachords on the musical foreground. Also, by characterizing these hexachords as "all-combinatorial," I have implied that a property of interest to composers of serial music was also of interest to Lutosławski. But, because Lutosławski rarely uses an ordered row to generate the pitch material of a composition - and often, in fact, describes Schoenberg's method in derogatory terms - it seems unlikely that he chose these hexachords for their combinatorial properties, *per se*. Instead, I now believe that Lutosławski used these hexachords because they have both inversional and transpositional symmetries. Indeed, two of the hexachords, (014589) and (012678), contain multiple transpositional and inversional symmetries, and it is these same two hexachords that appear prominently in almost all of Lutosławski's late music.

Because these hexachords contain two types of symmetry, they can be generated in two different ways, by means of either *inversional union* or *transpositional combination*. By inversional union, I refer to a property found in many texts on atonal theory and described succinctly by John Rahn as follows:[10]

> The union of any two inversionally related sets is an inversionally symmetrical set. Conversely, an inversionally symmetrical set may always be 'disunited' into at least one pair of inversionally related subsets.

By transpositional combination, I refer to a property defined by Richard Cohn as follows:[11]

> Transpositional combination (TC) is a binary operation whose input is set classes A and B. The operation adds each pitch-class in the prime form of A to each pitch class in the prime form of B. The result is the set class representing the union of all such sums.

More colloquially, transpositional combination describes a process by which a collection of pitches and a transposition of that collection are combined to create a larger collection. Cohn also defines a more specific case of transpositional combination in which a pitch collection is combined with transpositional levels that create an interval cycle. The larger sets that result from such a process are those sets that many twentieth-century composers seem to favor. For example, when pitch-class set {0, 2} is combined with levels of transposition that form the interval cycle {0, 3, 6, 9}, the resulting pitch-class set is {0, 2, 3, 5, 6, 8, 9, E}, which is one form of the octatonic scale. By the definitions above, if a set-class contains the property of inversional symmetry, it can be generated by inversional union, and if a set-class contains the property of transpositional symmetry, it can be generated by transpositional combination where the levels of transposition form an interval cycle. Among the set-classes that can be generated through either process are the octatonic, diatonic, whole-tone, and hexatonic

---

[10]John Rahn, *Basic Atonal Theory* (New York: Schirmer Books, 1980), 93.

[11]Richard Cohn, "Properties and Generability of Transpositionally Invariant Sets," *Journal of Music Theory* 35, no. 1 (spring 1991): 16.

collections.

    I will illustrate cases of transpositional combination using an analytic notation like that of Example 6, which reproduces a portion of the final *ad libitum* section in the *Partita*. At the top of the example, Cohn's notation shows the set-classes involved in the process of transpositional combination. In this case a form of set-class (03) participates in transpositional combination with a form of set-class (012) to generate a form of set-class (012345).[12] The score appears below Cohn's notation when practical. Below the score I illustrate the transpositional combination with musical symbols. In this notation, one of the set-classes appears as open note-heads with stems connected by a beam. This set-class repre-sents the levels of transposition. The set-class that travels through these levels of transposition appears as notehead(s) connected by a slur.

    I illustrate inversional union using a similar analytic nota-tion. Example 7 reproduces mm. 128 - 129 in the violin part of *Su-bito* (1992). Numerical notation at the top of the example shows that in this passage the larger pitch-class set {E, 1, 2, 4, 5, 7} is the result of the union of two inversionally related trichords, {E, 1, 4} and {2, 5, 7}. When referring to inversional union, I notate the pitch-class sets in normal form so that their inversional relationship is clear. Below the numerical presentation, I reproduce the score when practical. Beneath the score I present the pitch-class sets as verticalities on two staves. In this particular example the two pitch-class sets interlock in pitch space; that is, the highest notes of the lower pitch-class set appear above the lowest notes of the higher pitch-class set.

---

[12]Following Cohn, I shall use Forte's labels for set-classes in the notation of transpositional combination. In the music-analytic notation and the text, however, I will use numbers without commas in parenthesis: (013), (014), and so on.

Example 6: Transpositional Combination in *Partita:* Final *Ad libitum.*
2-3 * 3-1 = 6-1

Example 7: Inversional Union in mm. 128-129 of *Subito* (violin part).
{E, 1, 4} U {2, 5, 7} = {E, 1, 2, 4, 5, 7}

Subito by Witold Roman Lutosławski. Copyright © 1994 by Chester Music Limited (PRS). All rights for USA & Canada controlled by G. Schirmer, Inc. (ASCAP). International Copyright Secured. All Rights Reserved.
Reprinted by Permission

Example 8: Transpositional Combination in the violin part, *Partita,* II.
4-19 * 3-12 = 6-7 . Copyright information as in Example 5.

I maintain this interlocking of pitches in the verticalities that appear in the music-analytic notation. Next to the verticalities, however, I unfold the individual pitches of the entire pitch-class set as they appear in pitch space. An interval string below this version of the pitch-class set reveals any mirror symmetry that may appear in pitch space.

We hear evidence that Lutosławski generates hexachords using both inversional union and transpositional combination in the *ad libitum* that forms the second movement of the *Partita*. Evidence of inversional union appears immediately in the violin part. Here, the opening gesture consists of three pitches belonging to pitch-class set {E, 2, 3}. Immediately following, the violin plays a second gesture whose three pitches, belonging to pitch-class set {6, 7, T}, are an inversion of the opening gesture. Both pitch-class sets belong to set-class (014). The inversion is immediately apparent because it occurs in pitch space as well as pitch-class space. At the conclusion of this second gesture, the union of the two trichords produces the hexachord {2, 3, 6, 7, T, E} that will account for all of the pitch-classes in the violin part. A similar process of inversional union generates the pitches in the piano part. The opening gesture of the piano can be heard as the union of pitch-classes {9, 0, 1} with an inversion of these pitch-classes, resulting in the I-symmetrical tetrachord {9, 0, 1, 4}. This tetrachord is a form of set-class (0347), a subset of the octatonic collection that is prominent in other late works. In other words, Lutosławski, generates both set-class (014589) in the violin and set-class (0347) in the piano by means of inversional union; and in both cases, the process of inversional union involves set-class (014). The two forms of (014) that generate the violin's material are *partitioning* subsets of set-class (014589) because they have no pitch-classes in common; but the two forms of (014) that generate the piano's material are *non-partitioning* subsets, because they share at least one pitch-class.[13] As such, the piano completes neither its hexachord nor the aggregate until later in the *ad libitum* section. On the second system of the piano's score, the appearance of F4 in the piano expands that instrument's pitch material to a form of set-class (01459). Lutosławski withholds pitch-class 8 that will complete the hexachord for this *ad libitum* until the fourth system of the piano score, at which point the second part of this movement's two-part form begins. Since Lutosławski presented the violin's hexachord at the beginning of the movement, the withholding of the final pitch-class in the piano's hexachord also delays the completion of the aggregate so that it will coincide with the formal

---

[13]For a formal exposition of partitions in music see Robert D. Morris and Brian Alegant, "The Even Partitions in Twelve-Tone Music," *Music Theory Spectrum* 10 (1988): 74-101.

division of this movement.

It is in the second half of the *ad libitum* that the method of generating the hexachord in the violin part differs from that of the piano part. Here, Lutosławski creates the pitch material of the violin part through transpositional combination. At the beginning of the second section the violin performs repetitions of the tetrachord {E, 3, 6, 7}. At the opening of the next phrase Lutosławski transposes this tetrachord up four semitones to produce {3, 7, T, E}, and at the third phrase of this section a second transposition up 4 semitones produces {7, E, 2, 3}. In this section, hexachord (014589) results from the transpositional combination of set-class (0148) with set-class (048). We can show this process in Cohn's shorthand or in music-analytic notation as in Example 8.

At the same time that the violin creates its hexachord through the process of transpositional combination, the piano continues to form its hexachord through the process of inversional union. This becomes clear when considering how Lutosławski divides the piano's material between the hands. In each of the three phrases that make up the second part of this *ad libitum,* the right hand contains pitches belonging to a form of set-class (037) while the left hand contains pitches belonging to an inverted form of the same set-class. In the first phrase, for example, the pitches in the right hand, {9, 0, 4}, are an inversion of the pitches in the left hand, {1, 5, 8}. Example 9 encapsulates this inversional union.

Lutosławski's uses of both inversional union and trans-positional combination in the second movement of the *Partita* artic-ulate form. In the piano part, the participation of set-class (014) in a non-partitioning of a tetrachord results in the withholding of two pitch-classes from the hexachord that will account for the pitch material of the *ad libitum*. Lutosławski introduces the last of these withheld pitch-classes at the formal division of the movement.

Example 9: Inversional Union in the piano part, *Partita*, II.
{9, 0, 4} U {1, 5, 8} = { 0, 1, 4, 5, 8, 9}
(Copyright information included in Example 5).

Example 10: TC and IU in the final *Ad Libitum* from *Partita*, piano part.
{5, 8} U {7, T} = {5, 7, 8, T}   2-2 * 2-3 = 4-10

Example 11: Transpositional Combination in the second line of the final
Ad Libitum from *Partita*. 2-3 * 3-1 = 6-1.

In the violin part, Lutosławski articulates this formal division by a change from inversional union to transpositional combination.

By comparing this *ad libitum* to others in Lutosławski's output, we can understand why he considered it to be extraordinary. In no other work by Lutosławski is a single *ad libitum* co-extensive with an entire movement. *Ad libitum* sections in previous works were limited by the static register and pitch structure. Because of this limitation, Lutosławski relied on many *ad libitum* sections to articulate formal structures. In this *ad libitum* section Lutosławski loosens the restraints of his former compositions by allowing pitch-classes to appear in multiple octaves. He apparently becomes less concerned that the combination of the pitches performed by the participating instruments will result in a single chord. In order to guide the listener through the structure of this single *ad libitum* section, Lutosławski relies on two compositional procedures, inversional union and transpositional combination.[14]

We find evidence of transpositional combination and inversional union in the other *ad libitum* sections of the *Partita* as well, although these processes do not always have a clear role in defining form. In the third *ad libitum*, which appears before the coda of the last movement, the two processes highlight a series of increasingly dissonant interval-classes, which contribute to the climactic effect of this *ad libitum* section. Here, a form of set-class (012345) appears in the violin, while its literal complement appears in the piano. Example 10 illustrates the ways in which inversional union and transpostional combination generate the material in the beginning of the piano part. The opening chord with its mirror symmetry in pitch space suggests that pitch-class set {5, 7, 8, T} results from the inversional union of two minor thirds. Immediately following this chord, the same pitch-class set results from transpositional combination. These two processes highlight two different sets of interval-classes. In the case of the opening chord, where inversional union is evident, the highlighted interval-classes are ic 3, which forms each dyad, and ic 1, which is the interval at the registral center of the pitch collection. In the case where the same material is generated through transpositional combination, the highlighted interval-classes are ic 2, which forms each of the dyads, and ic 3, which forms the levels of transposition for those dyads. As inversional union and transpositional combination occur throughout this *ad libitum*, they often result in highlighting pairs of these three interval-classes, i.e. ic 1, ic 2, or ic 3.

---

[14]The articulation of the form of this *ad libitum* is not limited to the use of pitch. In particular, a two-part form is also supported by (1) a change from relatively quick rhythmic values to slower ones and (2) an alternation between a relatively high register and a low register, especially in the piano.

Transpositional combination dominates the formation of the pitch material in the second line of the piano part, where dyad {5, 8} appears in transpositions that form a chromatic trichord. Example 11 shows this process in Cohn's shorthand and in music-analytic notation. Here the highlighted interval-classes are ic 3, forming the individual dyads, and ic 1, forming the levels of transposition. A similar process of transpositional combination generates the repeated chords in the piano that close this *ad libitum*. In the first six repeated chords both the registers and Lutosławski's method of adding pitches to the chords suggests another instance of the transpositional combination of ic 3 and a chromatic trichord. In the final repeated chords, however, the addition of two pitches in the center of the chords creates mirror symmetry in pitch space, suggesting inversional union. This addition does not alter the total pitch-class content of the chords, but it does add more instances of ic 1 as a highlighted interval-class. Example 12 illustrates both transpositional combination and inversional union in these final chords. Before commenting further on the implications of the highlighted interval-classes in these final chords, I will turn to the violin part of this *ad libitum* section.

One of the clearest examples of transpositional combination in the violin part appears in the beginning of the third line. Here the chromatic tetrachord (0123) results from the transpositional combination of ic 2 and ic 1 as shown in Example 13. Readers may recall that these are two of the three interval-classes that are highlighted in the piano part of this section. In the final line of the violin part, we hear a similar type of ambiguity between transpositional combination and inversional union that we heard at the end of the piano part. In this case the hexachord can be analyzed as the transpositional combination of a form of set-classes (024) and (01), as shown in Example 14.

Example 12: T-Combination and I-Union in the piano part, final *Ad Libitum* from *Partita*.   2-3 * 3-1 = 6-1
{6, 7, T} U {5, 8, 9} = {5, 6, 7, 8, 9, T}

{0, 2}
(02)   (01)   {1, 3}
                        (02)

                                    {0, 1, 2, 3}
                                    (0123)

Example 13: T-Combination in the third line of the final *Ad Libitum*
from *Partita*. 2-1 * 2-3 = 4-1

{1, 2}   {3, 4}   {E, 0}
(01)   (01)   (01)

{E, 1, 3}   {E, 0, 1, 2, 3, 4}
(024)   (012345)

Example 14: T- Combination in the last line of *Ad Libitum* from *Partita*
2-1* 3-6 = 6-1. Copyright information in Example 5.

                        (03)   (03)   {1, 2, 4, 5, 7, 8, T, E}
(03)   (03)   (0134679T)

(04)   (04)

(06)   3 · 1 · 2 · 1 · 2 · 1 · 3

Example 15: TC and IU in the second movement of *Bukolika* no. 5.
(2-3 * 2-4) * 2-6 = 8-28
{7, T, E, 2} U {1, 4, 5, 8} = {1, 2, 4, 5, 7, 8, T, E}

However, both the manner in which Lutosławski places four of these pitches in a different register, and the contour of these four pitches, with one dyad ascending followed by one dyad descending, suggests inversional union as the basis of part of the whole hexachord. This lower tetrachord contains ic 1 both as the interval that participates in inversional union and as the center of pitch inversion. As was the case with the piano part, ic 1 in the violin part becomes most prominent at the end of the *ad libitum*.

In this *ad libitum* it is not as simple to coordinate the two parts into a single hypothetical score. However, the repeated passage at the end of the violin part suggests that both the final line of the violin and the repeated chords at the end of the piano part will be heard together. In both instruments, transpositional combination and inversional union highlight interval-classes in set-class (012345) so that ic 1 will predominate only at the end of the *ad libitum* section. The dissonance in ic 1 coupled with the heightened rhyth-mic activity in the violin part and the repeated chords of the piano part brings maximum tension to the end of this *ad libitum* section.

* * *

Transpositional combination and inversional union allow us to reconsider Lutosławski's entire output. Rather than viewing his music as a path from simplicity to complexity and back to simplicity, we can view his music through the filter of a pair of procedures that generates much of the pitch material found in compositions throughout his career. With these two processes in mind, I shall conclude by taking a look at some excerpts from Lutosławski's earlier works.

At the beginning of this essay, I referred to the second movement of the *5 Bukoliki* as an example of Lutosławski's earlier style. I mentioned that the left hand of this piano piece is structured by the octatonic collection, common to much music of the 20th century. Example 15 illustrates that the octatonic collection arises from both transpositional combination and inversional union in the left-hand part of this movement. The transpositional combination in the passage involves set-classes (0347) and (06). Set-class (0347), however, is also the result of transpositional combination, involving set-classes (03) and (04). The inversional union in the passage is evident if we place all of the notes of this left hand part in their registral order from lowest to highest. As Example 15 reveals, these pitches produce mirror symmetry in pitch space, suggesting inversional union.

The same two processes are evident in the harmonic aggregates in Lutosławski's works of the 1960s and '70s. Example 16 shows one of the harmonic aggregates in his "Wiatr" from *Five Songs*. The three tetrachords that make up this harmonic aggregate belong to the same set-class, and we can describe the formation of the harmonic aggregate as the transpositional combination of set-classes (0257) and (048). The reader may realize that this harmonic aggregate contains the property of parallel symmetry which I described above. All parallel-symmetric harmonic aggre-gates can be viewed as the result of transpositional combination. In a harmonic aggregate that appears later in this song cycle, inversional union is in evidence. Example 17 shows the final harmonic aggregate in "Dzwony cerkiewne." The interval string of this harmonic aggregate shows mirror symmetry that suggests inversional union, and indeed the harmonic aggregate is made up of two chromatic trichords that form the I-symmetrical hexachord (012678) in the upper register and two more chromatic trichords forming the literal complement of this hexachord in the lower register. All mirror-symmetric harmonic aggregates can be viewed as the result of the inversional union of two hexachords.

Finally, transpositional combination and inversional union generate much of the pitch material in Lutosławski's late works. In mm. 128 - 129 of *Subito* for violin and piano (1992), Lutosławski presents pitch-class sets in both the piano and the violin that are subsets of octatonic collections. We can also think of both pitch-class sets as products of inversional union. Example 18 shows that pitch-class set {E, 1, 2, 4, 5, 7} in the violin is the product of the inversional union of pitch-class sets {E, 1, 4} and {2, 5, 7}. Similarly, pitch-class set {9, T, 0, 1, 3, 4} in the piano is the product of the inversional union of pitch-class sets {T, 1, 4} and {9, 0, 3}. In the piano part, inversional union is highlighted by the duplication of pcs 3 and T in different octaves, which produces mirror symmetry in pitch space.

(0257)
(0257)
(0257)

(048)

4   <0, 2, 5, 7, 8, T, 1, 3, 4, 6, 9, E>

2-3-2 · 1 · 2-3-2 · 1 · 2-3-2

Example 16: Transpositional Combination in a Harmonic Aggregate
from the song *Wiatr*.   4-23 * 3-12 = 12-1

<1,3,2>   <8,7,9>   <4,6,5>   <E,T,0>

Example 17: Inversional Union in Harmonic Aggregate from the song
Dzwony Cerkiewne.
<1,3,2> U <8,7,9> = <1,3,2,8,7,9> = 6-7
<4,6,5> U <E,T,0> = <4,6,5,E,T,0> = 6-7
<1, 3, 2, 8, 7, 9>U<4, 6, 5, E, T, 0> = 12-1

Example 18: Inversional Union in *Subito,* mm. 128-129.
{E, 1, 4} U {2, 5, 7} = {E, 1, 2, 4, 5, 7}
{9, T, 0, 3} U {T, !, 3, 4} = {9, T, 0, 1, 3, 4}
Copyright information included in Example 7.

We have seen in *Partita* that transpositional combination generates pitch material in Lutosławski's late works as well. Two excerpts from his Symphony No. 4 (1992) will serve as illustrations from the end of his career. Example 19 reproduces the flute melody that appears at the opening of the Symphony No. 4. Here a form of set-class (014589) arises through the transpositional combination of set-classes (014) and (048). Shortly after this flute solo, set-class (048) participates in another process of transpositional combination, this time with set-class (036), to produce the larger set-class (01245689T). This occurs in a series of solos for horn, trumpet and clarinet that appear in Example 20.

Reference to inversional union and transpositional combination allows us to go beyond a description of Lutosławski's career as following a familiar arch from simplicity to complexity and back to simplicity. We are now in a position to argue that two procedures underlie music throughout his career. In his early music, transpositional combination and inversional union result in pitch collections like the octatonic.[15] In his later music, transpositional combination and inversional union result in harmonic aggregates with the properties of parallel or mirror symmetry, and in the latest music the same two processes create smaller pitch collections that have multiple I- and T- symmetries such as set-class (014589). Lutosławski's turn to these smaller collections may be seen as a response to the problems that he found in creating large-scale forms using only harmonic aggregates presented with the limited aleatory technique. Seen from this perspective, Lutosławski's distinctive voice is a consequence not of adapting the systems and fashions of the time but of finding personal solutions to compositional problems.

---

[15] A different view of the evolution of Lutosławski's compositional technique, resulting from a detailed style analysis of his entire oeuvre is presented in Martina Homma's doctoral dissertation, *Witold Lutosławski: Zwölfton-Harmonik - Formbildung - "aleatorischer Kontrapunkt. Studien sum Gesamtwerk unter Einbeziehung der Skizzen;* (Cologne: Bela Verlag, 1996). This monumental study is not available in English and was not consulted by the author [editor's note].

Example 19: Transpositional Combination in flute solo from Symphony no. 4, Rehearsal # 3. Symphony No. 4 by Witold Roman Lutosławski. Copyright © 1995 by Chester Music Limited (PRS). All rights for USA & Canada controlled by G. Schirmer, Inc. (ASCAP). International Copyright Secured. All Rights Reserved. Reprinted by Permission

Example 20: Transpositional Combination in Wind/Brass solos in the Symphony no. 4, Rehearsal #5. Symphony no. 4 by Witold Roman Lutosławski. Copyright information included in Example 19.

PART III

MUSIC

&

NATIONAL IDENTITY

The Dilemma of Twentieth-Century Polish Music: National Style or Universal Values

by Zofia Helman[1]

The National Style as a Compositional Problem

The history of twentieth-century Polish music has been marked by the clash of artistic poetics proclaiming different values in different periods. These clashes constitute turning points that can usually be traced to more general stylistic and aesthetic changes in European music; however, in Poland, these changes always had an intrinsically different nature from those in other countries and they manifested themselves in the preference for a national style or universal values.

The question of a national style arises not only from research aimed at identifying specific features in the music of a nation, but also from the strategies and choices adopted by individual composers. At least during the last two centuries, the question of a Polish national style was a problem in composition which came to be inscribed into the very history of Polish music. At times the national style was a product of specific ideological factors connected with a consciously created program; at other times, the national style became an intolerable burden paralyzing artistic freedom. Although the reasons and justifications for the compositional choices varied, they were inevitably intertwined with the historical and artistic circumstances of Poland.

The reasons for the tension between the national and the universal in Polish music date to the so-called "national schools" of the nineteenth century, when a positivist ideology assigned art a social and national mission during the period of Poland's partition (1795-1918). Initially formulated for literature, this mission per-

[1]This text is translated by Joanna Niżyńska and Peter J. Schertz from Zofia Helman, "Styl narodowy czy wartości uniwersalne - dylemat muzyki polskiej dwudziestego wieku," in *Dziedzictwo europejskie a polska kultura muzyczna w dobie przemian* [The European heritage and Polish musical culture in the period of transformations], Anna Czekanowska, ed.(Kraków: Musica Iagellonica, 1995), 175-200. Reprinted by permission.

vaded the entire artistic consciousness of the second half of the nineteenth century. Consequently music, like literature and painting, assumed the utilitarian-didactic tasks of sustaining the national consciousness, serving the ideal of a reborn independent Poland, and stimulating and supporting Polishness. Józef Sikorski proclaimed "the gospel of national thought" in opposition to "cosmopolitanism;" music was to be evaluated according to such criteria as its "social tendency" and "usefulness."[2] Behind these declarations lay the assumption that music must conform to the demands of its native audience:[3]

> Art must be domestic . . . . This is why a national-genre painter or a composer of songs which preserve the national spirit are dearer to people than a painter who is historical or religious in some universal sense or than a composer writing operas and symphonies for the whole world. The former show that they love humanity through their nation; the latter see their nation as a part of humanity. The latter might be even more sublime, burn with an even greater flame, but the former will be recognized and will influence people in a more beneficial and faster manner since its impact is more immediate. The motto of the former is "Art from Life and for Life," their task - to proselytize for national ideals and citizenship; the latter claim "Art for Art's Sake," their task - to proselytize for humanity, in other words, cosmopolitanism.

Such beliefs in the patriotic duty and social mission of art explain the tastes and preferences of the audiences and critics of the nineteenth century. Characteristically for the second half of the

[2]Józef Sikorski (1813-1896) was a music critic, theorist and composer. In 1857 he founded the musical weekly *Ruch Muzyczny* [Musical Movement] which was renamed in 1862 *Pamiętnik Muzyczny i Teatralny*. His reviews appeared in *Biblioteka Warsawska, Gazeta Polska, Bluszcz, Tygodnik Ilustrowany*. In 1870 he was one of the founders of the Warsaw Music Society (WTM).

[3]The quotation comes from Sikorski's article "Muzykalność i obywatelstwo" [Musicality and citizenship], *Ruch Muzyczny* no. 45 (1860), in *Antologia krytyki muzycznej XIX i XX wieku* [Anthology of music criticism of the 19th and the 20th centuries], Stefan Jarociński, ed.(Kraków: PWM Edition, 1955), 105-109 (the quotation is from p. 105). Sikorski developed these ideas earlier in "Myśli sztuki domowej dotyczące" [Thoughts concerning "home"arts], *Ruch Muzyczny* no. 13-14 (1859).

nineteenth century, Chopin's genius was admired by all ("our leading artist," comparable to the great poet-prophets [*wieszcz*] of Polish literature), although his music was often regarded as elitist. It was Moniuszko who exercised a more direct influence upon the musical culture of the time, "dominating the minds of his listeners and of composers willing to serve the audience."[4] In an article written for the five hundredth performance of *Halka*, Antoni Sygietyński declared that Moniuszko, "sang in the name of everyone and for everyone" while Chopin "sang" only "for the chosen ones."[5] Sygietyński describes Moniuszko's music as expressing the national temperament in the fullest manner because the composer was "equally noble and Völkisch, embracing in his heart the entire nation."

During the period of the partitions, it was difficult for artists to ignore the patriotic and ethical values of an art programatically created for the purpose of fortifying the hearts of Poles. Thus, the modernist revolt of the young generation at the turn of the twentieth century was less a revolt against the ideal of a national rebirth [*odrodzenie*] as against a xenophobic separation from Europe's artistic movements. The discussions within the literary movement Young Poland [*Młoda Polska*] established the "young" in opposition to the "old;" the participants in this movement emphasized the individual over the society; individuality over communal responsibility; philosophical speculation over pragmatism; the autonomy of artistic values over utilitarianism; and a universal perspective over a nationalist perspective. Artur Górski, writing under

---

[4]Adolf Chybiński (1880-1952) was a musicologist who received his doctorate in Munich, and was a professor of musicology in Lwów and Poznań. The article "Chopin a muzyka polska (w setną rocznicę urodzin mistrza)" [Chopin and Polish music: on the 100th anniversary of the birth of the master], published in *Widnokręgi* no. 1 (1910) is quoted from Jarociński, *Antologia*, 330.

[5] Antoni Sygietyński (1850-1923) was a music critic and piano teacher at the Warsaw Music Institute. His reviews appeared in *Ateneum, Nowiny, Prawda, Kurier Warszawski, Gazeta Polska, Nowa Gazeta*, etc. His review of Moniuszko's *Hrabina* [Countess] appeared in *Kurier Warszawski* no. 306-4 (1898) and the review of Moniuszko's *Halka*, quoted here, appeared in *Kurier Warszawski* no. 340 (1900): 345-6. The review was reprinted in Jarociński, *Antologia*, 272-276; quotations come from pp. 275, 272. Interestingly, his son, Tadeusz (1896-1955) was a composer and promoter of Polish folklore, the founder of the State Folk Ensemble "Mazowsze" and the author of numerous arrangements for this group.

the pen-name "Quasimodo," denied the validity of inherited paradigms which, in the name of the national tradition, shielded Polish culture from West European impulses. Górski declared:[6]

> such an understanding of "tradition" and the "national spirit" breaks us and we surrender to it from our youth. Other factors have contributed to the shape of the modern Polish soul and we want to express them in our art, even in the face of opposition by the entire older generation. This, in any case, is the only form of our resistance. All other activities we leave for your sober and lucrative transactions; in art alone we demand freedom. No real art, no great art can exist without the free expression of artistic individuality - otherwise art is created for the masses, as some sort of artistic industry.

The attitude of young composers toward the positivist tradition was no different than that of the members of Young Poland. For the composers, what had earlier been ironically labeled "cosmopolitanism" was a perspective on art derived from a system of universal values. The idea of a national art based upon utilitarian-didactic tasks ceased to be attractive. It is in this period that Karol Szymanowski wrote:[7]

> What wasn't called "National Art" during this past period of captivity! Under this name occurred a hopeless sinking into the whirlpool of past splendors; the dead ghosts of the past were conjured, the timid eye was closed to the roaring, rapid stream of contemporary life happening around us; under this name "going to the people" was also hidden, the peculiar hypnotism of mazurkas and Christmas carols, the collecting of awful pinkish folk paper cut-outs with green ribbons; under this name were also written German-academic fugues on the subject of

[6]Quasimodo [Artur Górski], "Młoda Polska" [Young Poland], *Życie* (1898). Reprinted in *Programy i dyskusje literackie okresu Młodej Polski* [Programs and literary discussions of the period of Young Poland], Series I, no. 212, Maria Podraza-Kwiatkowska, ed. (Wrocław: Biblioteka Narodowa, 1977), 96-125.

[7]Karol Szymanowski, "Uwagi w sprawie współczesnej opinii muzycznej w Polsce" [Remarks about contemporary musical opinion in Poland], *Nowy Przegląd Literatury i Sztuki*, no. 2 (July 1920), reprinted in *Karol Szymanowski: Pisma*, vol. 1, *Pisma Muzyczne* [Writings about Music] Kornel Michałowski, ed. (Kraków: PWM Edition, 1984), 33-46. Quoted from p. 39.

Niedaleko Krakowa [Not far from Kraków] or *Chmielu, chmielu zielony* [Hops, green hops]. Sometimes this "National Art" became a poisonous false tip on a fencing foil, striking unexpectedly the heart of the "ideological" enemy.

In spite of the popularity and positive reception of the first concerts of Spółka Nakładowa Młodych Kompozytorów Polskich [Publishing Cooperative of Young Polish Composers] critics reacted harshly to the young composers, rejecting their aesthetic stance and the modernity of their musical language. Various accusations were leveled against Szymanowski and the remaining members of Spółka Nakładowa: that they were betraying patriotic ideals, that they "slavishly" imitated the music of Wagner and Strauss, and that they overwhelmed artistic inspiration with technique.[8] Thus, the gap between the older generation and the generation of Young Poland grew. Szymanowski's letters to Zdzisław Jachimecki in 1910 and 1911 contain many bitter words about the leading figures of Polish music, including Paderewski. After Paderewski's speech celebrating the centenary of Chopin's birth on October 23, 1910 at the Lwów Philharmonic, Szymanowski wrote: "I don't care for this genre of patriotic commonplace." This letter contains not the brash pose of Young Poland, but reflections of Szymanowski's authentic sense of loneliness:[9]

> I am perfectly aware that there will always be an indestructible wall of different beliefs and different concepts of art and life between me and my society . . . I am not a cosmopolitan, but in our current atmosphere and mood I feel somehow foreign. As a musician I will be respected only so long as a direct line can be traced from Chopin to my own compositions (e.g., *Sonata,*

---

[8]Aleksander Poliński (1845-1916) was a music historian and critic, publishing reviews in *Kurier Warszawski, Tygodnik Ilustrowany, Echo Muzyczne i Teatralne.* In 1904 he became a professor of music theory in the Warsaw Institute of Music. He wrote the first history of Polish music, *Dzieje muzyki polskiej* (Lwów 1907), and published articles about composers from the renaissance to romanticism. The polemics are in his article "Młoda Polska w muzyce," *Kurier Warszawski,* no. 110 (22 April 1907), quoted in Karol Szymanowski, *Korespondencja* [Correspondence], vol. 1, Teresa Chylińska, ed. (Kraków: PWM Edition, 1982), 31-133.

[9]Letter published in Karol Szymanowski, Chylińska, *Korespondencja,* 244-245.

Preludes, Etudes). But, when I stand on my own feet, they will throw stones at me - as my recent concerts have proved.

Aleksander Poliński's accusation that Szymanowski's early work contained foreign influences affected the attitude of critics and, with time, musicologists listed as Szymanowski's musical predecessors almost all the important late Romantic composers. To perceive foreign influences as the genesis and sources of analyzed compositions involves a double movement, a double bind, as it were - on the one hand, historical-musical phenomena were treated from a positivist perspective, on the other hand, Polish music was regarded as an isolated system somehow threatened by these "foreign influences." Of course, the native art of Poland, being a part of European culture, was never created in true isolation but in close proximity to and in an ongoing dialogue with the artistic production of other nations. Only the tension between the native and foreign could inspire creative choices and strategies.

Obviously, the Young Poland works of Mieczysław Karłowicz and Szymanowski cannot be understood without reference to Wagner, Strauss, Reger and the entire canon of German modernism. In their artistic explorations, these composers did not so much break with the national tradition of Chopin, Moniuszko, and Noskowski, as enrich that tradition by borrowing from other music cultures. Therefore, the music of Young Poland should be analyzed in the broader context of European trends rather than from the perspective of an isolated Polish music. Hence, if the goal of the composers was to "catch up" with Europe, it was not the academic imitation of foreign patterns, but the creative use and transformation of various sources. By inscribing themselves into the dominant stream of European styles, they enriched their national art with new and original values.

The music of Young Poland does not, however, lack works which sustain continuity with the national tradition. This is mainly expressed by references to the heritage of Chopin (e.g., in the early piano music of Szymanowski), the use of Polish poetry for the texts of lyric works, and the literary programs of the symphonic works of Karłowicz and Ludomir Różycki. Perhaps less obvious are the hidden programs in Szymanowski's music, e.g. *Uwertura koncertowa* [Concert Overture] (based on Tadeusz Miciński's poem *Witeź*

Wlast [Prince Wlast]) and Symphony No. 2 (based on Stefan Żeromski's historical novel *Popioły* [Ashes]) - which are the result of literary inspiration rather than a manifestation of a *correspondance des arts*, especially since the composer eventually abandoned writing programmatic works derived from literary compositions.[10]

To join contemporaneous critics in classifying the works of the composers belonging to Young Poland as "national" or "universal" would be artificial, not to say absurd. From today's standpoint, a certain coherence of aesthetic beliefs derived from European modernists is the most distinctive trait responsible for their style. In Szymanowski's songs, this coherence forms the same ideological background whether the lyrics are by the poets of Young Poland or by German modernists; it is even present in his works inspired by Oriental exoticism as well as in the opera *King Roger*, a work springing from the most universal influences.

The debate over the nature of art burst out again in the period of the Second Republic (1918-1939). In 1915, on the very threshold of Poland's independence, Stefan Żeromski published the article "Literatura a życie polskie" [Literature and Polish life] in which he argued that for many generations Polish art had been characterized by traces of messianism and by "service for an unhappy fatherland, despite attempts at the turn of the nineteenth and twentieth century to liberate Polish art and literature from service to

---

[10]Leon Markiewicz, indicating a hidden literary program in *Uwertura*, refers to a review from *Scena i Sztuka*, no. 7 (1909); see Markiewicz, "Introduction," in *Karol Szymanowski: Dzieła* vol. 1, *Concert Overture, Op. 12* (Kraków: PWM, 1968). Some remarks on this subject can be found in Adolf Chybiński's review, "*Symfoniczny koncert polski* in Berlin," *Gazeta Lwowska*, no. 89,(19 April 1906) and no. 90 (20 April 1906): "This symphonic poem is as mysterious as its motto [Miciński's words]," quoted in Szymanowski, *Pisma muzyczne*, 94-96. The relation of Symphony No. 2 to Żeromski's *Popioły* is the subject of Ludwig Finsher's article, "Symphonie, Literatur un Philologie. Zur 2. Symphonie Karol Szymanowskis," in *Das Musikalische Kunstwerk: Geschichte, Ästhetik, Theorie. Festschrift Carl Dahlhaus zum 60. Geburtstag*, Hermann Danuser, ed.(Laaber, 1988). Szymanowski's own words on the subject in a letter to Żeromski are themselves significant: "I have a strange relation to your works: they touch me so deeply that each of them stirs me to compose; such was the case of *Aryman, Walgierz, Duma o hetmanie, Popioły* - unfortunately, I always end up with nothing (I do not consider the indirect influences, which can often be found in the intimate history of the creation of some of my works)," See Szymanowski, *Correspondence*, 218.

the society and to proclaim that they had a European right to freedom."[11] Yet, the situation had not changed and freedom of artistic expression remained an unfulfilled desire of the truly creative individuals. Szymanowski attributed a similar status to Polish music in the article "Uwagi w sprawie współczesnej opinii muzycznej w Polsce" [Remarks concerning contemporary musical opinion in Poland] and in his interview for the Warsaw newspaper *Kurier Polski*.[12]

Those critics of the older generation who opposed the European ideas and musical criticism of the 1910s revived the arguments used at the beginning of the century. Thus, Stanisław Niewiadomski wrote:[13]

> A popular understanding of the character cannot exist without dance rhythms and themes resembling our folk songs. Thus, the listener cannot recognize any Polishness in Szymanowski except for moments reminiscent of Chopin and for the above-mentioned nobility, which we used to consider as uniquely ours. And the reason why Polishness cannot be recognized in his music is simply that there are no dance rhythms and his melody and harmony contain too strong of a modern-international element to allow Polish strains to be recognizable.

Believing that national symbols are recognizable only when "the formal aspect of a given music is completely clear," Niewiadomski associated the question of a national style with "comprehensiveness," a quality of form. Traditional conceptions of musical nationalism were based on the established classical-romantic paradigm whose supporters sought to isolate native works from

---

[11]Stefan Żeromski, "Literatura a życie polskie" [Literature and Polish life], in Podraza-Kwiatkowska, *Programy i dyskusje literackie,* 710-711, 725.

[12]Szymanowski, "Uwagi" (1920), in Michałowski, *Pisma muzyczne,* 33-45. The interview published in *Kurier Polski* no. 310 (12 November 1922) is reprinted in Szymanowski, *Pisma muzyczne,* 58-62.

[13]Stanisław Niewiadomski, "Karol Szymanowski 'wspaniale osamotniony'" [K.S. "splendidly isolated"], *Rzeczpospolita,* no. 330 (3 December 1922), quoted in Szymanowski, *Pisma muzyczne,* 75-79. Niewiadomski's two essays on Chopin appear in the first part of this volume.

contemporary movements and foreign influences (both Wagnerian-Straussian influences, which were eventually accepted, as well as from French and Russian ones). Exhortations to speak "the tongue of your own nation without looking East and West"[14] contained the academism and blandness of "yesterday's" musical ideas, especially in light of the "nationalization of the repertoire," after which only the greatest works of the classical literature were performed while contemporary music from abroad was resisted.[15] Szymanowski responded to such developments with the demand: "Should a police regime and custom house really defend the in-dependence of Polish music? Are we really so afraid of foreign influences? Are we that weak?"[16]

Szymanowski, like the writers of interwar literary manifestos and programs, expressed the belief that the political independence of Poland should be followed by the liberation of Polish art from its didactic and patriotic tasks. The new art should aim more than ever before at the obliteration of the boundary between "Polishness" and "Europeanness," between a distinctive Polish art and the shared European tradition, which, after all, was the soil of Polish culture. In his article "Opuszczę skalny mój szaniec," Szymanowski wrote: "One should not . . . look for cosmopolitanism or, worse, for internationalism in my music. One can find

---

[14]Expression from an essay by composer Ludomir Rogowski (1881-1954), "O muzyce polskiej" [About Polish music], *Wiadomości Muzyczne*, no. 9 (1925). Rogowski's music was inspired by French impressionism, elements of Eastern cultures and early Slavic cultures. He often used pentatonic and whole-tone scales; by blending a whole-tone with a Persian scale he developed a new "Slavic" scale used in the Joyous Symphony. In his music criticism he advocated reconciliation of all Slavic nations (since 1926 he lived in Dubrownik, Yugoslavia).

[15]Expression from an essay by composer Ludomir Różycki (1884-1953), "O polską muzykę" [For Polish music], *Kurier Warszawski* (20 April 1925). Różycki was one of the members of the "Young Poland" group and a composer of orchestral music, ballets, and operas on Polish subjects, bringing together neo-romantic style and folk influences.

[16]Karol Szymanowski, "Zagadnienie 'ludowości' w stosunku do muzyki współczesnej" [The issue of "folk quality" and its relationship to contemporary music] published in *Muzyka*, no. 10 (1925): 8-13; reprinted in Szymanowski, *Pisma muzyczne*, 168-175; quoted from p. 170.

in it only 'Europeanness,' and this does not deny its Polishness; and to this we have all rights. Today's Polishness is, after all, different from yesterday's: It is free."[17]

This debate over Polish and universal values occurred in the year when Szymanowski's artistic attitude underwent an aesthetic change that led him away from the themes of his Young Poland period as well as from his fascination with Oriental exoticism and ancient culture. This change first manifested itself in the song cycles *Słopiewnie* and *Rymy dzieci ęce*, followed by *Mazurki*, *Stabat Mater*, and *Harnasie* . In contrast with the nineteenth-century national school, Szymanowski sought a new style based on the musical language of contemporary European trends and the simultaneous exploration of Polishness on a deeper level. This exploration began with the rejection of the superficial application of melodic formulas and dance rhythms appropriated from folklore.

In his articles, Szymanowski often employs such terms as "racial specificity," "racial properties," and "racial characteristics" - terms which neither the composer nor commentators on his writings have explained.[18] There is no need, however, to avoid the heavily burdened concept of race. Although the name of the nineteenth-century philosopher Hippolyte Taine does not appear in Szymanowski's texts, his letters attest that he studied Taine's *Philosophie de l'art* and *Voyage en Italie* and it may be assumed that Szymanowski derived his concept of race from Taine.[19] In this context, "race" would refer to a lasting psychic feature, a set of predis-

---

[17]Szymanowski, "Opuszczę skalny mój szaniec," [I will leave my rocky stronghold], partly published in *Rzeczypospolita* no. 6 (8 January 1923), reprinted in its entirety in Szymanowski, *Pisma muzyczne*, 80-88; quoted from p. 84. This essay is a response to attacks by the conservative, nationalistic music critics, Niewiadomski and Rytel.

[18]See Szymanowski's essay on Fryderyk Chopin in the present volume; the editor's introduction and her paper, "Chopin and the 'Polish Race: On Political Dimensions of Chopin Reception,'" read at *The Age of Chopin: A Sesquicentennial Chopin Symposium,* Indiana University, 1999; forthcoming in conference proceedings, Halina Goldberg, ed.

[19]Hippolyte Taine, *Philosophie de l'art,* (Paris, 1921); cf. Zofia Helman, "Les conceptions de Karol Szymanowski sur la musique," *Polish Art Studies* (Wrocław, 1987) : 317-318.

positions and primal characteristics deeper than national "character." Taine uses botanical analogies to compare race (*"avec ses qualites fondamentales et indelebile"*) with the seed, nation (*"avec ses qualites originelles, accrues ou limitées en tout cas appliquees et transformées, par son milieu et son histoire"*) with the plant, and art to the blossom.[20] The influence of Taine's work can be seen in Szymanowski's assertions that all manifestations of folk art are "permanent and fixed, ahistorical and the most direct expression of the spiritual characteristics of a 'race'" and that "in our understanding 'folklore' expresses the deepest primal characteristics of a given race in relation to aesthetic impressions."[21] Szymanowski saw in the folklore of the Tatran Highlanders the "purity of racial expression" in which the most primal characteristics were preserved and reinforced.   Following Taine, Szymanowski attributed a significant role in the development of Tatran art to the climate and natural environment; he finds in the Highlands the "primal wildness, the schematic roughness of the primitive" alongside a "steady hand leading to the choice of the simplest and sole path for expressing this rough material as an artistic idea."[22] According to Szymanowski, the art of great masters is also based upon "the fixed relation of the artistic individual to the characteristics of his race."[23]   For Szymanowski, the music of Chopin served as the best example of such a relationship, but he also mentions "the genius of race" in regard to French music in his article "Maurice Ravel."[24]

If Szymanowski indeed saw in primal, "racial" qualities atemporal ties that integrated the whole of a national music into a single entity, he did not explain what these qualities expressed and

---

[20]Taine, *Philosophie de l'art,* vol. 1, 226.

[21]"Zagadnienie 'ludowości,'" in Szymanowski, *Pisma muzyczne,* 172, 169.

[22]"O muzyce góralskiej" [On the *górale* music of the Tatra mountains], *Pani* 8/9 (1924): 8-10, reprinted in Szymanowski, *Pisma Muzyczne,* 103-108; quoted from p. 107.

[23]Szymanowski, "Zagadnienie 'ludowości,'" 172.

[24]Szymanowski, "Maurice Ravel," *Muzyka* no. 3 (1925): 94-96; reprinted in Szymanowski, *Pisma muzyczne,* 148-150.

how they determine the characteristics of a national music. We can say that he trusted more in his artistic intuition than in rational explanation. Szymanowski also saw in the art of Tatran folk culture the purest relics of a mythical pre-Slav culture, which he idealized. What is more important for understanding the influence of Tatran folklore upon his music, however, is that Szymanowski found in it an ideal model for creating a form to express a new attitude toward folklore in general. Drawing upon folkloric material, Szymanowski (like Stravinsky, Bartók, and Janaček) tried to create a new musical language through new rhythmic, tonal, textural, and auditory means. Szymanowski's aim was not just to quote or transform folk music, but to extract from it the primal, archaic traits of folklore as a point of departure for innovative musical ideas (as exemplified in the two cycles of *Pieśni kurpiowskie* [Kurpie Songs]).

Polish religious tradition (including that of the countryside) served as the second source of inspiration in the creation of Szymanowski's national style. Thus, in *Słopiewnie*, Szymanowski utilized a Franciscan theme typical of interwar Polish poetry; in *Stabat Mater*, he sought to create a Polish equivalent to the great European masterpieces utilizing the Latin sequence. In an interview, Szymanowski explained:[25]

> I tried here [in the *Stabat Mater*] to express concepts which became crucial to my understanding of what 'national music' is, as I perceive it. Since it was religious music in this particular case, it had to be as far from liturgical music with its exalted and (to me) dry academism as from the mechanical appropriation of authentic 'folk' music of this type.

By using a Polish translation (characterized, in the composer's words, by a folkish simplicity and naiveté) of the Latin, Szymanowski sought in his musical adaptation to make the religious experience more immediate and personal - less with the aim of emphasizing the formal dramaturgy than of expressing its internal emotional content. The fusion of Gregorian choral phrases with those from Polish religious songs (*Gorzkie żale* [Bitter sorrows],

---

[25]Szymanowski, "Na marginesie *Stabat Mater*" [On the margins of *Stabat Mater*], interview published in *Muzyka*, no. 11/12 (1926): 579-599, reprinted in Szymanowski, *Pisma muzyczne,* 370-373; quoted from p. 372.

Stała Matka boleściwa [The sorrowful mother stood]) contributed immensely to the Polish idiom of the work. No other composition of Szymanowski so perfectly combines the ideas of universalism and the national tradition. The same model may be applied to *Litania* [Litany], in which the Polish elements originate not in folk material, but in the poetical texts of Jerzy Liebert and in a lyrical expressiveness, which, as in *Stabat Mater*, reflects the contemplative character of religious experience.

Another important component in Szymanowski's national style was his use of the Chopin tradition. This tradition has often been indicated in criticism of *Mazurki* op. 50.[26] For Szymanowski, the reference to Chopin had a deeper meaning. The point was not to imitate formal solutions which had been devised in the past, but to continue the system of values embodied by the music of Chopin. According to Szymanowski, in the interwar period, Chopin became "the eternal example of what Polish music can achieve as well as the highest symbol of Europeanized Poland, which at the same time does not lose its racial specificity or its standing at the highest level of the European culture."[27] In his essay on Chopin, Szymanowski attempted to present Chopin as the artists of the interwar period saw him, namely as a master of construction and form rather than a Romantic ideal. These are precisely the elements which Szymanowski emphasizes in the works of his spiritual ancestor and these are the elements which lend Chopin's music an atemporal importance that transforms it into a living force influencing the development of twentieth century music. These same elements also became "a testament of the will to act which applies to all of us, to the fearless who will to explore the fuller form of Polishness."[28]

---

[26]Zofia Lissa, "Rozważania o stylu narodowym w muzyce na materiale twórczości Szymanowskiego" [Reflections about national style in music, on the material of Szymanowski's output], in *Z życia i twórczości Karola Szymanowskiego*, Józef Chomiński, ed. (Kraków: PWM Edition, 1960), 31-41; Tadeusz Zieliński, "Mazurki Szymanowskiego," ibidem, 117ff.

[27]Szymanowski, "Fryderyk Chopin," published in the present volume; quotation from Szymanowski , *Pisma muzyczne*, p. 98.

[28]Szymanowski, "Chopin," lecture given at an anniversary celebration at the University of Warsaw," 9 November 1930, published in *Wiadomosci Literackie*, reprinted in *Kwartalnik Muzyczny* and special issue of *Muzyka* (1932), cf.

Although Szymanowski never formulated a final version of his opinions, it is clear that he recognized the limitations inherent in the very concept of a national style. Some of his thoughts are known only from rough notes, which indicate that he very much realized the impossibility of leaving behind "the cursed circle of 'nationality' defined by living place, climate, social and cultural circumstances, language or genetic traits;" nonetheless, he claimed that "to postulate a national art is a dangerous misunderstanding."[29] His view obviously arises from the conviction that "the modern nation-state . . . should have its own aesthetics," yet these aesthetics should never limit "the uncompromising freedom of the artist."

Throughout the interwar period we can, of course, observe the continuation of Szymanowski's way of thinking. Composers often referred to the period of the Polish Renaissance and Baroque; moreover they frequently used Old Polish texts (for instance, Wespazjan Kochowski in Roman Palester's *Psalm V*; Jan Kasprowicz's translations of Mikołaj Copernicus's Latin texts in the motets of Tadeusz Zygfryd Kassern's *Septem sidera*; the liturgical texts in Michał Kondracki's *Cantata ecclesiastica*, 1937; the fifteenth-century Marian texts in Tadeusz Szeligowski's motet *Angeli słodko śpiewali*, 1934) and stylized their works in the spirit of the music of the past in order to show the universal sources of the Church tradition through the most praiseworthy pages of Polish history.[30] Folk music remained a point of departure for creative

---

Szymanowski, *Pisma muzyczne*, 256-263; quoted from p. 260.

[29]Expression quoted from Szymanowski's note about national art, published for the first time in Szymanowski, *Pisma*, vol. 2, *Pisma literackie* [Literary writings], Teresa Chylińska, ed. (Kraków: PWM Edition, 1989), 208.

[30]Roman Palester (1907-1989) was a composer who studied in Kraków, Lwów, and Warsaw and had a distinguished career in the interwar period, winning numerous prizes, and active in the International Society for Contemporary Music. He spent World War II in Warsaw and lost many music manuscripts in the Warsaw Uprising; from 1949 he lived in Paris and directed the culture department of the Polish section of Radio Free Europe. His early music adhered to neoclassical stye and drew from folklore; later pieces feature the development of an individual compositional language, use of 12-tone technique and post-serial structural methods. Cf. Zofia Helman, *Roman Palester* (Kraków: Musica Iagellonica, forthcoming). Tadeusz Kassern (1904-1957) studied composition in Lwów, Poznań and Paris. From 1948 he lived in New York where he taught in

explorations, although there was a shift from quoting folklore directly to generalizing the folk characteristics. Furthermore, young artists were less interested in the idiom of Polishness than in the exotic folklore of such border regions as Bieszczady mountains in the south-east Poland [Huculszczyzna], Lithuania, and Belarus. Despite Konstanty Regamey's (1959) view that Szymanowski's formulation and realization of a concept of a national style resolved the "cosmopolitan/national" antinomy which had affected Polish music since the nineteenth century, it must be acknowledged that the effects of this resolution were short-lived.[31] By the mid-1930s, some of Szymanowski's "followers" had simplified his ideas. For instance, in the 1934 article "Z zagadnień współczesnej twórczości muzycznej w Polsce," Jan Maklakiewicz revived nineteenth-century thinking by distinguishing between the "cosmopolitan" (which, he claims, contributes no positive values and focuses on the experimental) and the "national" (based on the musical culture of "our people").[32] In Maklakiewicz's article, the old antinomy returns with

---

the Dalcroze Institute. His compositions reveal influences of Szymanowski and interests in early music, Gregorian chant, folklore, jazz and neoclassicism. Michał Kondracki (1902-1984) studied composition in Warsaw (with Szymanowski and Melcer) and Paris (with Nadia Boulanger) and was one of the organizers of the Society of Polish Composers and the Polish Society of Contemporary Music. In the interwar period he was influenced by the folklorism of Szymanowski and Stravinsky, and wrote a series of articles on Polish folk music. Tadeusz Szeligowski (1896-1963) studied in Kraków (composition with Wallek-Walewski and musicology with Jachimecki) and continued his composition studies in Paris with Nadia Boulanger. From 1931 he was a professor of composition, successively in Vilnius, Poznań, and Warsaw. His eclectic style draws elements from Polish early music and folklore.

[31]Konstanty Regamey (1907-1982) was a Polish-Swiss composer and linguist. He studied Indian philology in Warsaw and Paris and lectured on the subject in Warsaw, where he was also active as a music critic, editing *Muzyka Polska* (1937-1939). From 1944 Regamey taught Oriental and Slavic philologies at universities in Freiburg and Lausanne. His compositions mix neoclassical traits with Oriental influences; in this area he was self-taught. Regamey's text is quoted from "Musikschaffen und Musikleben," in *Polen. Osteuropa-Handbuch* (Cologne-Graz, 1959).

[32]Jan Maklakiewicz, "Z zagadnień współczesnej twórczości muzycznej w Polsce" [From the issues of contemporary musical production in Poland], *Muzyka*, no. 1 (1934): 33-37. Maklakiewicz (1899-1954) was a composer who was also active

even greater force since he believes that the social impact of music should be addressed by a national policy which should, therefore, encourage popularizing music to create a useful repertoire for the mass audience. Maklakiewicz revived both the notion of the artist-as-activist [*społecznik*] as well as the theory of the organic work. His utilitarian idea of a popularizing music should, however, be distinguished from the growing number of manifestations of the nationalistic and totalitarian ideology in music. Nationalist ideologues adopted the concept of national music (with reference made to the tradition of Chopin and Szymanowski), even though Szymanowski, the composer of *Harnasie*, had no connection with this type of ideology.

The paradox lies in the fact that representatives of neoclassicism did more to perpetuate Szymanowski's vision than did "nationalists" (hence the neo-classicist movement was accused of "cosmopolitanism"). Szymanowski constantly reminded people that Poland lies in Europe, a connection as obvious to the young generation (many of whom had been educated abroad) as the need for freedom of artistic expression.

Although it stood in opposition to the nationalist program during the second half of the 1930s, neoclassicism accorded with Szymanowski's assumptions concerning the national style (for this reason, neoclassical works do not lack Polish elements). Many composers who proclaimed a "pure" music based on classical and baroque patterns, referred to folk music in their works (for example: Roman Palester's *Taniec z Osmodoły* [Dance from Osmodoła], 1933, and his ballet *Pieśń o ziemi* [Song of the Earth], 1937; Michał Kondracki's *Mała symfonia górska* [Little Mountain Symphony], 1930; Roman Maciejewski's *Pieśni i kurpiowskie na chór mieszany* [Kurpie Songs for Mixed Choir], 1929; and Zygmunt Mycielski's

---

as church organist, choral conductor and music critic. After studies with Roman Statkowski in Warsaw and Paul Dukas in Paris, he became a professor of the Warsaw Conservatory (1929-39), director of the Warsaw Philharmonic (1947-48), and professor of composition in Warsaw. His music continued the Szymanowski tradition by drawing ideas from Polish early music and history, as well as folklore and oriental subjects.

Pięćpieśni weselnych [Five Wedding Songs]).[33] Nonetheless, these composers opposed limiting themselves to folkloric motifs in the belief that Polish "exoticism" should not constitute the core of the national style. They were more interested in problems of composition and form - the elements which could contribute to the creation of a "new order." By adopting the popular idiom of contemporary neoclassicism, young Polish composers aligned themselves with the universal values of European culture while simultaneously defending the autonomy of music from the tendentiousness and utilitarianism of nationalist programs. Thus, the interwar neoclassicism obliterated the opposition of tradition to innovation on the one hand as well as the distinction between national and universal values on the other. Neoclassical composers referred to the classical repertoire as a means of demonstrating the connection between the new music and tradition, but this did not contradict their search for new means of expression; the past became a force for shaping the present. Similarly, the use of folk material in the themes of major works (following the example of Bartók and Szymanowski) somehow lent the source material an additional dignity.

In the late 1940s, the problem of a national style as an isolated structure based primarily on native folk traditions became an issue within the aesthetics of socialist realism. Once again the dilemma of a national art or universal values emerged in the history of Polish music. Although the choice of the former was determined for the composers, the meaning of a national art changed and assumed a different value than in earlier periods.

From today's perspective, we can see clearly both the superficiality of the program for Polish music instituted in the late

---

[33]Roman Maciejewski (1910-1998) studied piano, organ and composition in Berlin, Poznań, and Warsaw. From 1930 he lived abroad - in France, the USA and twice in Sweden where he settled in 1977. His earlier works continued the traditions of Karol Szymanowski; Maciejewski later developed his own style inspired by neo-romanticism and early music especially in *Missa pro defunctis - Requiem* (1959). Zygmunt Mycielski (1907-1987) was a composer and music critic who studied with Paul Dukas and Nadia Boulanger in Paris; at that time he served as president of the Society of Young Polish Musicians in France. After World War II Mycielski returned to Poland where he became an editor of *Ruch Muzyczny* and continued to compose in a post-neoclassical and post-tonal style.

1940s/early 1950s as well as the ways in which social realism diverged from a belief in the autonomy of artists. Two factors must be understood before examining this period. First of all, the institution of a national style was not a new program, not even in its attempt to engender greater musical appreciation and understanding among the masses or in its fight against elitism (both issues had been the subject of contention in the 1930s; it required only a change of label). Second, the program of social-realism was proclaimed at the very moment when interest in folklore as a source of artistic inspiration had drastically diminished and when the pre-war ideas had ceased to be attractive. After the establishment of a broadly understood national tradition and its musical expression during the interwar period, composers were reluctant to accept that music of a national character that related to "the life of the masses" could only be produced by using folk material.

Roman Palester and Stefan Kisielewski were the most notable composers during the first post-war period to point out the need to aim at a musical synthesis which would deepen music's relation to European culture. Kisielewski wrote:[34]

> The national music is not national because it consists of quotes from folklore . . . . To express in music the aesthetic ideals of one's nation does not need to rely on photographing its folklore and tediously adapting it : . . . If artists create according to the needs and characteristics of their individualities and if they simultaneously become familiar with technology and the contemporary state of musical evolution through which they acquire the universal technique allowing them to express themselves freely and in a manner comprehensible to the world - then we won't need to worry about the general image of Polish music; it certainly will not be false or poisoned with foreignness

---

[34]Stefan Kisielewski, "Muzyka narodowa i próby obrazoburstwa" [National music and attempts at iconoclasm], *Tygodnik Powszechny*, no. 91 (15 December 1948). Kisielewski (1911-1991), was a composer, writer, and influential journalist (critic of music, politics, society); he studied in Warsaw with Sikorski and Lefeld (composition, piano, and also Polish philology). Kisielewski participated in underground music life during the war; most of his compositions were lost during the Warsaw Uprising (1944). In 1945 he reactivated *Ruch Muzyczny*, and also served as a member of parliament, and director of a publishing company. His music adheres to a neoclassical style.

or choked with the stagnant atmosphere of its own isolation from the rest of the world.

Naturally, within the paradigm of social realism, world achievements and "universal technology" were identified with cosmopolitanism and formalism, i.e., as threats to the integrity of the national music. The theory of the interaction of music with the folk heritage was aimed at the creation of a music accessible to members of the working and peasant classes. The program of popularizing music and educating the masses also mandated the negation of all types of "elitism" in art (a program familiar from the pre-war era); but, in fact, the point was not so much the social utility of music as its function within the ideological sphere. This new understanding of the concept of "national" music soon found its adherents in Poland: in those years, banal adaptations of folk songs for various types of choirs were written as well as songs for mass rallies and monumental cantatas for official celebrations with lyrics written under the direct supervision of ministerial "Maecenases" (e.g. Alfred Gradstein's cantata *Słowo o Stalinie* [Word about Stalin]).[35] Social realism found its expression in applied music, which was nothing less than kitsch. Clearly, such music was not struggling for its own truths since its creation was permeated by both major and minor compromises with the reigning dogmas. These dogmas affected not only the extra-musical content, but also matters of form; nonetheless, the effect of these dogmas did not change the auto-nomous development of musical style, for some common norms of musical language applied and were accepted in the circle of com-posers.

Some of the movements which had started in the pre-war period continued to develop during these years. The vital tradition of Szymanowski and the examples of other highly appreciated composers from the time of Bartók did not carry negative conno-tations and permitted the search for authentic musical values. Some composers (such as Stanisław Wiechowicz and Tadeusz Szeli-gowski) continued in the national-folkloric mode of the pre-war

---

[35]Alfred Gradstein (1904-1954) studied with Statkowski and Melcer in Warsaw; he was a key representative of socialist realism and a composer of many mass songs.

years because it was closest to their artistic inclinations;[36] others, such as Andrzej Panufnik, Witold Lutosławski, and Artur Malawski, tried to expand and renew this trend, which served as the background for works which to this day have retained their original power (e.g., Lutosławski's *Concerto for Orchestra*, 1951, or Panufnik's *Sinfonia rustica*, 1948).[37] Some younger composers (for example, Kazimierz Serocki and Włodzimierz Kotoński) found it natural to refer to movements most appreciated in musical circles while simultaneously displaying an authentic interest in folklore (Serocki's Symphony No. 2, 1953; his Trombone Concerto, 1953).[38]

Some works by Palester demonstrate that the question of a national style remained a vital issue for composers of this period;

[36]Stanisław Wiechowicz (1893-1963) studied composition in Kraków, Dresden (Dalcroze Institute), St. Petersburg and Paris (Schola Cantorum). Active as a music critic and choral conductor, after World War II he taught composition in Kraków (to Penderecki, among others). Wiechowicz created an original variant of the national style, drawing from Polish folkmusic (melody, rhythm, articulation, formal principles - ostinati, repetitions, etc.).

[37]Andrzej Panufnik (1914-1991) studied composition and conducting in Warsaw, Vienna and Paris. His early compositions were destroyed during World War II; until his emigration to England in 1954, Panufnik was considered the most important Polish composer, and was the recipient of state prizes and a delegate to international congresses and events. His works reflect a fascination with geometry, symmetry, and structuralism, as well as inspiration from folklore and early music (esp. religious). Artur Malawski (1904-1957), a composer, violinist and conductor, studied in Kraków and Warsaw; after World War II he was a composition professor in Kraków (his students included Penderecki, Dobrowolski, and Semkow). Works from his first period are impressionistic, later influenced by Skryabin, Szymanowski, Prokofiev; after World War II Malawski developed a personal style with many references to Polish folklore.

[38]Kazimierz Serocki (1922-1981) was a composer and pianist who studied in Warsaw and Paris (with Nadia Boulanger). With Tadeusz Baird and Jan Krenz, Serocki formed the "Grupa 49" of young composers, he also was a co-founder of the International Festival of Contemporary Music "Warsaw Autumn" (1956). Serocki's early folk music inspirations and neoclassical leanings gave way to experiments in 12-tone technique, indeterminacy, sonorism, spatial music, electroacoustics, etc. Włodzimierz Kotoński (b. 1923), studied composition with Szeligowski in Warsaw, where he was later a professor of composition. Kotoński's fascination with the folklore of the Tatra mountains was later supplanted with interests in 12-tone music, sonorism, instrumental theatre, and especially, electroacoustic music (he produced the first Polish works for tape).

this is particularly evident in *Kołacze* [Cakes - a Wedding Poem] written during the war for a female choir and chamber orchestra to a text by Szymon Szymonowic, and the 1948/1949 *Wisła* [Vistula], a cantata for voice recitative, mixed choir, and instrumental band with a text by Stefan Żeromski. Unfortunately, these works were not broadly heard and thus they exerted only a minimal influence on other composers and on the public; nor was their impact reflected in musical criticism. The scores of these works were not published; *Kołacze* has yet to be performed and the cantata *Wisła* only premiered in Poland at the end of the fifties. Yet, in these works, Palester realized the national style by marking it as folkloric, so in a way, he perpetuated Szymanowski's ideas without following his immediate example. In *Kolacze*, Palester reaches out to the best traditions of Poland's Golden Age [i.e. the 16th century] through the poetry of Szymon Szymonowic, demonstrating his conviction that these traditions can be modernized and that composers should continue to combine native with universal elements. A modern vocal melodic style arose from Old Polish prosody and the unique phonic traits of the language. Although these melodies were free from folkloric associations and from the stylization of earlier music, this style nevertheless grew out of the characteristics and emotional features of the Polish language. The result was an idiosyncratic fusion of Old Polishness with the rich harmonic and rhythmic concepts of the contemporary language of music.

The cantata *Wisła* utilized a text written by Stefan Żeromski in 1918 to celebrate the independence of Poland. The fact that Palester composed this work exactly on the thirtieth anniversary of this event also carries a special significance. As the composer wrote about the genesis of the piece:[39]

> In the darkest period of the German occupation of Warsaw, I and a small circle of my friends - artists - were pondering what place, what landscape, what atmosphere best expresses the core of this strange phenomenon of the Homeland, a small part of which we all feel ourselves to be, and whose name is Poland.

---

[39]Roman Palester, "Nagroda Muzyczna Oddziałów Wartowniczych. Przemówienie Romana Palestra" [Music award of sentry divisions. An address by Roman Palester], Weekly Addition to *Ostatnie Wiadomości*, no. 43 (Mannheim, 23 October 1955).

Stefan Jaracz . . . claimed that the valley of the Vistula in Kazimierz best synthesizes everything which is associated in his heart with the concept of the Homeland. I admit that since that time I look with different eyes from the ruins of the castle through willow woods and the muddy waves of the Vistula as these attributes of Polishness spread out upon the far bank of the river: from the manor-house with its orchard growing to the edge of the river to the ruins of Janowiec castle, huge and enchanting in its stillness. A bit later I associated this image with the beautiful prose of Żeromski who, like nobody else, found the right words for creating the same image.

Thus, a moment of beauty, an almost painterly sensitivity to the charm of the homeland's landscape, is added to the cultural and intellectual tradition at the core of Palester's sense of nationality. Palester does not, however, aim to be "a painter of sounds" who tries to color the patriotic prose of Żeromski with folkloric motives. Rather, he tries to render the drama and expressive force of this prose by approaching it from the "inside." Since the whole text is in recitative, only in the choral sections can we see the relationship of its intonation with the Polish language; the musical declamation - free, flexible, and supple - fully renders the phonic characteristics of the Polish. Often based on diatonic phrases, Palester's melodies frequently evoke the character of folk tunes, but without stylizing or imitating them. In opposition to the choral plan, the instrumental plan is based on a twelve-tone theme, although it still displays a significant structural coherence and a certain dryness of sound [*suchość brzmienia*] arising from the make up of the orchestra (four French horns, two harps, two pianos, and percussion). In *Wisła*, then, the Polish tradition serves as a point of departure and the most important point of reference for the music, but Palester speaks a universal language by combining what is native and familiar to him with what is general and universal.

The late 1940s/early 1950s was the last period in Polish music when there was an "official" policy to suppress the awareness of the universal, transnational values which are the common source of art. In the chauvinistic conception of the national style, all inspirations not derived from the sphere of the native tradition and (more pertinently) to the officially-defined tradition, were regarded as a manifestation of "foreignness" which threatened the identity of the insular community. The iron curtain effectively cut off exchanges with the outside world and official criticism sought to engender distrust of new movements by characterizing them as "anti-humanistic" and "experimental." Under these circumstances, only a carefully practiced form of moderate neoclassicism could exist alongside of the national movement. However, the official attitude toward neoclassicism remained paradoxical. In the doctrine of social realism, the fixed genres and forms of the classical tradition in literature and music offered a framework on which "new content" could be grafted; at the same time, Western neo-classicism was regarded as "anti-realistic," "formalist" and, in its emphasis on the autonomy of art and "pure form," possessed of an aesthetic program clearly antithetical to the prevailing political ideology. Even the social realist and Western approaches to the classical tradition differed significantly as the former permitted no dialogue of any kind with the styles of the past. Nevertheless, neoclassical works were tolerated as long as they did not utilize too many innovative elements and legitimized themselves by their "national" character, which was not difficult to achieve. In this era, neoclassical compositions allowed composers to avoid the expression of ideological declarations in both their titles and the texts of their vocal works. Often composers revived the national tradition with adaptations of Old Polish music (e.g. Panufnik's *Divertimento na tematy Janiewicza, Koncert gotycki, Tryptyk jagielloński*, and *Suita staropolska*). Émigré composers such as Aleksander Tasman, Jerzy Fitelberg, Michał Spisak, Antoni Szałowski, Roman Maciejewski, and Szymon Laks also continued to work in the neoclassical style.[40] Overall, neo-

---

[40]Aleksander Tansman (1897-1986) settled in Paris in 1919, spent the war years in Los Angeles, and returned to France in 1946. Grzegorz Fitelberg (1879-1953) was Poland's most famous conductor dedicated to new music; he worked for Diaghilev's *Ballet russes* in 1920s, led the Warsaw Philharmonic, survived the war in Portugal and the U.S., and returned to Poland in 1947 to direct the Radio Orchestra in Katowice. His son, composer Jerzy Fitelberg (1903-1951) remained in the U.S. after the war. Szymon Laks (1901-1983) settled in Paris in 1926, but spent the war years in the Auschwitz concentration camp (surviving as a member of the camp orchestra). These four composers were of Polish-Jewish origin. Michał Spisak (1914-1965) studied composition in Warsaw and Paris (from 1937 with Nadia Boulanger) where he remained after World War II. Antoni Szałowski (1907-1973) had the same composition professors as Spisak and settled in Paris in 1936; his music reveals post-impressionistic influences in addition to

classicism was the predominant style in the first post-war decade of
Polish music, notwithstanding the doctrine of social realism. The
Stalinist years delayed the importation of new trends from the West
into Poland, but these trends were not lost to Polish music. The
regime of social realism did not change the way composers perceived the national tradition and its relationsto universal values.

The period after 1956 was characterized by the accelerated
adaptation of new compositional techniques and a new artistic
aesthetic. Adorno's *Philosophie der Neuen Musik* indicated new
directions for explorations.[41] The idea of progress in art became the
measure of art's truth and value. The proliferation of non-
conformist attitudes led to the development of new means to attack
both existing habits of reception and traditional systems of norms
and conventions. New and previously unthought of possibilities of
artistic experimentation arose. Composers associated with the avant-
garde sought to redefine not only the methods of musical creation,
but the very material of music. This wider world of sounds required
a new means of notation; the concept of the closed form was reevaluated; the old manner of performative art was brought into
question as were the old forms of reception; time and space in music
were presented in new relations. The old opposition of the national
style and universal values lost its relevance and attitudes now
polarized around the opposition of avant-garde and conservative
tendencies directed toward tradition.

The consciousness of the cultural unity of Europe became
a counterweight to an art imbued with national elements. In searching for their own cultural lineage, artists explored a broader tradition
than that indicated by the language that they speak or a particular
region, national history, or folk tradition. The spiritual ties to the
tradition of European universalism which had begun with ancient
Rome and Christianity grew stronger and came to constitute a value

---

neoclassical traits.

[41]Theodore Wiesegrund Adorno, *Philosophie der Neuen Musik*, Rolf Tiedemann,
ed. (Frankfurt am Main: Suhrkamp, 1975; orig. published in 1948, expanded in
1966). In English: *Philosophy of modern music*, trans. Wesley V. Blomster and
Anne G. Mitchell (London: Sheed and Ward; New York: Seabury, 1973). In
Polish: *Filozofia nowej muzyki*, translated by Fryderyka Wayda (Warsaw: PIW,
1974).

superior to any offered by national and ethnic particularism. Simultaneously, this sense of spiritual kinship began to embrace other cultural centers - traditional and contemporary non-European civilizations - with their value systems, philosophical thought, and rich artistic phenomena. What was distant and foreign suddenly became, in spiritual terms, close and familiar. The music of the sixties and seventies drew its inspiration from the cultures of different periods and cultural centers - from the classics of ancient Greece and from Europe, from the Old and New Testament and from the Koran, from modern Polish poetry and from German and French poetry. The works of Krzysztof Penderecki, Witold Lutosławski, Roman Palester, and Tadeusz Baird exemplify this movement. All of these composers refer not only to Polish traditions, but to those of different parts of the world. This movement drew upon Kochanowski and Słowacki as well as upon Milton, Shakespeare, and Goethe; Chopin and Szymanowski as well as the great masters of European music. The heroes of the stage were Miguel Manara (Palester's *The Death of Don Juan,* 1959-1961), Father Grandier (Penderecki's *The Devils of Loudun,* 1969), or Mary Stuart (Romuald Twardowski's opera of that name, 1979)[42] and not necessarily Sigismund Augustus, Queen Jadwiga, or Father Suryn. These works may be set in medieval France, Byzantium, or ancient Greece; the myth of Orpheus was a greater inspiration than Slavic legends. Composers developed a more intellectualized view of the world; artists treated existential problems, the drama of the human condition, the inner experiences of the individual, metaphysical issues, eternal questions about one's sense of being and the nature of good and evil. In the artists' adoption of themes from a broadly understood cultural heritage, we can discern a double aim: to show archetypes in a changed, modern situation; and to identify "always" with "now" via a transformation and delivery of well known *topoi.* The ending of Palester's *The Death of Don Juan* alludes to the universal and modern situation, not merely the particular and

---

[42]Romuald Twardowski (b. 1930) studied composition in Vilnius, Warsaw and Paris (with Nadia Boulanger); his music includes operas, ballets, symphonic and vocal-instrumental compositions.

historical as Oskar Miłosz presented it in his work.[43] Penderecki appends to the last chapter of Milton's *Paradise Lost* a vision of the future world full of allusions to contemporary events. In these years, Polish composers adopted the European tradition into their own experience and reflections; it became their natural environment, constituting their sense of identity. This tradition also became the source of redefinitions and reinterpretations, serving to express the particular and the contemporary.

In the 1970s and 1980s, the traditions of Polish music not only persisted but acquired new emphases in the changed relation between the national style and universal values. Both as a matter of inspiration and in regards to the realization of music, the two tendencies ceased to function as opposing forces. In contemporary Polish music, composers no longer suffer from a sense that they are unable to "keep up" with Europe; nor do they understand the national style as an obligatory program imposed from either above or from an internal need to make patriotic gestures.   In this new consciousness, Polish music - as that of any other nation - is not an isolated phenomenon torn from a broader cultural context. Szymanowski already possessed this sensibility when, on the threshold of the 1920s, he wrote: "One should not. . . look in my music for cosmopolitanism or, worse, for internationalism in my music. One can find in it only 'Europeanness,' and this does not deny its Polishness."[44]

In contemporary Polish music, the national tradition manifests itself in a variety of ways, from a new transformation of folk idioms to a general relation between vocal-instrumental music and speech patterns. Wojciech Kilar in *Krzesany*, for instance, pursues the idea of Szymanowski's *Harnasie*, but he does so through

---

[43]Oskar Miłosz is the author of the play that Palester's opera is based on. This work received the first prize at a competition of the Italian section of the International Society for Contemporary Music in 1961. Palester's name and music was banned in Poland till 1977 because of his émigré status and his work for the Free Europe radio station; the opera was not known in his home country.

[44]Szymanowski, "Opuszczę skalny..." in Szymanowski, *Pisma muzyczne*, 84.

new musical means such as the use of aleatoric improvisation.[45] Kilar focuses as much on stylistic elements as on rendering the emotional climate induced by the traditional music of the Tatra Mountains. In Kilar's *Kościelec 1909* and *Siwa mgła* [Grey Mist], the impact of folklore is less obvious, but the very reference to Karłowicz's symphonic poem demonstrates a new way of linking the national tradition with the contemporary world.[46] Witold Rudziński's opera *Chłopi* [Peasants] utilizes all the musical means of theater for the sake of presenting folk rituals and traditions as well as the intertwining of primal human desires with the eternal rhythm of nature.[47]

A different group of works employs modern means to evoke Old Polish traditions. Among these compositions are Henryk Mikołaj Górecki's *Muzyka staropolska* [Old Polish Music], *Trzy utwory w dawnym stylu* [Three Pieces in the Old Style], Symphony No. 2 (*Copernican*), Symphony No. 3 (*Symphony of Sorrowful Songs*), String Quartet No. 1 *(Already it is dusk)*; Kilar's *Bogurodzica, Przygrywka i kolęda*; and Panufnik's *Sinfonia sacra*.

In the political context of the 1970s and 1980s, compositions marked with the national character bore a special significance. Composers responded to the political situation of captivity with references to the Romantic tradition and its martyrological myth. Composers working in this mode include Krzysztof Penderecki (*Te Deum* with its quotation from the hymn "Boże, coś Polskę," and *Polskie Requiem*), Krzysztof Meyer (Symphony No.

---

[45]Wojciech Kilar (b. 1932) studied composition with Woytowicz in Katowice and Kraków and with Nadia Boulanger in Paris (1959-60). His early works were inspired by the folklorism of Stravinsky and Bartók; in the 1960s, 12-tone ideas (Webern, Boulez) were juxtaposed with borrowings from jazz. Since 1971, Kilar's music has followed an individual path of a simple, somewhat minimalistic style, with folk references and expressions of religious sentiment. He is also an established composer of film music.

[46]*Kościelec 1909* is dedicated to the memory of Karłowicz and the title refers to the place and date of his tragic and premature death, in an avalanche during a skiing trip in the Tatra Mountains.

[47]Witold Rudziński (b. 1913) studied in Vilnus with Szeligowski and in Paris with Nadia Boulanger and Charles Koechlin. Since 1957 he taught composition in Warsaw. The opera *Chłopi* (1974) is based on a novel by Reymont.

6, *Polish*), Andrzej Panufnik (*Katyń-Epitaph, Sinfonia votiva*), Paweł Buczyński (*Oratio MCMLXXXII*).[48] Quotations from Polish religious-patriotic songs or references in the titles, dedications, or commentaries of these works were intended to create social sensitivities and to create a semantic space in which the artist and audience might both inhabit. The intention of meaning becomes clear through the use of national symbols. The return of the national Romantic stereotype in a contemporary situation attests to the strength of its presence in the social consciousness (or subconsciousness) of the nation. In addition to the functional aspect of addressing the native audience, composers of this period thought it of crucial importance to attempt to place events in Poland into a universal context. Was this attempt successful? As usually happens in the history of music, the most sophisticated works do not succumb to an overemphasis in the direction of a "politically involved" art which explains itself by its own intention. In turn, the quality of the aesthetic form of autonomous works (works free from explicit intentions), makes those works even more expressive of their times (e.g. Lutosławski's Symphony No. 3, 1983).

The most widespread manifestation of national idiosyncrasies is the use of the Polish language. This means more than the introduction of "Polish" content and significance or the mere appropriation of a literary tradition; it also includes the phonic features of the text and the relation between ordinary vocal patterns and singing, with the result that some works significantly define a national idiom due to the impossibility of their translation into another language. Lyrics drawn from both old and modern poetry have played an important role in the work of a number of composers, including Tadeusz Baird (*Erotyki* with text by Małgorzata

---

[48]All these works express the national and religious fervor of a tumultous period in Polish modern history: the birth of the Solidarity movement aimed at the overthrow of Poland's Soviet-dominated government and the movement's suppression through the introduction of martial law (1980-83). Krzysztof Meyer (b. 1943) studied composition with Wiechowicz and Penderecki in Kraków and with Nadia Boulanger in Paris. Since 1987 he has been a professor of composition at the Hochschule für Musik in Cologne. In addition to composing, Meyer wrote monographs on Shostakovich and Lutosławski. Paweł Buczyński (b. 1953) studied composition with Tadeusz Baird in Warsaw and with Roman Haubenstock-Ramati in Vienna.

Hillar, and *Five Songs* with text by Halina Poświatowska), Roman Palester (*Three Poems* with text by Czesław Miłosz, *Monogramy* with text by Kazimierz Sowiński, and *Listy do Matki* [Letters to Mother] with text by Juliusz Słowacki), Kazimierz Serocki (*Oczy powietrza* [Eyes of the Air] with text by Julian Przyboś, *Serce nocy* [The Heart of Night] with text by Konstanty Ildefons Gałczyński), Marek Stachowski (the cycle *Ptaki* with text by Zbigniew Herbert), and Krystyna Moszumańska-Nazar (*Madonny polskie* with text by Jerzy Harasymowicz).[49] While the text's sonorous layer plays a significant role in contemporary vocal lyrical genres, the melodics of speech (its rhythm, the direction of line, and accents) is not always respected since expressiveness and meaning take precedence.

The above-mentioned works make clear that the Polish school of composition should not be defined solely on the basis of a superficial national idiom. Tadeusz Baird correctly grasped the core of this phenomenon in describing the music of Szymanowski:[50]

> With a few other artists from different fields, Karol Szymanowski reached the essence of Polishness in art in a deeper sense of the word by expressing the specific, best, and most distinctive traits of Polishness: spontaneity and emotionality, openness to new artistic ideas (and a willingness to be inspired by them), the primacy of content over a nevertheless sophisticated form, the conscious retention of tradition while simultaneously searching for a path into the future, and, last but not least, the Romantic tendency which is most typical for the

---

[49]Tadeusz Baird (1928-1981) studied with Woytowicz, Sikorski, and Rytel in Warsaw, where he became a professor of composition in 1974. Baird's early neoclassical style (*Colas Breugnon*), gave rise to an individual lyrical, colorful and romantic brand of atonality *(Four Essays, Viola Concerto)*. Marek Stachowski (b. 1936) studied with Penderecki in Kraków where he has taught composition since 1967. He has been a guest professor at many universities, and has received numerous compositional prizes, e.g. the UNESCO Rostrum of Composers (1974, 1979, 1990). Krystyna Moszumańska-Nazar (b. 1924) studied composition with Wiechowicz in Kraków, where she has been teaching composition since 1981. Her interests include electroacoustic and instrumental music.

[50]Tadeusz Baird and Izabella Grzenkowicz, *Rozmowy, szkice, refleksje* [Conversations, sketches, reflections] (Kraków: PWM Edition, 1982), 28.

Polish art and from which the most important and lasting works have been born - those works most rooted in the national memory.

National Style as a Systematic Category

There is a rich musicological literature analyzing the theoretical issues related to the concept of national style.[51] This literature also contains a descriptive element, focusing on changes in the works of individual composers.[52] In spite of great differences of opinion among authors, all acknowledge the existence of certain traits in the music of different nations, which have persisted since the Middle Ages.[53] In the music of Europe, which was predominantly affected by the fusion of cultures, these changes affected only the local character of a music which was otherwise coherent in its stylistic universality. This universality changed only at the turn of the eighteenth and nineteenth centuries. In the wake of the French Revolution, a sense of national differences arose and the conscious effort to form distinct national identities led to the fragmentation of universality into national schools. This desire to define a nation's cultural specificity was connected with the desire to be free from the

---

[51]See, for example, Guido Adler, *Der Stil in der Musik* (Leipzig, 1911); Ernst Bücken, "Geist und Form im musikalischen Kunstwerk," *Handbuch der Musikwissenschaft* (Potsdam, 1932), 116-129; Zofia Lissa, "O stylu narodowym w muzyce" [About national style in music], in Lissa, *Szkice z estetyki muzycznej* [Sketches of a music aesthetics] (Kraków: PWM Edition, 1965); Anna Czekanowska, "Do dyskusji o stylu narodowym" [Towards a discussion about national style], *Muzyka* no. 1 (1990): 3-18.

[52]Zofia Lissa, "Problemy polskiego stylu narodowego w twórczości Chopina" [Problems of Polish national style in Chopin's output], *Rocznik Chopinowski*, no. 1 (1956); Lissa, "Rozważania o stylu narodowym w muzyce na materiale twórczości Szymanowskiego" [Reflections on national style in music on the material of the music of Szymanowski], in *Z życia i twórczości Karola Szymanowskiego* [From the life and creative output of K.S.], Józef Chomiński, ed. (Kraków: PWM Edition, 1960); Anna Czekanowska, "Studien zum Nationalstil der polnischen Musik," *Kölner Beiträge zur Musikforschung* no. 163 (1990).

[53]Bücken, "Geist und Form," 116ff.

Italian, French, and German influences which dominated Europe at that time.

Carl Dahlhaus indicates that the roots of "musical nationalism" (a concept used by Dahlhaus in a purely descriptive, non-pejorative sense) are to be found in Herder's claim that the national spirit (*Volksgeist*) is the basic creative element and drive in art and other human endeavors.[54] During the nineteenth century, the *Volk* and *Volksgeist* were eventually identified with the concept of the nation without regard to how the concepts of the "folk" and "national" were initially marked. The roots of the nation were to be found in the folk and, thus, folk music was considered the strongest expression of the "national spirit" (echoes of this formulation can also be found in the twentieth century). According to Dahlhaus, Herder's false hypothesis became the basis for the "national schools" in nineteenth and twentieth century music. Whatever their genesis, these schools are so essential for understanding musical culture that music historians can not omit them in their reflections.

The opposition of Herder's concept of *Volkgeist* to the idea of universalism resulted, in the course of the nineteenth century, in the treatment of music as a national category. More broadly, this opposition resulted in the antinomy of "national" and "cosmopolitan" art. Although such an antinomy was crude (since it pejoratively marked everything which was not considered "national"), it nonetheless became a fixed distinction in some of the cultural milieus of Central and Eastern Europe.

A number of twentieth-century works attempted to explain the category of national style and its genesis more precisely. Szymanowski tried to define the essence of the phenomenon through the particular and stable "racial traits" of a given nation. Other authors of the interwar period (e.g., Stefania Łobaczewska, 1938) assumed the existence of a hypothetical "national character" - determined by a set of psychic dispositions, fixed and stable, shared by a community - which "at all times [shapes] all the artistic acti-

---

[54]Carl Dahlhaus, "Über die Idee des Nationalismus in der Musik des 19. Jahrhunderts," in *Colloquia musicologica Brno 1972 & 1973*, vol. 2, *Idea nationis et musica moderna* (Brno, 1979), 426ff.

vities of this community" regardless of the historical epoch.[55] On the other hand, in her first works on the subject of the national style Zofia Lissa (1936) sought the sources of national distinctiveness in the "psychic structure" of a people, which was manifested in its pure form only in folk music.[56] Hence, the national character of art is only apparent when art refers to folklore. In this theory, the tonal and rhythmic features of folk music are not as important as the emotional climate which is a direct expression of "the psychic structure of the nation." Searching for the "primal cause" of the distinctions among the arts of different nations in "racial features" or "psychic dispositions" does not constitute a significant change from the nineteenth century concept of the "national spirit." In both cases, artistic phenomena are thought to be formed by some sort of *entelechia* which contributes to the dichotomy between the national, native, familiar sphere, on the one hand, and the universal and foreign which threatens one's identity, on the other hand.

In her later works, Lissa (1964, 1965, 1970 and 1975) tried to resolve this issue in several different ways.[57] First of all, she renounced the idea of the "national character" as a fixed psychic configuration which determines artistic creation. This concept, Lissa claims, "has no justification in the psychology of nations: it is identified by the very analogy of the works, mainly by the homogeneity of art, which, in turn, is explained by the 'national character." Hence, we deal with a typical *definiens per definiendum*.[58] On the other hand, according to Lissa, it is possible to talk of common "psychic attitudes," defined as "fixed ways of reacting to perceived works of art and the readiness to react in specific ways

---

[55]Stefania Łobaczewska, "U źródeł współczesnej muzyki polskiej" [At the sources of Polish contemporary music], *Życie polskie*, vol. 3 (1938).

[56]Zofia Lissa, "O stylach narodowych w muzyce" [About national styles in music], *Sygnały,* no. 20 (1936), quoted from Jarociński, *Antologia*, 423-427.

[57]Zofia Lissa, "O suscnosti nacjonalnogo stilja," in *Voprosy estetiki*, vol. 6 (Moscow, 1964); "O stylu narodowym w muzyce," in Szkice z estetyki; "Prolegomena zur Theorie der Tradition in der Musik," *Archiv für Musikwissenschaft*, no. 3 (1975); "Prolegomena do teorii tradycji w muzyce," in *Nowe szkice z estetyki muzycznej* [New sketches in the aesthetics of music] (Kraków: PWM Edition, 1975).

[58]Lissa, "Prolegomena do teorii," 151.

to specific phenomena . . . . This is a type of emotional habit based
on specific intellectual habits."[59] Lissa relativized the question of
national styles by indicating that the historical nature of "psychic
attitudes" as being dependent upon the living conditions, historical
circum-stances, and cultural traditions of a nation. The stable,
though not fixed, construction of tradition both forms the basis of
the national styles in music and integrates the national community
in historical and spatial terms. Folklore, therefore, is not treated as
the sole ele-ment in a national style, but as one of several elements
in con-junction with other traditions, both of a musical and a non-
musical nature (e.g. language, literary tradition, religion, history,
and local topography). An important aspect of Lissa's work is the
attribution of a dynamic aspect to a national style: "Everything
which con-stitutes and determines this style is a complex of multiple
factors which change not only historically but also individually;"
hence, "the national style is constantly becoming, transforming, re-
creating."[60] The dialectics of these transformations depend on both
the development of historical styles in music and the attitude of the
audience - on their expectations and modes of receiving art. Thus,
artistic phenomena which audiences had not, at the time of their
creation, regarded as "familiar" may, with time, enter the national
tradition.

Anna Czekanowska also emphasizes the role of social communication in the reception and influence of the national style. The
permanence of national categories in music is determined by the
attitude of the listeners, their powers of integration, and an intuitive
sense of the mandates of the community; these factors exist
independently of the historical fluidity of formal/stylistic means and
their interrelation with the universal language of music in a
particular epoch.[61]

We can thus assume that relatively stable systems for
transferring national characteristics (in other words, media, as
Toma-szewski calls them, 1985) exist within the framework of a

---

[59]Lissa, "O stylu narodowym," 156, n. 27.

[60]Lissa, "O stylu narodowym," 147.

[61]Czekanowska, "Do dyskusji," 16-18.

national community.[62] These media serve (1) to create a sense of belonging and (2) to permit self-definition while stabilizing identities. The different choices of media depend on the historical period and the ways of their musical transference, in other words—the compositional technique and musical expression.

In theoretical works since the 1910s, the research category "national style" has not usually been identified with the history of music in a given nation. However, this category can greatly influence critical works by becoming the principle for organizing historical material. The historian who aims at the presentation of a nation's music (as a whole or in its stages) as a relatively stable and independent system tries, after all, to grasp relations of continuity in how features regarded as typical for a particular musical environment determined specific works. Especially in older approaches to the history of music (Poliński 1907, Reiss 1946), the "national category" functioned not only as the basis for an isolated, artificially constructed system of "Polish music," but also as the measure of value for musical compositions.[63]

Anna Czekanowska pursued a different approach by not attempting to envision the history of Polish music in its entirety from the perspective of national features.[64] The permanence of features regarded by some as national and their consistent appropriation by successive generations allow us to distinguish periods in which such national features were especially vital and functioned as carriers of essential values. From such a perspective, Czekanowicz singles out the period of the 17th century, the works of Chopin, Szymanowski, and contemporary composers from the whole history of Polish music. She, therefore, treats the history of music selectively and presents the manifestations of national traits in particular periods in a descriptive manner.

---

[62]Mieczysław Tomaszewski, "Kategoria narodowości i jej muzyczna ekspresja" [The category of nationality and its musical expression], *Ruch Muzyczny*, no. 6 (1985).

[63]Aleksander Poliński, *Dzieje muzyki polskiej* [The history of Polish music] (Lwów, 1907); Józef Reiss, *Najpiękniejsza ze wszystkich jest muzyka polska"* [Polish music is the most beautiful of all] (Kraków: PWM Edition, 1946).

[64]Czekanowska, "Studien zum Nationalstil."

There have also been attempts to demonstrate that the distinctiveness of the Polish national style is conditioned solely by autonomous musical factors. Thus, Irina Nikolska (1990) sees a shared dramaturgy of form in music from Szymanowski to the eighties.[65] This idiosyncratically Polish phenomenon (according to Nikolska) has appeared as a result of the composers belonging to the same national group and of the subconscious pattern of repeating the same archetype which constitutes the music of this group.

Putting aside the weight of conclusions arising from approaching music from the position of the national style, this approach implies the antinomy of native, tribal values with other values - foreign, universal (in other words values exogenic to what is primal, immanent, and endogenic). To define the relations between national, universal, and individual styles - a natural consequence of such a way of thinking - does not lead, however, to clear conclusions. According to Sochor (1979) music based on folk intonations and constituting the so-called national style remains under the constant influence of the universal language of music.[66] These external influences can affect the national style in different ways: they can destroy this style (when they are in discord with a type of folk intonations, e.g., dodecaphony), they can be neutral to it, or they can be adaptable to it. In her approach to the matter, Lissa is less categorical in emphasizing the mutual dependence of world music, the national styles, and the individual styles. According to Lissa, the elements of a national tradition determine the individual's musical style but are transformed within that style by the influence of the period. Subsequently, the characteristic features of great individualities (e.g., Chopin) enter the national tradition and constitute its future progress while at the same time enriching universal music.[67] Such thinking, however, mechanically presents the dialectics of continuity and change in the musical

[65]Irina Nikolska, *Ot Szimanovskogo do Lutoslavskogo i Pendereckogo* (Moscow, 1990).

[66]Arnold N. Sochor, "Nationales und Internationales in der Musik im Lichte der Marx-Leninistischen Ästhetik," in *Colloquia musicologica Brno 1972 & 1973*, vol. 2 *Idea nationis et musica moderna*, (Brno, 1979), 416.

[67]Lissa, "O stylu narodowym," 171-171, 178-179.

development of a given nation linearly, but cannot account for all the permutations. As often as not, the individual's style has stronger bonds with the universal style than with the national tradition.

Thus, continuity in the manifestations of the national tradition need not be the only factor in constructing the musical history of a given nation - nor are national features the only grounds upon which to constitute the nation's distinct identity. During some periods in the history of Polish music, no claims were made concerning the necessity to compose "national" music and, thus, the issue did not necessarily become part of the creative process. As a result, historical descriptions based on the chronological order of events in the musical culture of a given national community can take into consideration geographical and political criteria, but they do not have to be approached in isolation from universal trends in music. The history of a nation's music is then treated as an essential part of the universal history, as its active participant and not as its derivative or only as a constitutive element. From such a per-spective, it is not necessary to analyze the relations of continuity (in other words the analysis of posterior events through preceding events) in the musical history of a given community.

Within the mutual interactions between national and universal factors in the historical process of creating music, national idioms must be considered as "sub-styles" which are determined by the similarity of tradition and the conscious choices of some composers in particular cultures. Whether the composer's choices remain on the margins of universal music or enrich it with new aspects depends on individual talent, on the individual approach to composition, and on the mastery of artistic vision. The phenomena which can emerge from the field of national styles can be innovative (e.g. in the music of Mussorgsky, Bartók, Szymanowski) or only derivative - phenomena which are nothing but a simplification of the universal style. European music did not, as we know, develop in isolation from the soil of autochthonic folk music, but was always affected by unifying tendencies originating in the universal Latin culture. Thus in its basic meaning, the very concept of universalism denotes European culture as a unifying force from a common heritage and tradition, such as the Christian tradition, mythology, and the topoi of the universal/world literature. The pervasive os-motic tendencies towards unification were often stronger than the tendencies in the direction of national particularities. Universalism is also based on social communication understood more broadly than within strictly national cultures. Like the category of national style, universalism as an accepted system of reference cannot constitute a governing aesthetic quality. It can be epigonic, imitative, or creative depending on the individuality of the artist. Consequently, it seems that only the autonomous aesthetic quality determines lasting qualities, whether the character of the music is "national" or "universal."

Thus, the issue of the national style does not exhaust the complexities of historical-musical phenomena. The national style is, in fact, a historically determined category to which no ultimate meanings can be attached. It should not be used as an evaluative category - neither as a basis for aesthetic judgments nor as a recipe for originality and idiosyncrasy. Would it make sense to value Szymanowski's compositions from his "national" period over works of his middle period (*King Roger*, Violin Concerto No. 1, Symphony No. 3, *Myths, Masques*), even though his middle period was characterized by original artistic values? Such a division into works referring to the Polish tradition and the universal tradition is especially irrelevant in examining contemporary music - "Polishness" is not better represented by the former than the latter. Works based on the universal tradition (for instance, Penderecki's *Passion according to St. Luke* and *Paradise Lost*, Palester's *The Death of Don Juan* and Symphony No. 5, Lutosławski's *Parole tissées* and *Les espaces du sommeil*, or Baird's *Goethe-Briefe*) draw upon the grand themes of European culture understood in its entirety. The European-ness of such works should not, therefore, be regarded as an exogenic phenomenon, but as the spiritual environment of the artist with which he identifies and attempts to continue.

The nineteenth-century understanding of the national category as a kind of *entelechia* and a creative source obliterates the individuality of the composer and his creative role. The concept that a work of music is determined by national features conceals the artist behind his community as someone who, inspired by that community, expresses it, and represents it. One can agree with Dahlhaus who, in his criticism of the concept of nationalism, claims that Grieg's works are Norse not due to the "national spirit" but because Grieg, through his strong individuality, gave his nation an example of how to express "Norseness."[68] The same claim could be made about Chopin. The national expression of a composer is a conscious choice, not a result of the influence of unconscious forces.

Thus, even if in contemporary Polish music the tension between Polishness and universalism has become irrelevant, this does not mean that Polish music is threatened by the obliteration of all national values via a global unification. On the contrary, what is invaluable (in the national sense) will acquire an added dimension through universal, humanistic phenomena.

Translated by Joanna Niżynska and Peter J. Schertz

---

[68]Carl Dahlhaus, "Über die Idee des Nationalismus," 426-427.

Creating a Folk Music in the Polish Tatras

by Timothy J. Cooley

Approaching the Tatra Mountain town of Zakopane from the southeast along a street named T. Chałubińskiego, one encounters a monument to the street's namesake, Dr. Tytus Chałubiński (1820-89).[1] The monument (see Figure 1) features a pedestal topped with a larger-than-life bust of the renowned medical doctor from Warsaw. He was instrumental in developing Zakopane and this mountain region called *Podhale* [piedmont] as a tourist destination, originally for the intelligentsia beginning in the last quarter of the nineteenth century. He was also pivotal in shaping interpretations of *Górale* [Polish mountaineer][2] music-culture and the creation of what is today frequently represented as "authentic" Górale music. At the base of the pedestal is a second figure in smaller scale than the bust of Chałubiński. This is a full-body representation of a man dressed in traditional Górale costume, sitting with a small boat-shaped folk-violin in his left hand and a bow (now broken off) in his gesturing right hand. This life-size figure is Jan Krzeptowski Sabała (1810-1894), a legendary fiddler and storyteller from a village just to the west of Zakopane. Sabała was a companion and mountain guide for Chałubiński, and is today referred to by locals and visitors as a prototypical old-world Górale.

In this essay, I argue that the unique music-culture of Podhale is not simply the result of mountain isolation, the most frequent ethnographic trope about Podhale,[3] but also the product of

[1]Research in Poland for this essay was funded in part by the American Council of Learned Societies, Brown University, the International Research and Exchanges Board, and the Kościuszko Foundation.

[2]When writing in English, I use the plural Polish word "Górale" as both noun and adjective, singular and plural, rather than declining the word in the Polish manner. Derived from *góra* (mountain), "Górale" refers to all inhabitants of the mountainous areas. However, here I use the word specifically for people of the Polish Tatra region.

[3]See for example Sula Benet, *Song, Dance, and Customs of Peasant Poland* (New York: Roy Publishers, 1979[1951]), 130; Krzysztof Cwiżewicz and Barbara Cwiżewicz, "Music of the Tatra Mountains: The Trebunia Family Band" (compact disc recording with notes, Monmouth: Nimbus Records, 1995); Anna

subtle and not so subtle interactions between local musicians, researchers, and influential personalities from lowland Poland. With a summary of the musical ethnography of Podhale, I show that ethnographers documented an expanding and diverse music repertoire in Podhale through the mid-nineteenth century, and that only in the last quarter of the century do we find a narrowing of the repertoire to what is now interpreted as Górale music by most music scholars and by Górale musicians. Chałubiński and Sabała were pivotal in shaping this interpretation of Górale music-culture that was later codified in the period between the two World Wars, and the monument bearing their likenesses is highly symbolic of Podhale and the forces that continue to shape this music-culture.

Górale Music

In Polish publications since the 1920s, one finds fundamental agreement as to what Górale music is in terms of style and core repertoire.[4] For reasons I begin to make clear in this essay, Górale musicians today are in basic agreement with the

---

Czekanowska, *Polish Folk Music: Slavonic Heritage, Polish Tradition, Contemporary Trends* (Cambridge: Cambridge University Press, 1990), 84; Włodzimierz Kotoński, *Góralski i Zbójnicki: Tańce Górali Podhalańskich* (Kraków: Polskie Wydawnictwo Muzyczne, 1956), 18; and Louise Wrazen, "The *Góralski* of the Polish Highlanders: Old World Musical Traditions from a New World Perspective" (Ph.D. diss., University of Toronto, 1988), 48.

[4]The most prominent descriptions of Górale music from this period are by Adolf Chybiński, *O polskiej muzyce ludowej: Wybór prac etnograficznych* [About Polish folk music. Selection of ethnographic works] Ludwik Bielawski, ed. (Warsaw: Polskie Wydawnictwo Muzyczne, 1961); Stanisław Mierczyński, *Muzyka Podhala* [The music of Podhale] (Lwów: Książnica - Atlas, 1930) and *Pieśni Podhala na 2 i 3 równe głosy* [Songs of Podhale for 2 and 3 equal voices] (Warszawa: Wydawnictwo Związku Nauczycielstwa Polskiego, 1935); Włodzimierz Kotoński, *Piosenki z Podhala* [Songs from Podhale] (Kraków: Polskie Wydawnictwo Muzyczne, 1955) and *Góralski i Zbójnicki*; Jan Sadownik, ed., *Pieśni Podhala: Antologia* (Kraków: Polskie Wydawnictwo Muzyczne, 1971[1957]); and Aleksandra Szurmiak-Bogucka, *Górale, Górale, Góralsko Muzyka: Śpiewki Podhala* (Kraków: Polskie Wydawnictwo Muzyczne, 1959), *Wesele Góralskie* [Górale wedding] (Kraków: Polskie Wydawnictwo Muzyczne, 1974) and "Muzyka i taniec ludowy" [Music and folk dance], in *Zakopane: czterysta lat dziejów* [Zakopane: Four hundred years of history] vol. 1, Renata Dutkowa, ed. (Kraków: Krajowa Agencja Wydawnicza, 1991), 694-711.

fundamentally consistent descriptions of their music as represented in this literature. However, no such agreement existed before the 1920s. What I show in this study is that Polish ethnographers and music scholars, together with the locally prominent Górale musicians they worked with, collectively canonized a bounded repertoire and style that is today immediately distinguishable aurally as of Podhale. Following is a brief description of this repertoire and style.

The music style today recognized as being "Górale music" is characterized by related categories of vocal and instrumental music with typically short descending melodic phrases, often emphasizing a prominent augmented fourth above the tonic. Vocal music includes two basic related genres: *pasterski* [pastoral, see Example 1] and *wierchowa* [mountain peak song/tune]. Though the border between them is blurred, the two genres share many characteristics. Both usually contain two rhymed lines of text per verse with corresponding music. However, *pasterskis* are usually rhythmically free and *wierchowas* are (with rare exceptions) in duple meter.

All Górale instrumental music is based on song, though texts are not fixed and may be sung to different tunes, and new texts may be improvised. A typical ensemble consists of a lead violin responsible for the highly ornamented melodies, and one or more accompanying violins together with a three-stringed cello-like instrument called *basy*. Instrumental music is in duple meter clearly marked by the second violins and basy which are bowed vigorously on the beat, producing an audible distinction from most duple meter instrumental music from other regions of Europe in which the up-beat is frequently marked. Instrumental music can be performed for listening or for dancing. Music for listening includes instrumental versions of *pasterskis* and *wierchowas*, as well as *Sabałowas* (named after Jan Krzeptowski Sabała) and *staroświeckis* [of the old world]. *Wierchowas*, *Sabałowas*, and *staroświeckis* typically have five bar phrases in 2/4 meter, a distinguishing characteristic of music in Podhale, though not unusual in neighboring regions.

Music for dancing called *po góralsku* [in the Górale manner] follows a loosely organized cycle of dance/music genres. The cycle begins with an *ozwodna* [slowly], a five-bar phrase genre similar to *wierchowa* (Example 2).

Figure 1: Monument to Dr. Tytus Chałubiński (1820-1889) with folk musician, Jan Krzeptowski Sabała (1810-1894). Zakopane. Photograph by Timothy J. Cooley, 1992. Used by permission.

Pi-jes- go-rza-łec-ke pij do mnie, pij do mnie.
Jak cię noc-ka zaj-dzie, przyjdź do mnie, przyjdź do mnie.

You are drinking vodka, drink to me, drink to me.
When night finds you, come to me, come to me.

Example 1: Melody of the pasterski is from a field recording by Timothy J. Cooley; 19 July 1992, Poronin. Lead singer: Stanisława Szostak. Transcription by Timothy J. Cooley. Text transcribed and translated by Maja Trochimczyk.

Example 2: *Ozwodna,* performed by the troupe *Skalni,* on 19 August 1992, Zakopane. Recorded and transcribed by Timothy J. Cooley.

This is followed by a sequence of tunes/dances that may include additional *ozwodnas*, and *drobna*s [small] and/or *krzesany*s [striking]. The names of the dances (slowly, small, striking) refer to dance steps. *Drobnas* and *krzesany* are closely related tune types combining vigorous violin playing with elaborate and athletic dancing by a boy or man. Most typically they have four-bar phrases, but many feature unusual phrase structures. Each dance cycle ends with one of two tunes called *zielona* [green].

A separate dance genre called *zbójnicki* [robber's dance] is designated for a group of men and features specific songs and tunes. The legends of mountain robbers [*zbójniks*] are derived from the Slovak side of the Tatras, and the music of the zbójnicki reflects this origin. Performed in a circle that moves counter-clockwise, the dance cycle includes specific marches, the most characteristic punctuated by accompanying violins (second violin) bowing a typical eighth-note pattern emphasizing the up-beat (see example 3).

As mentioned above, the song poetry has two rhymed lines per verse. Typically, each line has twelve syllables and the second line is often repeated producing an ABB form. Alternatively, the poetry can be conceived of as having four lines of six syllables each. The poetry is often loosely organized around themes of love, sex, courtship and marriage; other prominent texts relate to place (especially the Tatra Mountains), to legendary robbers, and even to Górale music itself. Sadownik's 1957 study includes the most comprehensive collection of song texts in original dialect, and the notes by Cooley accompanying two compact discs released in 1997 contain the largest collection of dialect text transcriptions with English translations.[5]

History of Ethnographic Descriptions of Górale Music

The earliest descriptions of music and song in Podhale do not completely contradict the representations of Górale music that I have summarized above, but they present a more diverse and

---

[5]Sadownik, *Pieśni Podhala* [Songs of Podhale]; Timothy J. Cooley, "Fire In The Mountains: Polish Mountain Fiddle Music - Vol. 1 - The Karol Stoch Band" and "Fire In The Mountains: Polish Mountain Fiddle Music - Vol. 2 - The Great Highland Bands" (compact disc recordings with notes, Shanachie Entertainment, 1997).

unstable repertoire. They certainly do not suggest the unified representations of style and repertoire that emerged in the early
decades of the twentieth century and that remain the basis of
descriptions of Górale music. Here I survey the earliest references
to Górale music in the literature of the subject (published and in
manuscript) in an attempt to understand (1) what the music made by
Górale sounded like nearly two centuries ago, (2) how that music
changed as Podhale became more accessible to lowland Poland, and
(3) what (who) brought about the codification of Górale music by
the early twentieth century. This survey also serves as an English
language guide to the obscure nineteenth-century Polish publications
and manuscripts.

The first surviving examples of music from Podhale are
contained in Wincenty Gorączkiewicz's 1829 publication of thirty-
four "krakowiak" dance tunes. The final four dances of this
collection are based on tunes from Podhale. None of the tunes are
current in Górale repertoire, but at least two suggest common
structures in Górale music: a *krzesany* with four bars in 2/4 meter,
and a *wierchowa*-like tune with five bars in 2/4 time.[6]

In 1832, just a few years after Gorączkiewicz's arrangements were published, Seweryn Goszczyński (1801-76) toured
Podhale and eventually in 1853 published a travelogue, *Dziennik
podróży do Tatrów* [Diary of a journey to the Tatras].[7] Considered
by some to be the "father of Podhalan ethnography,"[8] Goszczyński
provides the earliest account of some of the contexts for Górale
music along with texts to seven songs, plus fractions of a few songs
he describes as being "in the spirit of krakowiaks" (p. 145). Unfortunately, tunes for the seven Górale songs are not included. The
song texts each have twelve syllables per line, each line being
divisible into two six syllable halves—by far the most common

---

[6]Gorączkiewicz, *Krakowiaki. Zebrane i ułożone na fortepiano* [Cracoviennes.
Collected and arranged for the piano] (Vienna, 1829). For reproductions of the
four tunes from Podhale in Gorączkiewicz, see Chybiński, *O polskiej muzyce
ludowej*, 167-69.

[7]Published in Petersburg by Nakładem B. M. Wolffa.

[8]Zofia Radwańska-Paryska and Witold Henryk Paryski, *Wielka Encyklopedia
Tatrzańska* [Great Tatra Encyclopedia] (Poronin: Wydawnictwo Górskie, 1995),
354.

poetic meter of Górale songs documented in the twentieth century. Goszczyński also lists the instruments used: violin, fiddle, bass [basy?], bagpipes, flutes and whistles, and notes that the violin, bass, and fiddles [*gęśle*] were most common for music in homes, and were necessary for dances. Shepherds preferred flutes, and they also used long wooden horns (alpine trumpets; p. 152). Ultimately, Goszczyński's travelogue does not inform us about the actual melodic and rhythmic sounds he experienced in 1832, but the poetic structures, instrumental ensembles, and contexts for music he does describe are compatible with music from Podhale in the following century.

The next contribution to ethnographic literature on Górale music is Ludwik Zejszner's *Pieśni ludu Podhalan, czyli górali tatrowych polskich* [Songs of the folk of Podhale, or Górale of the Polish Tatras]. Zejszner (1805-71) was not an ethnographer by profession, but a geologist and paleontologist. Nevertheless, his small book represents the first conscientious collection of Górale song texts. Zejszner did his collecting in Podhale in 1838, just a few years after Goszczyński visited Podhale, but his book was published in 1845, before Goszczyński's diary. Containing seven-hundred and thirty-seven song texts, Zejszner increases substantially our knowledge of early nineteenth-century Górale poetry, though he provides no transcriptions of melodies. The textual content and the poetic structure of the songs Zejszner recorded are similar to Górale songs today. Fully two-thirds of the over seven-hundred songs have twelve syllable lines, divisible into two six syllable halves, or six syllable lines. Another valuable contribution is Zejszner's description of Górale dancing. He observed that Górale dance was different from other Polish dances yet similar to Slovak dance, and his description enables me to conclude that at least in the early nineteenth century its general structure and format were very similar to Górale dance today.[9]

The next two records with information on music from Podhale are manuscript sources that do contain tune transcriptions. The first is dated 1851 and is credited to Gołaszcziński, an individual about whom nothing is known except what can be learned

---

[9]Zejszner, *Pieśni ludu Podhalan, czyli górali tatrowych polskich* (Warsaw: Drukarnia pod Fir. J. Kaczanowskiego, 1845), 34.

from the manuscript itself. Karol Hławiczka discovered the document in the Biblioteka Warszawskiego Towarzystwa Muzycznego [Library of the Warsaw Music Society] with the title "Śpiewy i tańcy ludu góralskiego pod Karpatami w obwodzie Sandeckim ułożone na Pianoforte i Violin przez Gołaszczińskiego 1851" ["Songs and dances of the Górale folk under the Carpathians in the Sandecky district arranged for piano and violin by Gołaszcziński 1851"]. The manuscript, if it still exists, is known to me only in a description by Karol Hławiczka published in 1936 in the journal *Muzyka Polska*, and by references to Hławiczka's description in the writings of Aleksandra Szurmiak-Bogucka, Kazimierz Bogucki, and Adolf Chybiński.[10]

Gołaszcziński's manuscript presents an image of song, music, and dance in Podhale that was expanding beyond the core repertoire and styles today considered Górale. None of the five tunes from his manuscript that are available are in the current repertoire, but three of the tunes are consistent with the *wierchowa/ozwodna* tune type. The remaining two tunes, on the other hand, are not tunes or tune-types performed in the core repertoire of Górale music today, and one is more similar to Orawa style tunes, a region bordering Podhale to the west. His description of dance also suggests regional variations on the periphery of Podhale. The dances he calls *drobny* (a particular dance step and tune type that is part of the *góralski* genre cycle) and the *kozak* (probably referring to the *zbójnicki* dance) are attributed to specific villages: Bukowina, Poronin, Zakopane, Kościelisko, Bystre—core villages in Podhale close to the Tatras. He goes on to describe Górale in the northwestern edge of Podhale around Czarny Dunajec

---

[10]I fear this manuscript may have been lost during the bombing of Warsaw during World War II. Though I have not yet confirmed this, it appears that the only music scholar to have worked with the actual manuscript is Hławiczka himself. Chybiński (writing before the war) and the Boguckis (writing after the war) use only information about the manuscript that can be found in Hławiczka's 1936 article: "Najstarszy zbiór melodyj pieśni i tańców podhalańskich" [The oldest collection of Podhale songs and dances], *Muzyka Polska* 3 no. 4 (1936): 253-63. For references to Hławiczka's article, see Szurmiak-Bogucka and Bogucki, "Stan badań nad folklorem muzycznym i tanecznym na terenie Polskich Karpat,"[The state of research into musical and dance folklore in the area of Polish Carpathian Mountains], *Etnografia Polska* 5 (1961), 278-79; Szurmiak-Bogucka, "Muzyka i taniec ludowy," 709; and Chybiński, *O polskiej muzyce ludowej*, 145, 170-71.

(bordering Orawa) as dancing these core Górale dances, but also dancing krakowiaks, *stajeras* (fast triple-meter dances), waltzes and polkas. Thus, we are provided with an image of dances (*góralski* and *zbójnicki*) that still make up the core dances considered specific to Górale as being in 1850 most common in the core Podhalan villages closest to the Tatras. We also learn from Gołaszcziński that other dances (including the Bohemian polka that became popular internationally only in the 1840s) were danced on the periphery of Podhale, especially in the northwestern edge which happens to be geographically the least rugged approach to the region.

A second manuscript source is a collection of a few songs dated 1857. This document consists of seven pages included in a larger folder entitled "Tecka po śp. Bronisławie Gustawiczu" ["Portfolio after the late Bronisław Gustawicz"] in the Ethnographic Museum in Kraków. The text and tune transcriptions are believed to be in the hand of Eugeniusz Janota, a naturalist and geographer who lived in the Tatras from 1852 until his death in 1878. The songs were collected in the small village of Rogoźnik, technically outside of the core of Podhale called *Skalny* [rocky] *Podhale*, though most ethnographies since the 1950s include this area in the ethnographic region of Podhale.[11] In this manuscript are tunes and poems that are similar to the core Górale repertoire (twelve syllable poetic lines and five bar melodic phrases), though with an altered tonality, as noted by Adolf Chybiński.[12] Where one expects an augmented fourth above the tonic in Górale music as understood in the twentieth century, Janota's transcriptions have a perfect fourth (see Example 4). Chybiński speculated that Janota was not familiar with "tonality" from Podhale, and that his transcriptions are flawed. However, I propose a different interpretation. Janota was working in Rogoźnik on the periphery of Podhale and in the broad valley that opens up into Orawa or northward towards lowland Poland. Perhaps the songs Janota transcribed reflect this transitional state; they are similar in poetic and melodic phrase length structure to songs common in Podhale but they adapt to a melodic tonality more common outside of Podhale.

---

[11]See for example Kotoński, *Góralski i Zbójnicki*.

[12]Chybiński, *O polskiej muzyce ludowej*,175-78.

Example 3: *Zbójnicki*, adapted from Mierczyński (1930).

Example 4: "Juhasi, juhasi," from Janota's transcriptions; with suggested corrections of the pitch "G" by added sharps (by Chybiński).

Example 5: *Słodyczkowa* published by Kleczyński (1888).

Chybiński's corrections to Janota's transcriptions produce a very different image of music from Podhale in the mid-nineteenth century. If one accepts Chybiński's argument that the fourth scale degree should be raised, Janota's transcriptions are very characteristic of Górale music of the twentieth century. If one rejects his edits, Janota's transcriptions take a much more ambiguous position with regard to establishing a core Górale repertoire. With the exception of the transcription reproduced above as example 4, they are not generally in the six-plus-six poetic meter style. For the most part, however, the musical meters are within the characteristic *wierchowa* or *ozwodna* genre: ten beats or five bars of 2/4 time. Melodically, the overall descending shapes suggest Górale tunes as documented by many in the twentieth century. However, without the raised fourth, they are not particularly Górale sounding, while with the raised fourth they become very characteristic.

At this point in the history of musical ethnography of Podhale, we have only brief glimpses of the music of Górale. These glimpses do not entirely contradict the image of Górale music presented later in the twentieth century; nor do they suggest an entirely stable repertoire and style. The best that can be said is that music from Podhale was recognized as significantly different from that of lowland Poland, and that it shared some of the stylistic qualities that were later identified with the music-culture of Podhale. The next document related to music in Podhale, however, complicates considerably our knowledge about the musical soundscape in Podhale in the second half of the nineteenth century.

Oskar Kolberg (1814-1890) was the most prolific collector of folk music in and around what is now Poland, and one of the most prolific collectors of all time anywhere. His collection of about 25,000 songs, more than half with melodies, is being published by the Polish Ethnographic Society [Polskie Towarzystwo Ludoznawcze], a project that began in 1961 and will include eighty volumes when completed. Volumes 44 and 45 are devoted to the mountain regions of Poland, including the Tatras. Based on fieldwork done primarily in 1857 and 1863, and on manuscripts and published works of others, these volumes contain 2316 songs, with and without tunes.[13]

Concentrating only on those songs that are provided with tunes, and excluding a number of tunes that Kolberg copied from an article by Jan Kleczyński that I discuss below, one-hundred and sixty-one tunes from volumes 44 and 45 are positively identified with Podhale. Only about half of these tunes are represented as being in duple-meter, a minimum requirement to conform to Górale music genres as defined by later musical-folklorists and ethnomusicologists. Another thirteen tunes are in mixed meter or unmetered and are conceivably in a Górale style as recognized today. Yet, after singing or playing through all of the tunes from Podhale in Kolberg's collection, I am able to identify only one that is still commonly played by Górale musicians in the twentieth century: Kolberg #1079, a tune today known as "Marsz Madziarski" [Hungarian March]. What is more interesting is that the other tunes Kolberg associates with Podhale are clearly outside the perimeters of Górale music as later defined. These tunes include an abundance of triple meter polonaises, obereks, mazurkas and waltzes - all genres not associated with Podhale, but common in lowland Poland.

Kolberg's monumental work suggests the existence of a music-culture in Podhale in the mid-nineteenth century containing a great variety of popular and folk genres and styles, from proto-Górale music to popular Polish and international dances and even German-language songs (not surprising, considering that Podhale was at the time a part of the Austrian-Hungarian empire). Most significant, he documents a time in Podhale when more and more people were traveling to the region seeking fresh air and even adventure. As in other parts of Europe, mountainous regions were becoming tourist destinations and no longer feared places to be avoided. This change is reflected musically with the increasing variety of genres found in Podhale.

---

[13]Oskar Kolberg, "Góry i Podgórze" [The Mountains and the Foothills], vols. 44 and 45 of *Dzieła Wszystkie* [Complete Works] (Wrocław: Polskie Towarzystwo Ludoznawcze, 1968).

Culture-Brokers in Podhale

The musical variety documented by Kolberg engendered an effort by the intelligentsia that frequented Podhale and by the Górale themselves to define what was and was not indigenous Górale music-culture. This trend is documented (and even encouraged) by Jan Kleczyński (1837-95), a younger contemporary and correspondent of Kolberg. Like Kolberg, he was also a sometime guest of Dr. Tytus Chałubiński, returning us to the monument with which I began this essay. His associations with the physician proved to be a key to the beginning of the process of reinterpreting Górale music-culture as a clearly delineated category that was ultimately codified in the second and third decade of the twentieth century.

Kleczyński published three articles about Zakopane and music in 1883 and 1884. In 1888 he published a longer piece that collected together music transcriptions from the earlier publications, totaling seventy-four tunes.[14] The narrative that accompanies the tunes published in 1888 provides a key for understanding Górale music-culture from the late nineteenth century to the present:[15]

> Whoever has found themselves on one of those beautiful trips to the mountains organized by Prof. Chałubiński, must have heard a march theme always played by the local "orchestra," that today has become the most liked of all Górale melodies [see Example 5]. . . . This theme is an old tune, however it was discovered by Prof. Chałubiński in his first years spent in Zakopane. Jędrzej Słodyczka plays this tune, an intelligent Górale from the village of Bystre, who when he was a little boy learned this melody from his grandfather. From him this melody is known as "Słodyczkowa. . . ." And so Słodyczka

---

[14]Jan Kleczyński, "Pieśń zakopańska"[Zakopane song], *Echo Muzyczne i Teatralne* 1 (1883): 9-10; "Zakopane i jego pieśni" [Zakopane and its songs], *Echo Muzyczne i Teatralne* (1884) no. 41: 419-21, no. 42: 429-30, no.44: 447-48, no. 46: 468-70; "Wycieczka po melodie"[An excursion for melodies], *Echo Muzyczne i Teatralne*, (1884) no. 56: 567-69, no. 58: 588-90, no. 60: 610-11, no. 62: 631-32, no. 64: 653; and "Melodye zakopiańskie i podhalańskie" [Melodies from Zakopane and Podhale], *Pamiętnik Towarzystwa Tatrzańskiego* 12 (1888): 39-102.

[15]In Kolberg "Góry i Podgórze," vol. 45: 447-49.

played this song, but it was not then a tune that belonged to
everyone, it was not popularized. Prof. Chałubiński influenced
the playing of this melody. He advised them how they should
play the basy, and today·it is the most liked tune.

This telling account of the popularity of a tune known as
"Słodyczkowa" is representative of the forces that encouraged
Górale musicians to shape their music-culture as they did over the
next many decades. We learn from Kleczyński that Professor (medical doctor) Tytus Chałubiński single-handedly influenced the
popularity of this tune, and that according to Kleczyński, he even
instructed Górale musicians on how they should play the basy part
to this tune. Today, over a century later, this same tune is known as
"Marsz Chałubińskiego" [Chałubiński's march] and is indeed a
popular part of the *zbójnicki* dance cycle. Kleczyński's account
also tells of Chałubiński's mountain outings with groups of Górale
musicians and dancers. In the evenings, even after strenuous hikes,
they would play music and dance while Chałubiński himself would
call for certain tunes, effectively exercising some control over the
music and dance as played by the Górale on his outings.[16] We are
left with the picture of Kleczyński and other Polish elite visitors to
Podhale being introduced to Górale music-culture through events
arranged by the region's most popular promoter, Dr. Tytus
Chałubiński - a lover of Górale culture who had no qualms about
suggesting ways to improve that culture. Kleczyński's writings
about Górale music-culture, then, are writings about Górale music-
culture as brokered by Chałubiński.

The brokered image presented by Kleczyński is the first
representation of Górale music-culture that contains many of the
same tunes found in subsequent representations from the twentieth
century. Of the seventy-four numbers transcribed and published in
his 1888 article, I found twenty-one also in twentieth century
sources, including Mierczyński (1930) and Kotoński (1956). This
contrasts sharply with the single tune I am able to identify positively
in Kolberg's roughly contemporary and much larger collection. An
additional twenty-three items in Kleczyński's edition fit models of
Górale music as described above. Kolberg, on the other hand, docu-

---

[16]Ibid., 447-48.

mented a much more diverse music-culture in which Górale music as it is defined today was only one type among other popular and folk styles of 19th-century Central Europe. While Kleczyński's representation is also diverse when compared to twentieth-century sources, well over half the tunes that he recorded fit into the realm of contemporary Górale music. Furthermore, his representation is more consistent with studies of music in Podhale that would be published forty, eighty, and more years later than it is with sources researched or published sixty to twenty years earlier. It is clear that Kleczyński is at the forefront of a trend in representing and creating a newly codified music culture known today as Górale music.

Kleczyński's involvement with Górale music-culture coincides with a pivotal period in Podhale when intensive tourism, almost exclusively by Polish intelligentsia, was actively promoted by Dr. Chałubiński (who established a sanatorium in Zakopane) and by others. A watershed moment for tourism in Podhale was the 1873 founding of the *Towarzystwo Tatrzańskie* [Tatra Society].[17] Since that time, the economy of Podhale has changed from a transhuman pastoral system to a more varied economy relying on a flow of cash from tourists. The demographics also changed from a region formerly (and still frequently, but I believe mistakenly) described as isolated, into a designated tourist destination drawing visitors from lowland Poland and the rest of the world. The permanent population of Poles from the lowlands has also risen in the major towns of Zakopane and Nowy Targ to the point that today they outnumber ethnic Górale.

Creating a Folk Music: Conclusions

The Warsaw physician Chałubiński and composer Kleczyński were instrumental in establishing an interest in Górale

---

[17]First called *Galicyjskie Towarzystwo Tatrzańskie*, but changed to *Towarzystwo Tatrzańskie* in 1874, then called *Polskie Towarzystwo Tatrzańskie* from 1920 to when the organization joined with *Polskie Towarzystwo Krajoznawcze* in 1950, changing its name to *Polskie Towarzystwo Turystyczno-Krajoznawcze* as it remains today.

music-culture beyond Podhale. Collectively they championed the music and musicians, published selected versions and arrangements of the music, and, at least in the case of Chałubiński, even suggested ways to improve this music. They and others before and after were creating a clearly defined and recognizable folk music genre.

The phenomenon of outsiders cooperating with and influencing regional musicians is not unique to Podhale. For example, Neil V. Rosenberg showed how festivals, promoted in part by American folklorists, were key to establishing bluegrass as a genre.[18] And just as the convergence of specific culture brokers and musicians at the right time created bluegrass, Górale music was formed by the timely meeting of musicians like Sabała, promoters like Chałubiński and scholars like Kleczyński. The *ruch regionalny* [regional movement] started by Chałubiński and his contemporaries continued through the turn of the century to World War II. Górale historian Tadeusz Gromada called this period Zakopane's "Golden Age," a period that eventually included Karol Szymanowski and other notable Polish composers.[19] The regional movement also encouraged an intellectual movement among ethnic Górale to value and promote their own folk arts, though this trend produced no ethnographic music scholarship by Górale. The movement was clearly lead by lowlanders who valorized Górale as unique Poles possessing a then rare quality of independence, and their music likewise was interpreted as unique and free of oppressive influences.

For this reason, mazurkas, obereks, and waltzes documented fifty years earlier by Kolberg were no longer fashionable in Podhale; rather, the stark tunes of Sabała and others were invested with great symbolic value by notable non-Górale such as Chałubiński, and composers Ignacy Paderewski and Karol Szymanowski. In fact it was Szymanowski who worked closely with Stanislaw Mierczyński for his still influential 1930 book *Muzyka Podhala*. This collection of 101 tunes did much to create a recognizable style of Górale music at a crucial moment in the history of Podhale and Poland. This style of music forged between the 1870s and 1930s by lowlanders working with prominent Górale musicians was projected

---

[18]Rosenberg, *Bluegrass: A History* (Urbana: University of Illinois Press, 1985), 11-12.

[19]Gromada, "Zakopane's Golden Age," *Tatrzański Orzeł* 28 no. 2 (1975): 6-8.

into the future - for Górale by memorializing it with an authoritative book representing respectful "fieldwork" with respected musicians, and for non-Górale with the same book that forms part of the canon of Górale music.

Music-cultures are symbolic systems with meanings and values mediated by people. In this sense, folk music traditions (like all music traditions) are made; they are human constructions, not the organic output of uneducated peasants, as some romantic nationalists have suggested.[20] If this view of music is correct, it is to be expected that these symbolic systems will change in meaning (and sound, though sound may be of secondary importance) as individual people make music, consume music, write about music, think about music, etc. Rather than searching for the pure origins of an admittedly interesting and unique music-culture, I have tried to show some of the processes by which individuals have changed the music-culture of Górale. In this case the individuals effecting change were outsiders (tourists, ethnographers, composers, etc.) to the music-culture, as well as prominent folk musicians within the music-culture. Together they codified certain genres and defined them as symbols of Górale. What Górale music-culture is today is as much a result of this conscious creation of a codified canon of repertoire as it is a byproduct of the migrations of peoples and tunes across Central and Eastern Europe. Then again, the opening of the mountains to tourists in the nineteenth century is a type of migration and travels to and from Poland by ethnomusicologists and other scholars for fieldwork resembles the traditional migrations of individual Górale across cultural and national borders for seasonal work. The monument to Chałubiński and Sabała that greets travelers at the southeast entry to Zakopane is a monument to migrations of all sorts. Statuary suggests stasis and permanence, but the juxtaposition of the physician and the fiddler on this monument symbolizes change. The monument reminds travelers of the dynamic relationships between migrating Polish intelligentsia and Górale a century ago that helped create the Podhale of today. Music-culture is an important part of that Podhale, and though it too

---

[20]See for example Béla Bartók, *Béla Bartók: Essays*, ed. Benjamin Suchoff (New York: St. Martin's Press, 1976), 173; and Cecil J. Sharp, *English Folk Song: Some Conclusions*, 3rd edition (London: Methuen & Co. LTD, 1954), 33-34.

has been memorialized and codified, it continues to change in response to a myriad of influences including the continued work of individual musicians, enthusiasts, and scholars.

Figure 2: Postcard illustrating the refrain of the national anthem, "March, March Dąbrowski, from Italy to Poland," from a set of postcards based on Juliusz Kossak's litographs published in an album celebrating the 100th anniversary of the anthem. Polish Music Center, Los Angeles.

Sacred/Secular Constructs of National Identity: A Convoluted History of Polish Anthems

by Maja Trochimczyk

An Anthem? Hymn? Song? -- Royal? National? Religious?

The convoluted history of texts and musics of national anthems is a testimony to conflicting visions of national identity - sacred and secular, militaristic and religious - that at times coalesced into a unified vision, and at other times competed with each other. The songs provide a sense of national belonging, a focal point for the definition of a national "soul." In this paper I will review a number of songs competing for the title of Poland's national anthem, with special attention paid to two of them - *Dąbrowski's Mazurka* (the current anthem) and *Boże, coś Polskę* [God Save Poland], its main rival. Before proceeding, though, I would like to pause for the issue of the definition and form of national anthems in general.

The Polish equivalent of the English term "national anthems" is "state hymns" - both terms have the same meaning if the nation and the state are one; if not - and this happened in Polish history - important differences arise. While the British *God Save the King/Queen* (first printed in the middle of the 18th century) is often described as the earliest national anthem, it should be, rather, called the first "state anthem." The wave of introductions of such hymns, often modeled upon the British hymn, or even using its solemn melody, culminated at about the middle of the 19th century.[1] Nonetheless, *God Save the King*, representing the type of the "ancient régime" anthem (i.e. associated with the old-world order

---

[1] In the introduction to *The National Anthems of the Allies* (G. Schirmer: New York, 1917), the editor thus describes the genesis of the 1833 Russian (Tsarist) anthem: "It was as a result of hearing the English National Anthem that Tsar Nicholas commanded General Alexis Lwoff, a member of the suite who had accompanied him on his travels, to write something to equal or even surpass *God Save the King*." It is also worth noting that the anthems of Switzerland, Denmark and Prussia used the British melody with different words.

centered on the supreme ruler and royal power),[2] was preceded by many older hymns that served as symbols of national identity in different countries, including the Dutch *Wilhelmus* of the 16th century and the Polish *Bogurodzica* of the 13th century.

In his classification of national anthems, Günther F. Eyck distinguished the following categories:[3]

(a) "ancient régime"- type of anthems discussed above;
(b) "resistance anthems" for which the French revolutionary hymn, *La Marseillaise,*[4] served as the exemplar (the *Mazurka* belongs to this group);
(c) "liberation anthems" (e.g. the Hungarian *Himnusz* and the Belgian *La Brabançonne*);
(d) "unification anthems" (e.g. of Germany and Italy);
(e) "anthems of contentment"(e.g. Sweden and Luxembourg).

Textual features provide the main criteria for this classification; with regard to the music, anthems may be divided into groups of:
1) stately, solemn hymns (*God Save the King/Queen*);
2) brisk, energetic marches (*La Marseillaise*);

---

[2]Günther F. Eyck, *The Voice of Nations: European National Anthems and their Authors* (Westport, CT: Greenwood, 1995). See also Ulrich Ragozat, *Die Nationalhymnen der Welt: Ein kulturgeschichtliches Lexikon* (Freiburg: Herder, 1982); William E. Studwell, "International Patriotic Songs: An Essay and Bibliography," *Music Reference Services Quarterly* 1, no. 4 (1993): 91-99; Robert Michels, "Elemente einer Soziologie des nationalliedes," *Archiv für Sozialwissenschaft und Sozialpolitik* 4 (1926): 317-61; Joseph Zikmund II, "National Anthems as Political Symbols," *The Australian Journal of Politics and History* 15 (1969): 73-80.

[3]See introduction to Eyck, *The Voice of Nations,* op. cit.

[4]For the revolutionary roots of *La Marseillaise* see Laura Anne Mason, *Singing the French Revolution: Popular Songs and Revolutionary Politics, 1787-1799.* PhD diss. (Princeton University, 1990). See also, Chantal Georgel et al., eds. *Marseillaise, Marseillaises: Anthologie des differentes adaptations depuis 1792* (Paris: Cherche-Midi, 1992); Herve Luxardo, *Histoire de La Marseillaise* (Paris: Bartillat, 1990); Arthur Loth and Pierre Briere-Loth, *La Marseillaise: Enquete sur son veritable auteur* (Paris: Nouvelles Editions Latines, 1992); Anton Hafeli, "Die Marseillaise: Zwischen absolutistischem Signal und revolutionarem Signet" *Dissonanz/Dissonance* no. 28 (May 1991): 4-13; Maurice Le Roux, "La musique de la Marseillaise," *Revue des deux mondes* no. 7-8 (July-August 1990): 165-178.

3) lively folk dances (Poland's *Mazurka*); and
4) elaborate aria-like structures with massive instrumental
introductions and complex formal outlines modeled upon
Italian operatic arias (anthems of many Latin American
countries, e.g. Chile).[5]

The texts of the anthems are quite limited conceptually, with
the predominance of ideas that vary "from martial assertion through
buoyant affirmation of patriotism to pleas for redemption by the
grace of God" (Eyck 1995, p. xiv). Most anthems have been
selected to serve in their official capacity as national symbols after
the mid-19th century, with the process largely reaching its
completion by the 1930s. However, frequent revolutionary
upheavals and political changes, such as the decolonization of
Africa, the emergence of Israel, and the disintegration of
Czechoslovakia, Yugoslavia and the Soviet Union continue to bring
revisions to the list.[6]

In 1917, when a collection of anthems of the allied countries
participating in World War I was published, neither the U.S. nor
Italy, nor Poland had a national anthem -- each country for a
different reason. Americans had not yet chosen between several
competing tunes, Italy still struggled with its heritage of disunity,
while the Polish state regained independence only in 1918. In 1943,
a similar collection of *National Anthems of the United Nations and
Associated Powers* was published to inspire patriotic enthusiasm
during World War II. Unlike its predecessor, this volume did
include the *Dąbrowski's Mazurka* which had been established as the

---

[5]The Chilean hymn (adopted ca. 1847; text by Eusebio Lillo, music by Ramon
Carnicer) includes an instrumental introduction and several orchestral interludes.
The reference to Italian opera as a model for anthems of the Latin American
countries first appears in the introduction to *Anthems of the United Nations: The
Inspiring National Songs the Allies are Singing on the Battlefields and at Home*
(New York: Edward B. Marks Music Corp., 1942).

[6]The literature of the "national anthem" is large, though mostly utilitarian. Some
titles have been quoted above. Two types of publications predominate: (1) edited
collections of anthems, with frequent textual and factual mistakes; a certain
subgroup of these collections is associated with war efforts, (2) historical studies
of individual anthems from different countries, with numerous studies of *La
Marseillaise* and many contributions from Latin and South America and the
Balkan countries.

official anthem of the independent Poland in 1926 (I discuss the significance of this date below). In the introduction to this war-time volume Schirmer defined the main characteristics of the national anthem as follows:[7]

> A national anthem is the expression in words and music of the very essence of the patriotic fervor of a people. Ardent and eternal as is the yearning for peace in all civilized nations, it is the perils confronted, the sufferings endured, the heroic sacrifices made *in time of war* which crystallize and intensify those feelings which human beings from time immemorial have termed, each in their own language, PATRIOTISM. Thus it is that almost all National Anthems are martial songs.

The current national anthem of Poland, *Dąbrowski's Mazurka,* fits Schirmer's description very well, as it was written to stimulate the enthusiasm of Polish soldiers for military struggle and praised their courageous participation in the Napoleonic wars. However, the military form of patriotism is not the only distinguishing feature of national anthems as a musical/poetic genre. Since the populations of most countries include at least some minorities, the ethnic "neutrality" of a song is a precondition for its establishment as an anthem of the whole nation. A 1942 collection of national anthems of the allied countries (published in the U.S.)[8] contains an interesting argument about this. The volume's editors credited their failure to find a vernacular hymn of India, that is an "indigenous song recognized by all Indians as their anthem," to the fact that no such "neutral" song existed on the Indian subcontinent -- its inhabitants spoke 24 different languages and did not share a common cultural experience that an anthem could express.

Regardless of specific beliefs and concepts contained in the texts of the anthems, these mass songs share another feature, that of the rhetorical form. The songs usually use a plural form of the personal pronoun, "we;" they also identify common enemies and

----

[7]*National Anthems of the United Nations and Associated Powers,* English texts by Lorraine Noel Finley, notes by Robert Schirmer (Boston: Boston Music Co., 1943), iii.

[8]*Anthems of the United Nations,* 1942, op. cit. The editors are not named in this volume.

goals, as well as allies (human or divine) who would assist "us" in achieving these objectives and vanquishing "our" foes. Thus, these texts transform the performers of the anthems into the members of one group, unified by the ideas and notions expressed in their texts.[9] In the case of some national anthems, this process is far from straightforward, but it can only occur when the nation or group is given a space for expressing such sentiments and notions. A late 19th century edition of *Songs of Eastern Europe*, for instance, placed Polish folk-, and art-songs among Austrian songs, preceded with that country's national anthem.[10] The editor, Jacob Kappey, apparently did not consider the Poles to be an ethnic group of equal prominence and displaying a comparable sense of national identity as the Bohemians or the Hungarians. The music of both these groups was included in separate sections, each beginning with the "national song" (e.g. "The war-song of the Hussites" for Bohemia). For Kappey and his 19th-century English-speaking audience the issue of Polish national sovereignty that could be expressed through the choice of a national anthem did not yet exist.

A Multitude of Anthems: Religious-National Symbols

The absence of concern for Polish sovereign identity apparent in Kappey's *Songs of Eastern Europe* is surprising if one were to consider the visibility and prominence of Polish anthems, religious and secular, in such orchestral compositions as Richard Wagner's *Polonia* (1836), Augusta Holmes's symphonic poem

---

[9]Thierry Charnay analyzed the process of forging a group identity using the example of four French revolutionary songs. He concluded that their texts demonstrated a process of entering and leaving a state of intersubjectivity which developed between two speakers, or enunciating subjects; the encounter between the addresser and the addressee permitted the fabrication of a new collective subject. See: Thierry Charnay: "Enonciation et chanson revolutionnaire," in *1789-1989: Musique, histoire, democratie* (Paris: Maison des Sciences de l'Homme, 1992), 429-444.

[10]Jacob Adam Kappey, ed. *Songs of Eastern Europe: A Collection of 100 Volkslieder of Austria, Bohemia, Hungary, Serbia, Turkey, and other Countries* (London: Boosey; New York, W. A. Pond [n.d.]). Chopin's *Melody* is included among the "Austrian" songs - this is a strange choice considering that this composer was born in the part of the country occupied by the Russians, not Austrians.

Pologne (1883), or Edward Elgar's overture *Polonia* (1915).[11] Each of these works was composed after a particularly tragic moment in Poland's history, during a different stage in its struggle for survival. Elgar's piece is of particular interest considering that this occasional composition, written for a benefit concert for the Polish Victims Relief Fund in London, made use of melodies published in *Three Polish National Hymns* in Russia (Moscow, n.d.): *Z dymem pożarów* [With the Smoke of the Fires], also known as *Chorał*, associated with the 1846 mutiny of peasants against the gentry in Galicia; *Nie masz to wiary* [There is no Such Faith], also known as *Marsz Żuawów*, March of the Zouaves, sung during the January Insurrection of 1863; and *Dąbrowski's Mazurka*, a secular patriotic song written in 1797, after the country lost its independence.[12] Of these three songs, the *Mazurka* became the national anthem, the *Chorał* remained in some religious songbooks, and the third one disappeared from the popular repertory. In time, the importance of the various candidates to the title of the "national anthem" shifted; different songs served as the national hymns of Poland at different historical moments. The 1996 collection of *Polish National Anthems*,[13] for instance, contains the following five patriotic songs (listed in the order of appearance in the publication):

---

[11]Jadwiga Paja-Stach, "Polish themes in *Polonia* by Edward Elgar," *Musica Iagellonica* 1 (1995): 147-158; Robert Anderson, "Paderewski and Elgar's *Polonia*," *Musica Iagellonica* 1 (1995): 141-146. For a discussion of the hymn's settings by other composers, see: Ferdinand Gajewski: "Chopin's *Dąbrowski's Mazurka*," *The Journal of the American Liszt Society* no. 32 (July-December 1992): 38-41; F. Gajewski: *Jeszcze Polska nie zginęła*: The Apotheosis of Dąbrowski's Mazurka," *Studi musicali* 19 no. 2 (1990): 407-419; F. Gajewski: "Liszt's Polish Rhapsody," *The Journal of the American Liszt Society* no. 31 (January-June 1992): 34-37. The first Gajewski article discusses music by Kurpiński and Chopin, the second presents Liszt's use of *God Save Poland* and *Mazurka* in *Salve Polonia*.

[12]An excellent source of texts and melodies of these songs as well as information about their authors and history may be found in Wacław Panek, *Polski Śpiewnik Narodowy* (Polish National Songbook; Poznań: Grupa Wydawnicza Słowo, 1996).

[13]Włodzimierz Sołtysik, ed. *Polskie Hymny - Polish National Anthems* (Warsaw: Triangiel KOMO-GRAF, 1996).

(1) *Bogurodzica* [Mother of God], a 13th c. Marian hymn, and one
    of the earliest documents of the Polish language;
(2) *Gaude, mater Polonia,* [Rejoice, Mother Poland], a 13th-c. Latin
    hymn to St. Stanislaus, the Patron Saint of Poland;
(3) *Polish National Anthem - Dąbrowski's Mazurka,* 1797;
(4) *Boże, coś Polskę* [God Save Poland], written in 1816 and revised
    several times;
(5) *Rota* [The Oath], a 1908-10 patriotic song permeated with Christian
    and anti-German sentiments, written by Maria Konopnicka and
    set to music by Feliks Nowowiejski.

The selection of hymns for *Polish National Anthems* emphasizes the traditional links between Christianity (or rather, Roman-Catholicism) and Polish statehood. Incidentally, such blurring of religious and political issues is the norm, not an exception in the history of anthems. Sołtysik, the editor of this collection, seems to have attempted to influence this history by selecting a number of anthems from a larger pool of candidates. His choice articulates the late 20th-century perception of the historical importance of various songs in Poland; his annotations highlight the "common knowledge" even more emphatically, by claiming, for instance, that the *Dąbrowski's Mazurka* maintained an un-questionable primacy over its competitors throughout its existence; this is a dubious statement, as I will argue further.

The Polish Children of Mary

In *Polish National Anthems* the position of pride is given to *Bogurodzica* [The Mother of God] which had played the role of the first musical symbol of the independent Polish kingdom. This hymn, with its title providing an exact translation of the Greek expression *Theotokos*, originated in the 13th century, while its earliest extant sources date back to the 15th century.[14] As one of the earliest written documents of the Polish language, *Bogurodzica* has a firm place in Polish cultural history - it has been discussed as an instance of the most archaic form of the Polish language, the first preserved document of Polish poetry, and an example of medieval, religious

---

[14] Jerzy Woronczak, "Bogurodzica," in Woronczak, ed. *Bogurodzica* (Wrocław: Zakład Narodowy im. Ossolińskich, 1962), 11-17.

"high art" music. According to the research of Professor Hieronim Feicht, whose extensive essay on this topic appeared in 1975,[15] *Bogurodzica* has textual links with the Czechs (some scholars attributed it to St. Adalbertus, the Czech-born bishop and patron of Poland) and Eastern Christianity (the language is obscure and strongly differs from modern Polish). Its musical connections link the hymn with early French songs (*Par dessor l'ombre d'un bois* by Jehan de Braine), liturgical drama, folk music, and the plainchant of the Latin Church, especially tropes to the Kyrie *Cunctipotents Genitor Deus*. The *Bogurodzica* melody, though, is too complicated for congregational singing (see Ex. 1).

Bogurodzica is a religious hymn, a simple prayer for personal happiness on earth and for a blessed life in heaven. It is written in the first person/plural ("we") as a group petition addressed to Mary asking her for intercession; the text does not mention issues of national identity. As such, *Bogurodzica* expresses pan-European Christian ideals. Despite its religious focus, this chant, through the centuries of its existence, became a symbol of issues often only loosely associated with its spiritual meaning. Poland's 15th-century historian Jan Długosz called the song "carmen patrium" (the song of the homeland];[16] he also referred to this song as "the battle hymn of St. Wojciech" (i.e. St. Adalbertus) and described its appearances during major events of Polish history.[17] The attribution of the authorship of this anthem to St. Wojciech was common in the medieval and renaissance periods; for instance, it accompanied a version of *Bogurodzica* printed in Jan Łaski's introduction to *The Statutes of the Polish Kingdom* (1596).[18]

---

[15]Hieronim Feicht, "Bogurodzica," in *Studia nad Muzyką Polskiego Średnio-wiecza* (Studies of the Music of the Polish Middle Ages; Kraków: PWM Edition, 1975), 131-232.

[16] Juliusz Kleiner and Włodzimierz Maciąg, *Zarys dziejów literatury polskiej* (An outline history of Polish literature), 2nd revised edition (Wrocław: Zakład Narodowy im. Ossolinskich, 1974), 13.

[17]Woronczak, op.cit., 21.   [18]Kleiner and Maciąg, op. cit., 14.

Example 1: *Bogurodzica* [Mother of God], 13th-century anonymous religious hymn in Polish. The oldest two strophes. Transcription according to Hieronim Feicht, "Bogurodzica," in *Studia nad muzyką polskiego średniowiecza* [Studies of the Music of the Polish Middle Ages] (Kraków: PWM Edition, 1975), 131-232. Reproduced from Włodzimierz Sołtysik, *Polskie Hymny - Polish National Anthems* (Warsaw: Triangiel, KOMO-GRAF, 1996). Used by permission.

The hymn was sung by the Polish troops during the battle against the Teutonic Knights held at Grunwald in 1410 (one of the landmark events in Polish history, defending national independence against encroaching dominance by the militant religious order) and during the battle with the Turkish army at Varna in 1444 (when the European armies were defeated and the young Polish king Vladislaus IV died). It also served as a coronation anthem for the Iagiellon dynasty of Polish kings through the sixteenth century. Only this later association with royalty and battles, and nothing in its content, place this chant among Poland's national anthems. This "hymn of the nation" must have been very popular since, despite the many wars that ravaged Poland, it survived in sixteen manuscripts dating from the period between the 15th and the 18th century. There have been four distinct versions of the song, which were also transmitted in many corrupt copies; the number of strophes ranged from two (the earliest ones) to over a dozen, with many late additions (see Example 1).

In more recent times, *Bogurodzica* has usually been printed in patriotic-religious hymnals and popular church songbooks as the first, most ancient and revered song. As a liturgical chant, *Bogurodzica* has been included in Vespers and Marian services. It is still being sung in Polish churches, especially in the monastic orders, but the language is too obscure and the music too difficult for the hymn's widespread use in congregational singing. *Bogurodzica's* shift to the role of a historical monument may be credited both to the archaicism of the language and to the complexity of the music -- with a monophonic, modal melody that is not easily harmonized and adjusted to the major/minor tonal system. Nonetheless, throughout its history the chant has served two main roles: it has been used as a sign of national identity (as the earliest example of written Polish language and as the traditional national anthem) and as a sign of devotion to the Mother Mary, a symbol of Poland's all-pervading Catholicism. The many religious, national, literary and musical meanings of this anthem can be divided into the following categories (Table 1).

No.	Type	Description
\multicolumn{3}{c}{TABLE 1. The various meanings of *Bogurodzica*}		
1A	Religious (historical dimension)	A document of the use of the vernacular in Christian liturgy
1B	Religious (social dimension)	A supra-temporal prayer with general pan-European, Christian content
1C	Religious (individual dimension)	A current expression of individual piety and trust in Mary's maternal protection
2A	National (monarchic dimension)	Coronation anthem, a proto-national anthem associated with the crowning ceremonies of the Polish kings
2B	National (military dimension)	Battle hymn of the Polish army fighting against the enemies of the nation (Turkey, Teutonic Knights)
2C	National (symbolic dimension)	A symbol of traditions of the Polish kingdom as a once-powerful Christian monarchy
3A	Literary (historical dimension)	A document of artistic use of the Polish language in poetry (literary achievement)
3B	Linguistic (historical dimension)	A document of the history of the Polish language
4A	Musical (historical dimension)	A document of musical composition, in its European context, relationships, and with its artistry and complicated transmission history
4B	Musical (symbolic dimension)	A symbol of the cultural survival and continuity of Polish music in continuous development from its emergence in the Middle Ages

The Marian hymn was used both on solemn church/state occasions and on the battlefield. The confluence of militaristic and religious meanings entered popular imagination after its portrayal in *The Teutonic Knights* by Henryk Sienkiewicz immortalized the image of Polish knights going to battle with their mortal enemy while calling on Mary's benevolence and support. Sienkiewicz wrote:[19]

> At any moment the battle would extend and flare along the whole line, so the Polish companies began to sing the old battle hymn of Saint Wojciech. A hundred-thousand iron-clad heads looked up to heaven, and from a hundred-thousand breasts, there issued one thundering voice:
>
> > *'Mother of God, blessed virgin*
> > *Mary, famed by God himself!*
> > *From thy Son, o gracious lady,*
> > *Mother stainless, mother only,*
> > *Gain us pardon for our sins!*
> > *Kyrie eleison!'*
>
> And straightaway strength came into their bones, and their hearts prepared for death. There was measureless victorious force in those voices and in that hymn, as if thunder had really begun to roll in the sky.

Bogurodzica was by no means the only patriotic-religious song of pre-modern Poland. Its Latin counterparts included two church hymns: *O gloriosa Domina* and *Gaude, mater Polonia*. According to a 17th-century writer, Jan Chryzostom Pasek, the Polish army led by King John III Sobieski sung the hymn *O gloriosa Domina* at the Vienna battlefield in 1682. Their victory ended the

---

[19]Henryk Sienkiewicz, *The Teutonic Knights*. Trans. Alicja Tyszkiewicz and Mirosław Lipinski (New York: Hippocrene Books, 1993), 769. First published in 1900 as *Krzyżacy*. I discuss the use of *Bogurodzica* in this novel, the Alexander Ford film based on it, and several contemporary compositions in "*Bogurodzica* Reborn: A Medieval Anthem in Contemporary Polish Music," in *The Yearning for the Middle Ages,* Dorothea Redepenning and Annette Kreutziger-Herr, eds. (forthcoming).

Turkish invasion of Western Europe and the siege of Vienna.[20] At
that time the Latin hymn to Mary served as the anthem of the Polish
hussars [cavalry], but soon it was forgotten.

Another Latin hymn, *Gaude, mater Polonia*, has had a
more extensive career at religious-patriotic occasions (see Ex. 2).
Its text praised St. Stanislaus, a bishop whose 1072 death was the
result of a confrontation with the king, Boleslaus the Bold [Bolesław
Śmiały]. (The parallels with the fate of St. Thomas Beckett are
rather obvious.) *Gaude, mater Polonia*, although the name of the
country appears in its title, asserts the primacy of religious authority
over royal power. It grew in popularity after an 1867 arrangement
by Teofil Klonowski was published; the hymn is currently included
in many collections and is a favorite with choirs.[21]

Bogurodzica, Gaude, mater Polonia, and *O, gloriosa
Domina* locate the Mother of the nation at the center of attention
(even if her function is only to intercede on the petitioner's behalf).
A different interpersonal dynamic is established in a text directed
straight to the "male" deity - as in the 19th-century anthem by
Alojzy Feliński's *Boże, coś Polskę* [God Save Poland]. This chant,
still expressing a passivity of devotion, calls upon God to act and
bring about a change that is eagerly awaited.

God Save Poland

With its refrain of "God bless our homeland" *Boże, coś
Polskę* still is a favorite prayer for the country sung in all Polish
churches. It became a hymn of the nation during the January
Uprising against the Russians in 1861-63, but its genesis does,
paradoxically, link Poland and Russia. The hymn's original refrain
included the words "God bless the king"-- referring to Tsar
Alexander the First, who, after the defeat of Napoleon became the

---

[20]Jan Chryzostom Pasek, *Pamiętniki Jana Chryzostoma Paska*. Ed. Bronisław
Gubrynowicz (Lwów: Gubrynowicz, 1898). Selections edited by Roman Pollak
published as *Pamiętniki* (Warszawa: Państwowy Instytut Wydawniczy, 1984).

[21]On a Polskie Nagrania CD (ECD 034, *Boże, coś Polskę)* this hymn closes the
collection performed by the State Folk Ensemble, "Mazowsze"; it also appears
on a CD issued by Schola Cantorum Bialostociensis, Białystok, n.d.

first ruler of a newly established Kingdom of Poland (1815).[22] Feliński entitled his 1816 creation *Hymn na rocznicę ogłoszenia Królestwa polskiego z woli naczelnego wodza wojsku polskiemu do śpiewu podany* [Hymn for the first anniversary of the announcement of the Kingdom of Poland; by the will of the Supreme Commander given, for singing, to the Polish army]; yet the hymn was rarely sung and initially rather unpopular. However, changing the reference in the refrain from "king" to "homeland" transformed Feliński's text (with a new melody, ca. 1828) into a symbol of national resistance embraced by patriots from various strata of the society. Its second melody (see Ex. 3), sometimes erroneously ascribed to Karol Kurpiński, or to a borrowing from a religious song, *Serdeczna Matko* [Beloved Mother], or to a quote from an aria by Jean Pierre Solie, was actually taken from a Cracow song, "Bądź pozdrowiona Panienko Maryjo" [Hail to you, Blessed Virgin Mary]. The provenance of this melody was authoritatively established by Dioniza Wawrzykowska-Wierciochowa (see note no. 22).

Since its 1828 publication, the revised hymn, known as "The Prayer of the Polish Army," gradually increased in popularity in Poland and abroad, especially in France. In 1861 Charles de Montalembert, who translated the song into French, rhapsodized about *God Save Poland*, calling it a "song inspired with hot flames of faith, suffering, patriotism, a song nurturing all the depths of noble feeling," with its "truly heavenly chords" and the "unstoppable velocity of sorrow and love" that the text expressed.[23] In the same year, the hymn was banned by the Tsarist government and its Polish representatives; in order to subversively keep the favorite hymn in the communal memory, Poles used its melody for a Church song, *Serdeczna Matko*. A 1860 French edition titled this religious song "Hymne polonais."

---

[22]See Dioniza Wawrzykowska-Wierciochowa, "O melodiach pieśni *Boże, coś Polskę,*" *Muzyka* 31 no. 3 (1986): 57-82. The new melody of the hymn was first published in a rare edition, "Pieśni i piosneczki narodów" collected by Father J. Orobz, (Poznań, 1828) where the hymn bears the title "Prayer of the Polish Army."

[23]Charles de Montalembert, "Une Nation en dueil" (Paris, 1861), 6-7.

Example 2: *Gaude Mater Polonia* [Rejoice, Mother Poland], 13th century anonymous religious hymn (to a text by Wincenty of Kielce). Transcription according to Włodzimierz Sołtysik, *Polskie Hymny - Polish National Anthems* (Warsaw: Triangiel, KOMO-GRAF, 1996), 7. Used by permission.

Boże, coś Polskę

Example 3: *Boże coś Polskę* [God Save Poland], text by Alojzy Feliński and Antoni Górecki (19th century), music from the Marian song *Bądź pozdrowiona, Panienko Maryjo* [Hail to you, Virgin Mary], 18th-century). From Wacław Panek, ed., *Polski śpiewnik narodowy* [Polish National Songbook], Poznań: Grupa wydawnicza Słowo, 1996, 114. Used by permission.

The same label, i.e. "hymn narodowy" [national anthem] was used for *Boże, coś Polskę* in popular hymnals of the Catholic Church.[24]

It is interesting to compare the changeable parts of the refrain of *God Save Poland* as it evolved since the text's inception. The first strophe, describing the past blessings that God bestowed on the country remains unchanged - as "eternal" as its transcendental addressee. It is "our" needs and requests expressed in the final line of the refrain that are modified to reflect the changing political situations and priorities:[25]

Boże, coś Polskę /przez tak liczne wieki
> *O, God who, through so many centuries,*

otaczał blaskiem potęgi i chwały,
> *surrounded Poland with the brilliance*
> *of power and glory,*

coś ją osłaniał tarczą swej opieki
> *who has protected it with the shield*

od nieszczęść które przygnębić ją miały
> *of your defense, against the disasters that*
> *were meant to defeat it.*

Ref: Ref:

Przed Twe ołtarze zanosim błaganie:
> *To your altars we carry a prayer:*

[followed by variants]   [followed by variants]

---

[24]See, for instance, Jan Siedlecki, ed. *Śpiewnik Kościelny z Melodjami na 2 Głosy* (Lwów-Kraków-Paris: Priests Missionaries, 1928).

[25]The 1816 verse is quoted from D.Wawrzykowska-Wierciochowa (1986, op. cit.), versions from the 1830 and 1996 from W. Sołtysik, *Polskie Hymny*, op.cit., and the variant from 1989 from *Śpiewnik Pielgrzymkowy* (Warszawa: Ośrodek Dokumentacji i Studiów Społecznych, 1989), 251.

Naszego Króla zachoway [sic] nam Panie!   (1816)
> *Save our King, Lord!*

[or]
Naszą Ojczyznę racz nam wrócić Panie!   (1830)
> *Return our Homeland to us, Lord!*

[or]
Ojczyznę, wolność, pobłogosław Panie!   (1989)
> *Bless our Homeland and freedom, Lord!*

[or]
Ojczyznę wolną pobłogosław Panie!   (1996)
> *Bless our free Homeland, Lord!*

The original prayer on behalf of the King was soon replaced by a request to regain independence, sought in a series of unsuccessful uprisings (1830, 1848, 1863) but realized only in 1918. The contemporary versions of *God Save Poland* (1989-1996) ask for God's blessings for a free country, though there also exists another version popular in the 1980s (after the suppression of the Solidarity movement): "Ojczyznę wolną racz nam wrócić Panie!" ["Return our free homeland to us, Lord"]. The Polish People's Republic (1944-1989) was officially an independent country, but the Solidarity supporters considered it an occupied zone of "Soviet influence" and prayed for its freedom.

Two other occasional and quasi-religious songs that contended for the title of Poland's anthem merit mention here: *Chorał* with a text by Kornel Ujejski (1846) and *Rota* by Maria Konopnicka and Feliks Nowowiejski (1908-10). The *Chorał* [Chorale - With the Smoke of the Fires] expressed sorrow at the peasants' uprising against the gentry (1846). Kornel Ujejski set the text as a prayer, asking God that such events from which "one's hair turns grey" - as the first strophe has it - would never happen again. Nonetheless, with its incipit of "with the smoke of fires, and with the ashes of fraternal blood" it was not an appropriate text to celebrate Poland's independence - although it served as a national hymn in the Austrian part of the divided country (where the lynching of the gentry by their oppressed serfs was the most severe).

A stronger candidate for the title of national anthem was *Rota* [The Oath] by Maria Konopnicka (1908) to the music by Feliks Nowowiejski (1910, see Ex. 4).

Tempo marsza, z zapałem

Canto

1. Nie rzu-cim zie - mi, skąd nasz ród, nie da-my po - grześć mo — wy,
2. Do krwi o - sta-tniej kro - pli z żył bro - nić bę - dzie - my du - cha,

Pf

po - lski my na - ród, po - lski lud, kró - lewski szczep Pia - sto — wy! Nie da - my, by nas
aż się roz-pa - dnie w proch i pył krzy - ża - cka za - wie - ru — cha! Twierdzą nam bę - dzie

gnę - bił* wróg, tak nam do - po - móż Bóg! Tak nam do - po - móż Bóg!
ka - żdy próg, tak nam do - po - móż Bóg! Tak nam do - po - móż Bóg!

Example 4: *Rota* [The Oath]. Text by Maria Konopnicka, music by Feliks Nowowiejski, op. 38 no. 2. Quoted from Włodzimierz Sołtysik, ed., *Polskie Hymny - Polish National Anthems* (Warsaw: Triangiel, KOMO-GRAF, 1996). Used by permission.

Unfortunately, its textual compass was too limited for it to prevail. This song expressed the sentiments of the Polish farmers in the Prussian-occupied part of Poland who were forced off their land: "We shall not leave the land of our forebears" they sang in resistance. *Rota* became very popular after 1910, the year when the Grunwald Monument was unveiled in Cracow and anti-German feelings reached their peak.

The notable feature in the texts of all the religious hymns mentioned above is the confluence of Catholicism and nationalism, with a particular "Polish" flavor of focusing on the Blessed Virgin Mary. Note the predominance of Marian hymns, such as *Bogurodzica, O gloriosa Domina*, and the relationship of *Boże, coś Polskę* to two Marian songs. Of interest, from the point of view of European medieval culture, is the custom of using Mary's image as a "shield" on the battlefield, i.e. singing *Bogurodzica* at Grunwald and Varna, or *O gloriosa Domina* during the siege of Vienna. A similar practice of using icons of Mary as "shields" in battles existed throughout medieval Europe.

The Secular Hymns: Love of Patria, not Mater Dei

During the 17th and 18th century Poland did not have a royal dynasty that would ensure a continuity of rule; the kings were elected by all the gentry gathering for Sejms [National Assemblies], and the country was gradually disintegrating into chaos. When Poland reached the lowest point in its history and was divided between Austria, Russia and Prussia (1773, 1791, 1795), a resurgence of interest in defining and protecting national identity led to the creation of a number of songs, which, in time, competed for the title of the "national anthem." In the 1770s, the patriotic poet-bishop, Ignacy Krasicki wrote a hymn addressed to *Święta Miłości Kochanej Ojczyzny* [Holy love of the beloved homeland] which is, to this day sung at the Military Academy [Szkoła Rycerska] as its anthem. Appropriately so, since the text calls for ultimate sacrifices for the sake of the country, including the offerings of poverty and death.[26] Krasicki's subsequent hymn, written for the first anniversary of the proclamation of the 3rd May Constitution (in 1792) is more joyous in nature and is set to a popular, memorable melody. Either of these songs could have become the Polish anthem, had the country survived and had the Constitution remained its highest law. Unfortunately, history proved otherwise; and the hopes felt at the moment of defining the country's first fully democratic Constitution gave way to disillusionment and despair when Poland was divided in a series of partitions, the last of which (1795) removed the country from the map of Europe.

　　After the failure of the final effort to save Poland, the 1794 Kościuszko's Insurrection, Poles scattered around Europe, with many emigrating to France to join the forces of Napoleon Buonaparte, with the hope that the valiant dictator would help restore their country. It is because of this connection that the current national anthem of Poland still contains a reference to Buonaparte, and speaks of marching from Italy to Poland, under the leadership of general Jan Henryk Dąbrowski. Józef Wybicki, the general's close associate, was one of the co-organizers of the Polish Legion in Italy and the author of the anthem; he penned the six strophes of what he called *Pieśn legionów polskich we Włoszech* [Song of the Polish Legion in Italy] in July 1797.[27] For the melody

---

[26]Dioniza Wawrzykowska-Wierciochowa, "*Święta miłości kochanej ojczyzny* Ignacego Krasickiego jako pierwszy świecki hymn narodowy polski" (Ignacy Krasicki's "*Święta miłości kochanej ojczyzny* as the first secular Polish national anthem) *Muzyka* 37 no. 2 (1992): 83-89. The hymn first appeared as a part of Krasicki's verse-novel *Myszeidos* [Mouse-boy] in 1773-74. Its two melodies were composed, respectively by Józef Elsner (tune from a stage play *Pospolite ruszenie* produced in Warsaw in 1807, published in 1831) and by Wojciech Sowiński in Paris (published by Launer in 1831).

[27]The most extensive study of the history of the anthem is by Dioniza Wawrzykowska-Wierciochowa, *Mazurek Dąbrowskiego. Dzieje polskiego hymnu narodowego* (Warszawa: Wydawnictwo Ministerstwa Obrony Narodowej, 1974). See also, by the same author: *Polska pieśń rewolucyjna* (Warszawa: Wydawnictwo Związkowe, 1970). A short, popular version (without notes and attribution of sources of illustrations): *Pieśń nadziei i zwycięstwa. Dzieje polskiego hymnu narodowego* (Warszawa: Wydawnictwo MON, Publishing House of the Ministry of National Defense, 1985). Other popular works draw from Wawrzykowska-Wierciochowa's research, e.g. Stanisław Hadyna, *Droga do hymnu,* 2nd ed. (Warszawa: Pax, 1989); Jan Kopczewski, *O naszym hymnie narodowym* (Warszawa: Nasza Ksiegarnia, 1988).

he used a folk mazurka from the Podlasie region; the music was later mis-attributed to Michał Kleofas Ogiński or to Wybicki himself (see Ex. 5: *Dąbrowski's Mazurka*). The Polish Legion, led by General Dąbrowski, had hoped to come with the Napoleonic troops "From Italy to Poland" to liberate their country, and the Mazurka's text made this hope explicit. Inspired by the song's catchy refrain, "March, march Dąbrowski" the troops marched on in the service of Napoleon: to defeat the papal forces at San Leo in Rome, to invade the Marian Sanctuary at Loreto, to fight against Spain, and to perish at San Domingo and Haiti (1802-1803). The Polish troops fought and won with Napoleon, expecting as their reward a restoration of independence to their country. A short-lived "Duchy of Warsaw" was born from this hope, to die in 1815 and lay buried for the next one hundred years.

    Dąbrowski's Mazurka belongs to a type of anthem-march associated with the French *La Marseillaise*, written for the marching troops of the French revolution. These marches are usually fast and energetic, filled with enthusiasm for the new world order that their texts call for. While the Polish anthem shares these features of a "call to arms" -- to fight for Poland's independence, it is a swift, boisterous dance in a triple meter, not a steady march. Eyck, who noted that the *Dąbrowski's Mazurka* became, like the *Marseillaise* popular among radicals challenging the existing social order, also noted its presence on such far away battlefields as Bull Run and Gettysburg (Eyck, op. cit., p. 66). The lively tune, and the inspiring texts, with the first strophe beginning: "Poland's not dead as long as we live" immediately captured the attention of the soldiers, Poland's emigrés and the country's inhabitants. The patriotic song was banned in 1815 (after the defeat of Napoleon), and again in 1860. Yet it lived on in numerous variants, sung during the successive uprisings against the Russians (the November 1830, the January 1863), as well as the 1848 Spring of the Nations. The characteristic liberty with which the words were changed to suit the occasion did not have a counterpart in the changeability of the music. The main sentiment expressed in the first phrase of the song, i.e. the hope that the country would survive because of the will and courage of its people, also remained stable in the various versions.

    In the early 19th century the song served as the hymn of the student union [Związek Burszów, 1816-1830]. At the time the text read: "March, march, the youth/ go first as it should be/ following your leadership/ we will become a nation again." Students embraced the song as their anthem again in 1863, when many escaped conscription to the Russian army by hiding in the Kampinos forest near Warsaw, and by starting the January Uprising [1863 refrain: "March, march to the forest"]. At the end of the 19th century, the song served as the anthem of those proclaiming the need to rebuild the country by hard work, coupled with the fight for its independence [1893 refrain: "March, March, the Poles, to fight and to work"]. While the text of the hymn was modified to suit new occasions and socio-political contexts even the name of "Dąbrowski" appearing in the current title did not survive all the changes. In many war-time versions "Dąbrowski" was replaced by names of various generals or military leaders such as Chłopicki or Skrzynecki (leaders of 1830), Langiewicz or Czachowski (leaders of 1863), Piłsudski (leader of the Polish Legion of 1914) or Sikorski (the commander of the Polish Army in Scotland during World War II, Piłsudski's main adversary and competitor). A 1942 collection of "the inspiring national songs the allies are singing on the battlefields and at home" printed the following variants of the Polish national anthem:

Już Skrzynecki nam dowodzi, *Already Skrzynecki leads us*	And a hero meritorious
już wre walka sroga. *into the raging battle*	Will our guide and captain be.
Polska wolna się odrodzi, *Free Poland will be reborn*	He will render us victorious,
bo pobijem wroga. *Because we will defeat our enemy.*	He will grant us liberty.

The differences between the italicized literal translation (underneath the Polish text on the left) and the actual English text included in the volume (right) reveal a shift of emphasis of the collective subjects' emphasis -- from hope in themselves under the leadership of a hero (Piotr Skrzynecki, one of the leaders of the November 1830 uprising against the Russians), to the hero himself.

Example 5: *Mazurek Dąbrowskiego* [Dąbrowski's Mazurka]. Polish National Anthem. Text by Józef Wybicki, music - anonymous. Official piano arrangement by Kazimierz Sikorski. Reprinted from Włodzimierz Sołtysik, ed., *Polskie Hymny - Polish National Anthems* (Warsaw: Triangiel, KOMO-GRAF, 1996), 17. Used by permission.

This publication is interesting because it sought to promote the unity of the Allies without giving justice to their national musical symbols. It certainly did not reflect the contemporaneous state of Poland's anthem, which was, after 1926, fixed in a four-strophe form, with the original refrain referring to Dąbrowski (see Example 5 for the music):[28]

1. Jeszcze Polska nie zginęła / kiedy my żyjemy.
   Co nam obca przemoc wzięła / szablą odbierzemy.
   Poland is not yet lost / while we live.
   We will fight (with swords) for all /
   That our enemies had taken from us.

Ref:

Marsz, marsz Dąbrowski	*March, march Dąbrowski*
z ziemi włoskiej do Polski!	*from Italy to Poland!*
Za twoim przewodem	*Under your command*
złączym się z narodem.	*we will reunite with the nation.*

2. Przejdziem Wisłę, przejdziem Wartę, / będziem Polakami.
   Dał nam przykład Bonaparte, / jak zwyciężać mamy.
   We will cross the Vistula and Warta Rivers, /
   we will be Poles, / Bonaparte showed us / how to win.

Ref. Marsz, marsz....

3. Jak Czarniecki do Poznania / po szwedzkim zaborze,
   Dla Ojczyzny ratowania wrócim się przez morze.
   Like Czarniecki to Poznan, after Swedish annexation,
   We will come back across the sea to save our motherland.

Ref. Marsz, marsz...

4. Już tam ojciec do swej Basi / mówi zapłakany
   Słuchaj jeno, pono nasi / biją w tarabany.
   Father says to his Basia in tears: "Listen only,
   It seems that our people are beating the drums."

Ref. Marsz, marsz...

---

[28]Quoted from *Polskie hymny - Polish National Anthems*, 22. Translation by the author.

The fourth strophe, seemingly with little connection to the remainder of the text (apart from emphasizing that the arrival of the victorious troops is imminent), has often been omitted in various popular editions of the anthem. The reference to Buonaparte in the Polish anthem sounds as anachronistic as the homage to Spain in the Dutch hymn, *Wilhelmus*. Yet it remained, while two other strophes have been cut from Wybicki's text (identifying Russians and Germans as the enemy, and the Kościuszko troops as the model of courage).

The valiant text and the lively, memorable melody endeared *Dąbrowski's Mazurka* to patriots and independence activists from other Slavic nations throughout the 19th century. After the defeat of the November Uprising in 1831 Polish troops scattered throughout Europe and brought the beloved song with them. German revolutionaries published posters "Noch ist Polen nicht verloren;" translations of the song into French and Swedish followed. In 1834, Tomasik, a Slovak poet who had lived in Kraków and knew the song from there, wrote the Czech version of the text: "Hej, Slované, ještě naše, Slovanská řeč žije...." In 1833 Ljudevit Gaj created a Croatian version and in 1840 Handrij Zejler penned a Serbian version of the text. The music remained the same in all the variants. In 1848 the first Congress of Western and Southern Slavic Nations met in Prague and adopted *Hej, Slovane* as the Panslavic Hymn. After 1945 it became the anthem of Yugo-slavia.[29]

Religious *versus* Secular: Two Visions of National Identity

It is this character of stimulating individual and communal self-confidence, as well as the absence of any Marian or Christian (or indeed religious) references in the text of the *Dąbrowski's Mazurka* that made it a prime candidate for the anthem of a secular, multi-ethnic state. Its main competitor, *God Save Poland*, brought prayers for the country to the Church's altars; it expresses the passivity of a believer, not the active stance of a soldier, a politician, or a pro-independence organizer. A brief comparison of the

---

[29]This anthem appears in the entry on "anthems" in *The New Grove Dictionary of Music and Musicians,* Stanley Sadie, ed. (London: McMillan, 1980).

conceptual areas touched upon these two anthems reveals their contrasting approaches to the common thematic thread of hope for national independence. *God Save Poland* affirms the old world order of unified Christian Europe, while the *Mazurka* looks forward creating an egalitarian society following a human leader. The religious hymn does not refer to acts of violence, the secular is a military song; the religious is free of concrete historical references, the secular mentions people and their acts; the religious places all the hope in the supreme power of the Deity, the secular incites enthusiasm and contributions from the people; the religious is conservative/passive/focused on nurturing the secular revolutionary/active/valiant. The music augments this contrast, with the descending outline, slow tempo, and stately compound duple meter of the *God Save Poland* and the uplifting melody, fast tempo, and lively triple meter with frequent dotted figures of the *Dąbrowski's Mazurka*.

While the *Mazurka's* references to Bonaparte may seem misguided they did not alienate ethnic and religious minorities, such as the Jewish population of Poland and "free-thinking" Poles without a religious affiliation. The delay between the achievement of Poland's independence (1918) and the establishment of the *Mazurka* as the country's official anthem (1926)[30] highlights the conflict between "religious" and "secular" ideals of national identity that are expressed in the country's anthem. This conflict is one of the aspects of the political struggle between the right-wing National Democratic Party (known as "Endecja") led by Roman Dmowski who was favorably inclined towards *God Save Poland*, and the left-wing coalition focused around Piłsudski's PPS [Polish Socialist

[30]*The Okólnik Ministerstwa Wyznań Religijnych i Oświecenia Publicznego* (Directory of the Ministry of Religious Faiths and the Public Enlightenment) of 15 October 1926 (signed by S. Gayczak, the vice-secretary of state) provided all schools in Poland with the officially approved text and music of the anthem. This is the earliest document confirming the official status of this song. Published in *Dziennik Urzędowy Ministerstwa Wyznań Religijnych i Oświecenia Publicznego* (1926), 391-392. I thank Dr. Mariola Szydłowska for providing me with all the details about this publication.

Party) supported by ethnic minorities who favored the *Mazurka*.[31]

In 1920-21, during deliberations in Poland's parliament, Sejm, the *Mazurka* option encountered opposition from the "Endecja."[32] In their quest for a religious anthem, the National Democrats had a powerful adversary in Józef Piłsudski - a key figure in Polish politics in the 20th century, the leader of the Polish Legions during World War I, one of the engineers of Poland's independence, and the country's dictator after the 1926 *coup d'etat*. Of importance for the *Mazurka's* ultimate victory in this "battle of the anthems" was its close association with the charismatic persona of Piłsudski. His name even appeared in a version of the *Mazurka's* text: the soldiers of the Polish Legion, which was created in 1914 under the protection of the Austrian Army, sang the refrain of *Dąbrowski's Mazurka* as "March, march, Piłsudski...." When Piłsudski led Poland to a victory in the defensive war against the Bolshevik invasion (1920) the *Mazurka* was a favorite with the Polish troops. Needless to say, Piłsudski fully embraced the militaristic ideals of armed struggle professed in the *Mazurka's* text, even though he withdrew from politics for several years, during which the first democratically elected president of Poland, Gabriel Narutowicz, was assassinated (1922).[33] Paradoxically, only the May 1926 coup d'etat engineered by Piłsudski cleared the way for the *Mazurka* to be officially sanctioned; this occurred five months

[31]Roman Dmowski (1864-1939) and Józef Piłsudski (1867-1935) were adversaries since the 1910s, when Dmowski followed a conciliatory path towards national sovereignty through serving in the Russian Duma, while Piłsudski allied himself with the Austrian government and military-revolutionary tactics. Neither man receives a very positive potrayal in Norman Davies's *God's Playground: A History of Poland*, vol. 2, *1795 to the Present* (New York: Columbia University Press, 1982), 52-56.

[32]According to information received from the Piłsudski Institute in New York, 1999. Panek quotes an article of 1914, published by Czesław Jankowski in *Przegląd Warszawski* as the earliest voice in favor of selecting *God Save Poland* as the national athem. See Panek, *Polski śpiewnik narodowy*, 91.

[33]Gabriel Narutowicz (1865-1922), Poland's first democratically elected president, was supported by the left-wing parties, including PPS, and by the Jewish, Ukrainian, and Byelorussian communities, but was not accepted by the religious-patriotic zealots, including his assassin, Eligiusz Niewiadomski (a relative of composer, Stanisław) and his backers from Dmowski's National Democratic Party (Davies, *God's Playground*, op. cit., 426).

after the coup. The Directory of the Ministry of Religious Faith and the Public Enlightenment of 15 October 1926, provided all schools in Poland with the approved text and music of the anthem (see footnote no. 30 above). Half a year later, the Directory of the Ministry of Interior Affairs (26 February 1927) officially approved the anthem's text; on 2 April 1927 the Ministry of Religous Faith and Public Enlightenment approved the piano arrangement of the *Mazurka* and published the score.[34] The title of the anthem was listed for the first time in the Constitution of the Polish People's Republic in 1976; the Sejm approved the official text and music of the anthem in 1980.

Such fierce competition between various patriotic songs for the role of the anthem is not unusual. During World War II two songs were alternately used as the anthem of Canada, *O, Canada* and *The Maple Leaf Forever*; the latter was more popular, but the former eventually prevailed. Its success may be attributed to the fact that its music was penned by a French composer and its text was devoid of overt references to "Britain's shore" and "Britannia's flag" that marked the text of *The Maple Leaf Forever* and were unfavorably received by the largest ethnic minority in Canada, that of French Canadians.

During the war, the newly established Polish hymn was used for national propaganda by people from widely divergent political orientations. The Polish armed forces associated both with Great Britain (the official Polish government in exile) and with the Soviet Union (Polish communists backed by Stalin) continued to sing the anthem in the battlefields in France, Great Britain, Italy and Germany. The song appeared at various important moments, such as the battle of Monte Casino, the Moscow Congress of the Communist Union of Polish Patriots in 1943, and the broadcast of the first Polish radio station in Lublin (1944; this station was backed

[34] The "Okólnik Ministerstwa Spraw Wewnętrznych" [Directory of the Ministry of Interior Affairs) issued on 26 February 1927 was published in *Dziennik Urzędowy Ministerstwa Spraw Wewnętrznych*" no. 1-2 (1927): 58. The second "Okólnik Ministerstwa Wyznań Religijnych i Oświecenia Publicznego" [Directory of the Ministry of Religious Faith and Public Enlightenment) issued on 2 April 1927 appeared in *Dziennik Urzędowy Ministerstwa Wyznań Religijnych i Oświecenia Publicznego* (1927): 183-184. Copies of these documents are held at the Iagellonian Library, Kraków, Poland. I thank Dr. Mariola Szydłowska for her assistance in checking details about these references.

by the Soviets).

One of the little known appearances of *Dąbrowski's Mazurka* after the outbreak of World War II and the defeat of Poland by the German army occurs in a war-time piece by Polish-Jewish composer, Aleksander Tansman, *Polish Rhapsody* (1940-41).[35] Tansman subtitled his orchestral composition "a homage to the defenders of Warsaw" and attempted to express their hope for an imminent end of the war by contrapuntally juxtaposing two national anthems in the work's climax: the British anthem, *God Save the Queen* and the *Mazurka*. The *Rhapsody* became very popular in the West as a sign of solidarity with the brave Poles. Its absence from concert programs after Poland became one of the satellite countries of the Soviet Union is self-explanatory. Poland now had another anthem to weave political counterpoints with.... Yet, the *Mazurka* survived it all.

The Hymn of the Republics, and Beyond...

After the war, the Soviet-dominated government of the Polish People's Republic demonstrated considerable political skill when it preserved the *Mazurka* as the anthem of the "socialist" country (1944-1989). The 1926 text remained unchanged and the only revision was a new harmonic setting by Kazimierz Sikorski (1948). The government also promoted serious studies of the anthem's history, and sponsored "a veritable renaissance of its author" - the dedicatee of monuments and commemorative tables (Eyck, p. 67). Wybicki's life and achievements became the subject of a number of monographs and biographies; the monumental and detailed source-study of the history of the anthem by Dioniza Wawrzychowska-Wierciochowa (1978) has corrected many oft-repeated mistakes. The publisher of this 500-page volume was Poland's Ministry of National Defense. The 1976 Constitution of the Polish People's Republic (infamous for its reference to "eternal" friendship with the Soviet Union, a denial of sovereignty) reaffirmed the role of the anthem. Thus, the *Mazurka* continued to serve as the official symbol of Poland, reminding Poles about the duty to be

---

[35]Janusz Cegiełła, *Dziecko Szczęścia. Aleksander Tansman i Jego Czasy,*[The child of luck. Aleksander Tansman and his times], vol. 2 (Łódź: Publishing House 86Press, 1996), 41-42.

active, valiant and courageous for the sake of their homeland. Its affective power was not diminished by its use by the distrusted socialist government.

While *Dąbrowski's Mazurka* was firmly established as a governmental sign of national sovereignty, it was not the anthem of choice for the 1980 Solidarity movement The union's activists chose another song for its unofficial hymn: *Żeby Polska była Polską* [Let Poland be Poland] by a satirist-turned-dissident-turned-politician, Jan Pietrzak (1976). Written after the social unrests in the industrial cities of Radom and Ursus, this song is not a call to armed struggle, and not a prayer for the country, but rather a meditation on the past wars and battles, fought by generations of Poles to "Make Poland, Poland."

After the change of government in 1989, the new leaders of the Republic of Poland (since 1989) not only retained *Dąbrowski's Mazurka* as an anthem, but also sponsored a renewed research and publication effort to promote its image. A 1993 film, produced by Edmund Zbigniew Szaniawski for the Military Company "Czołówka" [Avant-Garde], placed a new emphasis on the *Mazurka's* appearances in the Polish-Soviet war of 1920 and at allied battlefields of World War II. The hymn's peaceful aspects, if seldom present, here were completely ignored. Moreover, in a direct contradiction of the anthem's secular character, the film located the song in a variety of religious contexts.

Meanwhile, *God Save Poland* came to prominence again as it continued to be sung in the country's Catholic churches and during patriotic demonstrations. The presence of religiously-tinged patriotism in Poland after the triumph of the Solidarity movement is obvious in everyday musical practice and in recordings. For instance, the State Folk Ensemble *Mazowsze,* one of the cultural "emblems" of the Polish People's Republic, attempted to revamp its "socialist-folk" image by issuing a CD entitled *Boże, coś Polskę* (Polskie Nagrania, ECD 034, 1994). Its 20 tracks begin with *Bogurodzica,* and with *Gaude, mater Polonia* and are framed by recorded bells from the Częstochowa monastery, the sanctuary of Jasna Góra. Some of our "old friends" appear here: *Chorał, Rota,* and Krasicki's Hymn for the First Anniversary of the 3rd May Constitution. Religious themes predominate: the collection contains thirteen items, including nine Marian songs. With its pastoral cover portraying a crowded wooden village church, the CD articulates a myth of folk religiosity and popular patriotism that is dear to many Poles.

The links between the military and the religious dimensions of Polish national anthems have been strengthened in the 1990s, as may be seen in the contents of a CD issued by the Representative Ensembles of the Polish Army. This recording juxtaposes *Bogurodzica* and *Dąbrowski's Mazurka* with several religious pieces (e.g. Moniuszko's *Litany of Ostra Brama* addressed to Mary from a Vilnius sanctuary, and some contemporary works).[36] Despite these efforts to "Christianize" the *Mazurka* by placing it in a religious context, the 1797 anthem remains entirely secular since its text does not refer to God, Divine Providence, Mary, nor any other religious persona, nor concept. As such it represents the non-religious aspect of the Polish quest for independence and sovereignty, with the hope placed not in divine intervention, but in the people's abilities, courage, and strength.

This presentation of the complex historical roots of Poland's anthems articulates the shifting priorities of Poles who created, transformed, and selected anthems from an array of songs designed to serve the country as its national symbols. The convoluted history of *Dąbrowski's Mazurka, God Save Poland* and other Polish anthems articulates the intersection of national, political and religious interests in selecting a country's most potent musical "recognition sign." It is clear, for instance, that the contents of the majority of published anthologies of Polish anthems display a particular (sacred/military/secular/"socialist") bias that depends on the hidden agenda of the producers of these publications. However, national bias is not absent from the work of historians, as Norman Davies observes in his study of "Europe;"[37] indeed this particular problem with history-writing goes back to the difference between Tucidides's Greek nationalism and Herodotus's enlightened impartiality. While true "objectivity" and freedom from biases may be

---

[36]CD-recording *Białym orłem wzleć* [Fly with the white eagle] of the S. Moniuszko Concert Orchestra of the Polish Army, with the Choir of the Academy of Catholic Theology, Warsaw, produced by the orchestra (MCD 002, 1996).

[37]See Norman Davies's polemics about the definition of Europe in the introduction to his monograph *Europe: A History* (London and Oxford: Oxford University Press, 1996).

extremely difficult to achieve, or even totally impossible, the least one can do is critically examine one's inherited traditions with the hope of recognizing the patterns of the past which continue to replicate themselves in the present.

APPENDIX

Appendix:
Stefan and Wanda Wilk Prizes
for Research in Polish Music

by Brian Harlan

Description of the Competitions

The Stefan & Wanda Wilk Prizes for Research in Polish Music are sponsored by the Polish Music Center (PMC) and the Flora L. Thornton School of Music of the University of Southern California, Los Angeles. They are intended to stimulate research on Polish music in academic circles outside of Poland. The prizes are awarded to authors of the best books or papers reflecting original research on some aspect of the music of Poland, preferably on a less known topic or composer.

In the spring of 2000 the yearly essay competition, Wilk Prizes for Research in Polish Music, held since 1986, was replaced with two competitions held in alternating years: Wilk Essay Prizes for Research in Polish Music (odd years) and Wilk Book Prizes for Research in Polish Music (even years). The prize is to be awarded to the best book on Polish music published outside of Poland by an author who is not usually working in Poland. The books may be written in English, French or German. The prize consists of $2,000 and a framed certificate. The Essay Competition is divided into two categories. The winning essay by an author who is a student receives a prize of $500. All professional scholars and musicians may compete for a prize of $1,000. Both competitions are open to all authors based outside of Poland. Between 1986 and 1999 the competition took place annually and in some editions the prizes were divided between two contestants (the list of prize winners follows); in 1992 and 1996 the prizes were not awarded.

For more information about the competitions contact the Polish Music Center at the Flora L. Thornton School of Music, University of Southern California, Los Angeles, CA 90089-0851. Tel.:213-740-9369; Fax:213-740-3217; E-mail: polmusic@usc.edu; URL: http://www.usc.edu/go/polish_music.

The Wilk Prizes and the Polish Music Center

The Stefan and Wanda Wilk Prizes for Research in Polish Music were established in 1986 by Dr. Stefan and Mrs.Wanda Wilk, the founders of the Polish Music Reference Center at the University of Southern California, as one aspect of their efforts to disseminate knowledge about Polish music.[1] The PMRC (renamed Polish Music Center in the summer of 2000) is a research and information center devoted to gathering and disseminating knowledge about all aspects of Polish music.The idea of establishing a Polish music research and resource center was conceived by Dr. Stefan and Mrs. Wanda Wilk in 1981. In order to realize this goal, they donated the initial $100,000 to the Stefan and Wanda Wilk Endowment Fund. In 1984, an agreement was signed with the University and the School of Music; the PMRC became a reality. The official dedication ceremony took place in 1985, in the presence of Witold Lutosławski and other distinguished guests. The endowment grew over the years with gifts from the PMRC's founders as well as with major donations from Witold Lutosławski, Dr & Mrs. Zbigniew Petrovich, Dr & Mrs. Clark Halstead, Helena Nowicka, M.D., Dr & Mrs. Kenneth Harris, and Lottie Harasimowicz (in 1999 the Fund reached the value of over $1,600,000).

Wanda Wilk was appointed the first Director of the Center and introduced many programs. In 1982 she initiated a book series devoted to Polish music (Polish Music History Series); since 1986 she has organized and administered the Wilk Prizes for Research in Polish Music. Ms. Wilk enlarged the Center's collection of books, scores, recordings, and manuscripts, as well as organized many concerts featuring compositions by Polish composers. During her eleven years as Director, Ms. Wilk answered numerous inquiries regarding Polish music, assisted musicians in selecting a Polish repertoire, helped scholars to locate resources, and informed the American public about the existence of what she called a "golden

---

[1]For biographical notes about Dr. and Mrs. Wilk see the entries in *Polish Americans in California*, vol. 2, Gene Harubin Zygmont, Artur Zygmont, Gillian Olechno-Huszcza, Henrietta Simons, eds. (National Center for Urban Ethnic Affairs and Polish American Historical Association, 1995).

treasure trove of Polish music." In the fall of 1996, Dr. Maria Anna Harley (since the fall of 2000: Maja Trochimczyk), of McGill University, Montreal (Canada), was appointed the new director of PMC and assistant professor of music history and literature in the USC School of Music. In October 1997, during the *Górecki Autumn* Festival and in the presence of many distinguished guests the formal announcement was made by USC President, Prof. Steven B. Sample, to name the newly created position the "Stefan and Wanda Wilk Directorship" of the Center. After her 1996 retirement as director, Ms. Wilk has continued to support the activities of PMC as its Honorary Director, the Editor of the Polish Music History Series (until volume 6), and the President of the Friends of Polish Music - a fund-raising and support group for the Center.

The Polish Music Center is active in many areas. It publishes a book series (Polish Music History Series, six volumes since 1982), an online monthly bulletin with current news, the *Polish Music Newsletter*,[2] and a semi-annual online journal dedicated to scholarly studies of Polish music, *Polish Music Journal* (ISSN 1521-6039; published since 1998).[3] The Polish Music Collection held in the PMC library includes scores, books, recordings, periodicals, unpublished essays and dissertations, and ephemera (concert programs, reviews, press clippings, etc.). A special part of the PMC holdings is its Manuscript Collection kept on deposit in the Special Collections Department of the USC Libraries. The Manuscript Collection initially consisted of 22 works by 6 composers (Witold Lutosławski, Tadeusz Baird, Stanisław Skrowaczewski, Grażyna Bacewicz, Joanna Bruzdowicz, and Marta Ptaszyńska). In the fall of 2000 the collection expanded to over 100 manuscripts by 28 composers (additional donations of scores, sketches, and letters by Krzysztof Baculewski, Krzysztof Knittel, Zygmunt Krauze, Hanna Kulenty, Szymon Laks, Roman Macie-jewski, Bernadetta Matuszczak, Krzysztof Meyer, Krystyna Moszumańska-Nazar, Jan Oleszkowicz, Roman Palester, Edward Sielicki, Ryszard Sielicki, Elżbieta Sikora, Jarosław Siwiński,

---

[2]ISSN 1098-9188;<http://www.usc.edu/go/polish_music/news.html> ; published since 1996.

[3]ISSN 1521-6039; <http://www.usc.edu/go/polish_music/PMJ>.

Władysław Słowiński, Aleksander Tansman, Romuald Twardowski, Tadeusz Wielecki, Barbara Zakrzewska, Anna Zawadzka, and Lidia Zielińska). The Manuscript Collection continues to grow and is expected to double in size by the end of 2001 through numerous new donations.

The Center maintains a web site on Polish music <http://www.usc.edu/go/polish_music>. The site includes essays, directories, catalogs, links, and information about over forty Polish composers. Finally, the Center also organizes conferences, festivals, and lecture series held on USC campus and during meetings of scholarly organizations. The list of special events at USC includes:

• *Szymanowski Centennial* (October 1982; this event, organized by Wanda Wilk, Jim Samson, and Włodzimierz Kotoński, actually pre-dated the creation of the PMRC);

• residences by composer Witold Lutosławski (1985, 1993);

• recitals by composer-pianist Andrzej Dutkiewicz (1988, 1990), composer-percussionist Marta Ptaszyńska, pianists Adam Makowicz and Nancy Fierro, violinist Arnold Belnick, and others;

• *Górecki Autumn* - Festival and scholarly symposium dedicated to Henryk Mikołaj Górecki (with the composer in residence and the premiere of his *Symphony no. 3* under his baton; October 1997);

• *A Day With Women's Music* including a concert, scholarly symposium and a composers' round-table; with the residency of the composer Hanna Kulenty and the world premiere of her *Sixth Circle* for trumpet and piano (April 1998);

• *Polish/Jewish/Music!* International Conference with the participation of over twenty scholars from five countries (November 1998), proceedings forthcoming;

• *The Heritage of Chopin* series of lecture-recitals by Polish pianists, Barbara Hesse-Bukowska and Michał Wesołowski (February-March 1999);

• *Polish Music Manuscripts: Exhibition and Concert*, presenting the holdings of the Manuscript Collection and some of these pieces in performance (October 2000).

Winners of the Wilk Essay Prizes in Polish Music (1986-1999)

Competition No. 1 - 1986

Professional Prize:

Charles E. Brewer, University of Alabama, Tuscalloosa.
Popular Polyphony and the University of Kraków: The Music of PL-Kj 2464 and Related Sources.

> Published as *Collectio cantilenarum saeculi. XV: Rkp. Biblioteki Jagiellonskiej Kj 2464/Manuscript Kj 2464 of the Biblioteka Jagiellonska,* in the series *Źródła do historii muzyki polskiej* no. 30. (Kraków, Poland: Polskie Wydawnictwo Muzyczne, 1990).

Student Prize: Not awarded.

Competition No. 2 - 1987/8

Professional Prize: Not awarded.

Student Prize:

Stephen C. Downes, Goldsmith's College, University of London.
Tonal Processes in Szymanowski's Piano Sonata in A, op. 21.

> Paper based on Downes's M.M. Thesis, University of London, Goldsmith's College, 1987. Published in *After Chopin: Essays in Polish Music,* ed. Maja Trochimczyk (Los Angeles: Polish Music Center at USC, 2000). Dr. Downes's doctoral dissertation, *Szymanowski as Post-Wagnerian: The Love Songs of Hafiz, op. 24* appeared in the series *Outstanding Dissertations in Music from British Universities* (New York: Garland, 1994).

Competition No. 3 - 1989

Professional Prize:

Dr. Jeffrey Kallberg, University of Pennsylvania.
Hearing Poland: Chopin and Nationalism.

> Published in *Ninteenth-Century Piano Music*, Larry R.
> Todd, ed. (New York: Schirmer, 1990), 221-257. Prof.
> Kallberg is an expert on Chopin's music. His most recent
> book is: *Chopin at the Boundaries: Sex, History, and
> Musical Genre.* Series: *Convergences: Inventories of the
> Present* (Cambridge, Mass.: Harvard University, 1996).

Student Prize:

Tomasz Czepiel, Hartford College, Oxford, England.
*The Musical Establishment at the Court of Zygmunt August (1530-
1572).*

Competition No. 4 - 1990

Professional Prize: Not awarded.

Student Prize:

Anthony Gatto, University of Texas, Austin.
Bartók and Lutosławski: Observing a Lineage.

Competition No. 5 - 1991

Professional Prize: Divided between two contestants.

Dr. John Rink, University of Surrey, England.
Tonal Architecture in Chopin's Early Music.

> Published as: "Tonal Architecture in the Early Music," in
> *The Cambridge Companion to Chopin*, Jim Samson, ed.
> (Cambridge: Cambridge University Press, 1992), 78-97.

Dr. Richard Zielinski, Mercer University, Georgia.
Szymanowski's 'Stabat Mater.'
>Excerpt of Zielinski's D.M.A. dissertation, *Karol Szymanowski's Stabat Mater* (University of Illinois, 1990). Published as "Sources and Material's of Szymanowski's *Stabat Mater*," in *After Chopin: Essays in Polish Music*, ed. Maja Trochimczyk (Los Angeles: Polish Music Center at USC, 2000).

Student Prize: Divided between two contestants.

Martin R. Osborne, University of Southern California.
Witold Lutosławski: A Stylistic Analysis of the 'Trois poèmes d'Henri Michaux.'

Steven Zohn, Cornell University.
Witold Lutosławski's 'Chain 3:' Aspects of Form and Closure.

Competition No. 6 - 1992

Professional Prize: Not awarded.

Student Prize: Not awarded.

Competition No. 7 - 1993

Professional Prize:
Dr. Ann K. Mc Namee, Swarthmore College.
Grażyna Bacewicz's Piano Sonata No. 2.
>Published as "Grazyna Bacewicz's Second Piano Sonata (1953): Octave Expansion and Sonata Form," *Music Theory Online* 0 no.4 (1993) <http://smt.ucsb.edu/mto>
>A different version was published as "Piano Sonata II (1953) by Grazyna Bacewicz," on McNamee's web site *Analyses of Music by Women*, with sound samples and examples in five formats, <http://mcnamee.graham.com>

Student Prize:

Barbara Milewski, Princeton University.
'Jasiu i Kasia:' Folk Characters in Chopin's Mazurkas.

Competition No. 8 - 1994

Professional Prize:

Dr. Maria Anna Harley, McGill University, Montreal, Canada.
At Home with Phenomenology: Ingarden's 'Work of Music' Revisited.
> A short version published in: *International Journal of Musicology* 6 (1998): 9-24. Full text in *After Chopin: Essays in Polish Music*, Maja Trochimczyk, ed. (Los Angeles: Polish Music Center at USC, 2000).

Student Prize: Not awarded.

Competition No. 9 - 1995

Professional Prize:

Dr. Michael L. Klein, State University of New York at Buffalo.
Lutosławski's 'Partita for Violin and Piano:' A New Perspective on his Late Music.
> Published in *After Chopin: Essays in Polish Music*, Maja Trochimczyk, ed. (Los Angeles: Polish Music Center at USC, 2000).

Student Prize:

Joseph W. Rovan, Jr., University of California, Berkeley
Continuities and Reflections: A Comparison of Witold Lutosławski's Third and Fourth Symphonies.

Competition No. 10 - 1996

Professional Prize: Not awarded.

Student Prize: Not awarded.

Competition No. 11 - 1997

Professional Prize: Divided between two contestants.

Tyrone Grieve, University of Wisconsin, Madison.
Perspectives on Paul Kochański's Collaborative Work with Other Composers as Reflected Through his Personal Manuscript Collection.
> Published as: "Kochański's Collaborative Work as Reflected Through his Manuscript Collection," *Polish Music Journal* 1 no. 1 (Summer 1998):
> <http://www.usc.edu/go/polish_music/PMJ/archives.html>

Jill Timmons and Sylvain Fremaux, Linfield College, Oregon.
Alexandre Tansman: The Man and the Artist.
> Published as: "Alexandre Tansman: Diary of a 20th-Century Composer," *Polish Music Journal* 1 no. 1 (Summer 1998):
> <http://www.usc.edu/go/polish_music/PMJ/archives.html>

Student Prize:

Timothy J. Cooley, Brown University.
Authentic Troupes and Inauthentic Tropes.
> Published as: "Authentic Troupes and Inauthentic Tropes: Performance Practice in Górale Music," *Polish Music Journal* 1 no. 1 (Summer 1998):
> <http://www.usc.edu/go/polish_music/PMJ/archives.html>

Competition No. 12 - 1998

Professional Prize:
Asst. Prof. Halina Goldberg, Indiana University, Bloomington.
Chopin in Warsaw Salons
    Published in *Polish Music Journal* 2 no. 1 (Summer 1999):
    <http://www.usc.edu/go/polish_music/PMJ>

Student Prize:
Dorota Zakrzewska, McGill University, Montreal, Canada.
Alienation and Powerlessness: Adam Mickiewicz's 'Ballady' and Chopin's 'Ballades.' Polish Music Journal 2 no. 1 (Summer 1999).

Competition No. 13 - 1999

Professional Prize: Divided between two contestants.

Prof. James Parakilas, Bates College.
"Nuit plus belle qu'un beau jour": Poetry, Song and the Voice in the Piano Nocturne.

Dr. Sandra P. Rosenblum, independent scholar.
Chopin's Music in Nineteenth-Century America: Introduction, Dissemination, and Aspects of Reception

Student Prize: Not awarded.

Winners of the Wilk Book Prize in Polish Music (2000)

The Book Prize is divided equally between two books:

Prof. Jeffrey Kallberg, University of Pennsylvania.
Chopin at the Boundaries: Sex, History, and Musical Genre.
(Harvard University Press, 1996).

Dr. Martina Homma, Cologne, Germany.
Witold Lutosławski. Zwölfton-Harmonik, Formbildung, "aleatorische Kontrapunkt." Studien zur Gesamtwerk unter Einbeziehung der Skizzen. (Cologne: Bela Verlag, 1996).

Polish Music History Series

The Polish Music History Series (PMHS) was launched in 1982 by Wanda Wilk for the Friends of Polish Music (FPM) at the University of Southern California (USC) School of Music in Los Angeles. It is dedicated to composers, scholars, and performers of Polish Music who made their contribution to the commonwealth of music in the western world, but who have generally been neglected by music historians. The objective of the series is to fill this gap in American literature. Wanda Wilk, the first director of the Polish Music Reference Center (1985-1996) served as the Editor of the series till 1999.

A short guide to the music of Karol Szymanowski was published for the composer's Centennial celebration at USC in 1982 as the first number of the series. This was followed by two monographs, the first in English, on the outstanding composer Grażyna Bacewicz (1909-1969), whose works for chamber orchestra and string quartets are part of the standard repertoire in Europe. Bacewicz wrote seven string quartets, seven violin concertos, two piano quintets and several symphonic works worthy of being heard. The first monograph (1984) was written by Judith Rosen, a specialist on women composers. It includes a foreword by the renowned composer Witold Lutosławski, a list of works and a discography. The second book on Bacewicz (1985) is an analytical study of her chamber and orchestral music by Prof. Adrian Thomas, British musicologist. The fourth monograph in the series is *Polish Music Literature (1515-1990)*, a selected bibliography compiled by the eminent Polish music bibliographer, Kornel Michałowski and revised with additions by Gillian Olechno-Huszcza, who was at that time (1991) the archivist at the Polish Music Reference Center.

Monograph no. 5 (1993) is the biography of Karol Szymanowski written by the Polish specialist on this composer, Dr. Teresa Chylińska. The monograph presents an overview of Szymanowski's life and works, with some information about his first performances in the U.S. Volume six is the last one prepared under the editorship of Wanda Wilk who retired from her position of the PMRC Director in 1996. This volume, edited by Dr. Maja Trochimczyk, is also the first book in the series to list the Polish

Music Center as its publisher (this change more faithfully reflects the circumstances of the production of the series). Dr. Trochimczyk serves as Wanda Wilk's successor in the position of the PMC Director and, due to the nature of her duties, has taken over the role of the Editor of the series beginning with volume seven, a collection of essays on Szymanowski's songs edited by Zofia Helman, Teresa Chylińska and Alistair Wightman.

Since 1998 the PMHS is distributed by the Pendragon Press, New York. (P.O.Box 190; Hillsdale, NY 12529-5839; phone: 518-325-6100, e-mail: penpress@taconic.net). Titles in the series may also be ordered directly from the Polish Music Center.

The Polish Music History Series is an ongoing project at USC made possible through contributions, large and small, from Polish and non-Polish friends across the United States and Canada, to whom we are most grateful. Donations to cover the costs of translating, editing, and printing successive volumes of the series may be made to the Polish Music Fund at USC (a restricted fund designated solely for the support of the Polish Music Center).

The PMHS editorial board consists of: Dr. Teresa Chylińska, Kraków Poland; Dr. Maciej Gołąb, University of Warsaw, Poland; Prof. Adrian Thomas, Cardiff University of Wales, United Kingdom; Dr. William Thomson, Los Angeles, California; Wanda Wilk, Los Angeles, California; and Dr. Maja Trochimczyk, Editor-in-Chief.

Notes about Contributors

Timothy J. Cooley (b. 1962), an ethnomusicologist, received his Ph.D. from Brown University in 1999 for the dissertation on "Ethnography, Tourism, and Music-Culture in the Tatra Mountains: Negotiated Representations of Polish *Górale* Ethnicity." His publications include *Shadows in the Field: New Perspectives for Fieldwork in Ethnomusicology*, (co-editor with Gregory F. Barz. New York: Oxford University Press, 1997); "Music of the Polish Tatra Mountain *Górale* in Chicago" forthcoming in *The American Musical Atlas.* Edited by Jeff Todd Titon. (New York: Schirmer Books); and the entry on "United States of America (European-American music: Polish)." co-authored with Janice Kleeman and forthcoming in *The New Grove Dictionary of Music and Musicians,* revised edition,(London: Macmillan). Cooley also wrote extensive liner notes on early Górale music for a two volume CD set recorded in Chicago, *Fire in the Mountains: Polish Mountain Fiddle Music*, vols. 1 & 2. (Newton, New Jersey: Shanachie Entertainment Corp. 1997). His recent conference presentations include "Skanking in the Tatras: An Unlikely Mix of Polish Fiddle Music and Jamaican Reggae" (Society for Ethnomusicology, Pittsburgh, PA, October 1997) and "Multiculturalism in the Isolation of the Polish Tatras" (International Council for Traditional Music, Nitra, Slovak Republic, June 1997). In 1998-2000 Cooley has taught ethno-musicology at the University of California, Santa Barbara.

Stephen C. Downes (Lecturer in Music, University of Surrey) studied at the University of Exeter and Goldsmiths' College, London. His M.Mus. dissertation on Szymanowski's Op.21 won the student section of the Wilk Prize in 1988. In 1994 his doctoral dissertation, *Szymanowski as Post-Wagnerian*, was published by Garland, New York. His articles and reviews on Szymanowski, Kar owicz, appeared in British scholarly journals: *Music Analysis, Journal of the Royal Musicological Association,* and *Music & Letters*, for example "Themes of Duality and Transformation in Szymanowski's *King Roger*," *Music Analysis* 14 no. 2-3 (July-October 1995): 257-291; "Szymanowski and Narcissism," *Journal of the Royal Musical Association* 121 no. 1 (1996): 58-81. At present, Downes is a co-editor (with Paul Cadrin) of *Szymanowski Handbook*, with entries on all notable people associated with Szymanowski's life and music.

Mateusz Gliński (1892-1976) was a musicologist, conductor and composer, author of several arrangements of Chopin's works. He worked as the editor of *Mazowiecki* (since founding the journal in 1924 until 1938) and published, among other works, *Hymn to Poland*, an arrangement of a Chopin melody (Minneapolis, Minn.: Polanie Pub. Co, 1957). His musicological writings include *Chopin the Unknown* (Windsor, Canada: Assumption University of Windsor Press, 1963) and polemical articles about Chopin's correspondence to Delfina Potocka (Gli ski favored its authenticity, but was later proven wrong). Cf. Zofia Gli ska, ed., *Testament Mateusza Glińskiego* [The Testament of Mateusz Gli ski] (London: Oficyna Poetów i Malarzy, 1982).

Maria Anna Harley, see Maja Trochimczyk.

Zofia Helman (b. 1937) studied musicology at the University of Warsaw where she received her doctorate in 1967 for *Aspects of Karol Szymanowski's Compositional Techniques*. In 1980 she completed a pioneering study of *Neoclassicism in Polish Music of the 20th Century* (published in Polish in 1985, by PWM Edition). In 1999 her monograph of Polish composer Roman Palester (who was blacklisted by the communist government in Poland) was published by Musica Iagellonica in Kraków. Helman edited five volumes of *Complete Works* of Karol Szymanowski for PWM Edition (*Stabat Mater*, 1965; *King Roger*, 1973; *Demeter i Agawe*, 1975; *Veni Creator* and *Litania do Marii Panny*, 1975; *String Quartets*, 1976). She published numerous articles on the music of Szymanowski, as well as Baird, Chopin, Jana ek, Lutos awski, Poulenc, Palester, Prokofiev, Penderecki, Stravinsky, Tansman, Wagner, and compositional techniques of the 19th and 20th centuries (her publications appear mostly in Polish; also in German, French and Italian). Since 1959 Helman lectured at the Institute of Musicology, University of Warsaw; since 1990 she has been a full professor there, between 1991 and 1997 she served as the Institute's director. Her doctoral seminar in Music Theory and Analysis was instrumental in introducing ideas of Heinrich Schenker (tonal analysis), music semiotics and semiology (Jean-Jacques Nattiez), and critical methods borrowed from studies of literature (Lotman, Bakhtin) to Polish musicology.

Michael L. Klein is Assistant Professor of music theory at Temple University (he previously taught at the University of Texas, Austin. Klein received his undergraduate degree from the Eastman School of Music (1985), Rochester, a M.M.degree (1987) and a Ph.D. in music theory from the State University of New York, Buffalo (1995). His research currently focuses on the music of Witold Lutos awski and on intertextuality, particularly in the works of 20th century composers. He has presented papers on the music of Lutos awski at conferences of the Music Theory Society of New York State, the Society for Music Theory, and at an international Lutos awski conference in Pozna , Poland. A forthcoming article in the *Indiana Theory Review* discusses Lutos awski's use of register. In addition to his work as a theorist, he is an active pianist who has performed chamber music concerts in the U.S., Canada, Switzerland, and Japan. The paper published in this volume summarizes the findings from his doctoral dissertation, *A Theoretical Study of the Late Music of Witold Lutosławski: New Interactions of Pitch, Rhythm, and Form.*

Maria Konopnicka (1842-1910) was a poet, writer, author of books for children, literary critic and translator. In 1884-1886 she served as the editor of a women's journal, *Świt* [Dawn]. Between 1890-1900 she lived in western Europe and was involved with Polish émigré communities. In 1901-1902 she organized protests against persecutions of Polish school-children by the Prussian government; in 1905-1907, she organized assistance for Polish prisoners jailed by the Tsarist government after the revolution of 1905. After her poetic debut in 1870, she published numerous collections of poems, short stories and essays. Her poetry reveals inspirations with folk poetry, sym-bolism and experimental trends of the turn-of-the-century. Konop-nicka's social and political conscience finds expression in several of her stories and poems, e.g. "Rota" which became a hymn of the Polish farmers persecuted by the Germans and one of the candidates for the national anthem. Her

312   Contributors

volume *Linie i dźwięki* [Lines and sounds; 1897] contains many poems about music.

Witold Lutosławski (1913-1994) is usually considered the most important Polish composer of the second half of the 20th century. Lutoslawski was trained as a pianist (1924-27 with J. Smidowicz, 1932-1936 with J. Lefeld), violinist (1927-1932; with L. Kmitowa), and composer (1929-1937; with Witold Maliszewski). He also studied mathematics at the University of Warsaw (1931-33) and was later active as a conductor, especially of his own music. Lutos awski's early works adhere to neoclassical style; after 1945 he turned to Polish folklore, especially in the Concerto for Orchestra (1954) - a work bringing together neoclassicism and folklorism in a perfect synthesis. The development of an individual style of textural composition based on his own 12-tone method and the technique of controlled aleatorism took place in the late 1950s (*3 Postludia*, 1958-1960). *Jeux vénitiens* (1961) marks the triumphant appearance of Lutos awski on the international stage. His subsequent compositions of the 1960s through 1980s belong to the canon of modernist music: *Trois poèmes Henri Michaux* (1963), String Quartet (1964), *Paroles tissées* (1965), *Livre pour orchestre* (1968), Symphony no. 2 (1967), Cello Concerto (1970), *Les espaces du sommeil* (1975), *Mi-parti* (1976), Symphony no. 3 (1983), *Chain I* (1983), *Partita* for violin and piano (1984), *Chain II* (1986), and Piano Concerto (1988). Lutos awski's late style is characterized by textural reduction and an increase in expressivity: Symphony no. 4 (1992), *Chantefleurs and Chantefables* (1991). A recipient of a great number of honorary doctorates and awards (UNESCO International Rostrum of Composers, 1959, 1964, 1968; Grawemeyer Prize, 1984; Polar Prize, 1993; Kyoto Prize, 1993), Lutos awski did not hold a teaching position; but gave lectures during summer courses and festivals of his music.

Stanisław Niewiadomski (1859-1936) was a composer and music critic of a conservative orientation (frequently attacking Szymanowski). Niewiadomski studied with Karol Mikuli (Lwów), F. Krenna and J. I. Paderewski (Vienna), and S. Jadassohn (Leipzig). In 1886-1887 he directed the Lwów Opera, in 1887-1914 he was a professor of Lwów Conservatory. He spent World War I in Vienna, and since 1919 lived in Warsaw where he was a professor of the Warsaw Conservatory and music critic. As a composer, Niewiadomski continued Moniuszko's tradition of art songs setting Polish poetry (for solo voices and chorus). He was the author of a large number of neo-romantic songs to texts by Polish poets, e.g. Adam Asnyk, Adam Mickiewicz, Maria Konopnicka (including a version of the patriotic anthem *Rota*). In terms of musical style, his songs are closely linked to Polish folklore; Niewiadomski published arrangements of folk songs and soldier's songs. His output includes also two symphonies and four overtures, as well as some piano pieces. Niewiadomski was the founder and first president of Society of Music Writer and Critics (founded in 1924). His articles appeared in *Gazeta Muzyczna, Kurier Lwowski, Gazeta Narodowa, Echo Muzyczne i Teatralne, Rzeczpospolita, Kurier Polski, Muzyka, Orkiestra*, etc. In addition to many essays on Chopin, he wrote booklets on *Fryderyk Franciszek Szopen: największy muzyk polski* [F.F.Ch. - greatest Polish musician] (Warszawa : Wydawnictwo Komitetu Dni Szopenowskich w Polsce, 1933) and *Stanisław Moniuszko* (Warszawa: Gebethner i Wolff, 1928). His writings on music include a textbook on the elements of music (1909), a history of music (1927), and the first Polish translation of Hanslick's *On the Beautiful in Music* (1903).

Zygmunt Noskowski (1846-1909) was a composer and conductor. He started his music training by studying the violin (his second teacher was Apolinary K tski at the Warsaw Institute of Music, 1864-6); at the same time Moskowski studied with Stanis aw Moniuszko (harmony) and F. Ciaffei (voice). In 1872-75 Noskowski studied composition with Ferdinand Kiel in Berlin. He was active as an orchestral musician (Teatr Wielki in Warsaw), singer, pianist, music critic, and conductor. In 1881-1902 he directed the Warsaw Music Society (WTM) and conducted in many of its concerts; after the creation of the Warsaw Philharmonics, Noskowski was its second conductor. Since 1886 he taught at the Warsaw Institute of Music, with students including Melcer, Rogowski, Rytel, Szeluto, Fitelberg, Kar owicz, Ró ycki, and Szymanowski. His output includes works for different instrumental and vocal settings, with many piano miniatures and songs, revealing influences of Schumann and Liszt. The symphonic poem *Steppe* (1896-97) remains his most popular orchestral composition and marks a departure from his earlier fascination with conservative-romantic models (Mendelssohn) - expressed in 3 symphonies, orchestral overtures and variations. Chopin's influence does not appear in his earlier music; instead it marks Noskowski's later inclination to use Polish folk-song and popular melodies as source material for his music. Symphonic variations *From the Life of the Nation* [Z ycia narodu] are based on the theme from Chopin's Prelude in A major (1901); piano pieces include *Fantazja Góralska* (1885), *Polish Suite* (1890), *Folk Wedding Songs* (1890-1900). Noskowski wrote many cantatas on religious and national themes, choral arrangements of folk songs, *Songbook for Children* to poetry of Maria Konopnicka and incidental music for the theatre. His publications include press articles and reviews, textbooks on harmony (1903), counterpoint and fugue (1907), methods for the violin (1885) and piano (1894), and a collection of Lithuanian folksongs, edited with J. Baudoin de Courtenay (1892-1900).

Karol Szymanowski (1882-1937), Poland's most eminent composer after Chopin and Moniuszko is credited with creating a modern national style. Growing up in an artistic environment created by his family that belonged to Polish gentry, Szymanowski started composing before beginning a formal education in music; he studied with Noskowski in Warsaw (1901-1904) and joined the Young Poland group of composers and musicians (1905, with Fitelberg, Szeluto, Ró ycki, and others). Szymanowski's earlier works reveal influences of Chopin and Skryabin, as well as late romantic German music, i.e. Strauss, Wagner, Reger (especially two symphonies, and *Love Songs of Hafiz*). This "neo-romantic" phase lasted until 1914; the years of World War I (1914-1918) mark a turn towards an "impressionistic" style, inspired by the music of Debussy and Ravel (Symphony no. 3, "The Song of the Night") and, in the area of music for violin, marked by a collaboration with violinist Pawe Kocha ski (*Mythes* for violin and piano, Violin Concerto no. 1). At that time Szymanowski's interests shifted to ancient and oriental cultures; he traveled to Sicily and North Africa in 1914 and expressed these new interests, combined with the impressionistic influences in his songs (*Songs of Infatuated Muezzine, Songs of a Fairy-Tale Princess*) and the opera *King*

Roger (1918-1924). A profound shift in his aesthetic orientation in the 1920s directed Szymanowski towards "national style" - integrating modernist compositional techniques (Bartók), with Chopin influences (*Mazurkas* for piano), stylizations of the music of the Tatra mountains (ballet *Harnasie,* Violin Concerto no. 2) and of the Kurpie area (*Kurpie Songs*), as well as echoes of Polish religious folklore (*Stabat Mater* for choir, soloists, and orchestra, *Veni Creator*). Szymanowski's turn to contemporary French music, Polish folklore, and early music as sources of inspiration had a great impact on the future development of music in Poland. Involved in polemics with music critics of a more conservative orientation, Szymanowski published many articles and interviews. Two volumes of his literary and musical writings have been issued by PWM Edition; an English translation of his writings on music is being prepared by Toccata Press.

Maja Trochimczyk (b. 1957 in Poland; in 1987-1999 known as Maria Anna Harley) is Assistant Professor of Music History and the Sefan and Wanda Wilk Director of the Polish Music Reference Center at the Flora L. Thornton School of Music, University of Southern California, Los Angeles. After receiving two M.A. degrees in Poland (in sound engineering from the F. Chopin Academy of Music in Warsaw, 1987, and in musicology from the University of Warsaw, 1986) she completed her dissertation on *Space and Spatialization in Contemporary Music* (McGill University, Montreal, Canada, 1994). Trochimczyk has focused on the study of music by Polish composers (Bacewicz, Górecki, Lutos awski) while continuing to pursue her interests in 20th-century music (Bartók, Andriessen, Schafer, Xenakis), spatial music and constructs of Polish national identity (anthems, immigrant communities and musicians, dance groups). A recipient of research grants from Social Sciences and Humanities Research Council of Canada, Southern California Studies Center, Jewish Community Foundation, Ars Musica Poloniae Foundation, she has published over 30 articles and book chapters in an international array of books and journals, e.g., *Journal of Musicological Research, Musical Quarterly, American Music, The American Journal of Semiotics* (US), *Contemporary Music Review, Tempo, Organized Sound* (UK), *Interface - Journal of New Music Research* (Belgium),

Muzyka (Poland), *Studia Musicologica* (Hungary), *Women Composers: Music Through the Ages* (USA), *Lutosławski Studies* (UK), and *Crosscurrents and Counterpoints* (Sweden). She has also given presentations at over 40 musicology and interdisciplinary conferences in six countries. Her current responsibilities include editing books (on contemporary Dutch composer Louis Andriessen, Henryk Górecki, and on Polish-Jewish music) and a peer-reviewed online musicology journal, *Polish Music Journal,* which she co-founded in 1998 (<http://www.usc.edu/go/polish_music/PMJ>).

Richard Zielinski has pursued his educational and artistic endeavors with a commitment to excellence. At Indiana State University, Zielinski served as Director of Choral Activities and Coordinator of the Voice and Choral Division; conducts the *Concert Choir, ISU - Terre Haute Masterworks Chorale* and *Sycamore Singers;* taught choral methods and conducting; and administered the graduate program in choral conducting. As Founder and Artistic Director of the *Summer Sing Along Music Festival* (Fond du Lac, Wisconsin), Zielinski conducts the *Fond du Lac Philharmonic Orchestra*, and the *Festival Chorus.* Having received awards from the National Endowment for the Humanities, the Kosciuszko Foundation, and the Wilk Prize for Research in Polish Music, Zielinski has studied conducting internationally under the tutelage of Jan Szyrocki (*Szczecin Techinical Institute Choir*) Maestro Henryk Czy (*Warsaw Philharmonic Orchestra*) and Stefan Marczyk (*Szczecin Philharmonic Orchestra*). In the United States, he has studied conducting with Donald Neuen, Don V. Moses, and David Efron and was a finalist in the Leopold Stokowski Conducting Competition. Dr. Zielinski is also the Choral Editor for the *Musicator,* the official publication for the Indiana Music Educators Association, a state unit of the Music Educators National Conference.

Władysław Żeleński (1837-1921) was a composer and composition professor of a neo-romantic orientation, the most eminent Polish author of operas after Moniuszko. He studied the violin, piano and composition (with Mirecki since 1854). He began composing early, at the age of 20 conducting the premiere of his overture. In 1859-1862 Żeleński studied philosophy in Prague (he began these studies at the Iagellonian University in Kraków) receiving his doctorate in 1862; at the same time he also studied piano and organ. Żeleński continued his music education in Paris, returning to Poland in 1871, where he was a professor of harmony at the Warsaw Institute of Music since 1872. In 1888 he organized the Cracow Music Society and became its director. In addition to composing, he published a number of articles in the periodical *Czas*.

In his instrumental music, Żeleński drew from romantic music tradition and elements of Polish folklore (2 symphonies, overtures *In the Tatras* and *Forest Echoes*, Suite of Polish Dances, Piano Concerto in A minor, op. 60). His second opera, *Goplana* (to the libretto based on Juliusz S owacki's *Balladyna*, 1896) is the most outstanding work in his output. Żeleński composed four operas, over 100 songs, and numerous choral works. He also published music texbooks (elements of music, 1897, harmony and principles of composition, 1899).

* * *

Index

compiled by Dr. Linda Schubert

Todd, Larry R.: 302

Tomasik: 287

Tomaszewski, Mieczysław: 2 n5, 4
n9, 17 n1, 23 n1, 47 n1, 73 n7, 237,
238 n62

Treitler, Leo: 106

Trochimczyk, Maja: 1, 12, 14, 23
n1, 45, 60 n19, 60, 82, 86, 91, 107
n29, 108 n31, 247, 263, 299, 301,
303, 304, 308, 309, 315

Turowicz, Maria: 95 n12

Twardowski, Romuald: 229

Tyszkiewicz, Alicja: 274 n19

Ujejski, Kornel: 74, 279

Vladislaus IV (king): 272

Varèse, Edgard: 181

Varga, Balint Andras: 183 n9

Viardot, Pauline: 21 n7

Voltaire [Wolter]: 74

Wagner, Cosima Liszt: 132

Wagner, Richard: 22, 52, 55-58, 65,
115, 118, 124, 132, 156, 209, 210,
213, 267, 311, 315

Wallek-Walewski, Bolesław: 219
n30

Walsh, Stephen: 183 n9

Warsaw Conservatory: 84 n5

Waters, Edward N.: 24 n4

Wawrzykowska-Wierciochowa,
Dioniza: 276, 278 n25, 282 n26/27,
291

Wayda, Fryderyka: 228 n41

Weber, Carl Maria von: 18, 67

Webern, Anton: 231 n45

Weinstock, Herbert: 80 n7

Weiss, Karel [Weis]: 82

Weissmann, Adolf: 82

Wesołowski, Michał: 300

Wiechowicz, Stanisław: 222, 232
n48, 233 n49

Wightman, Alistair: 3 n6, 111, 143
n4, 144 n5, 145 n9, 146, 147 n13,
308

Wilk Prizes: 7, 9, 11, 297-298, 301-
306, 309, 316

Wilk, Stefan: 11, 298

Wilk, Wanda: 11, 162 n31, 298-
299, 307, 308

Willimann, Joseph: 80 n6

Windakiewicz, Helena: 157

Wintle, Christopher: 118 n25, 123
n31

Witwicki, Stefan: 74

Władysław Żeleński: 2

Wodzińska, Maria: 74

Wola, Żelazowa: 5